FORMAL PHILOSOPHY

FORMAL PHILOSOPHY

edited by

Vincent F. Hendricks

John Symons

Automatic Press ♦ $\frac{V}{I}$ P

Automatic Press ◆ $\frac{\vee}{\text{I}}$P

Information on this title: www.formalphilosophy.com

First published 2005

Printed in the United States of America
and the United Kingdom

ISBN-10   87-991013-1-9   hardback
ISBN-10   87-991013-0-0   paperback

Typeset in LaTeX 2_ε
Cover photo and graphic design by Vincent F. Hendricks

Contents

Preface

In the spring of 2005 we had the opportunity to work collaboratively on problems related to the application of epistemic logic and elements from formal learning theory to traditional epistemological questions. Given the nature of this topic, our conversations regularly turned to the more general question of the relationship between formal methods and philosophical investigation. We realized that some of the philosophers we most admire had never explicitly articulated their views on these questions and it occurred to us that it might be worth asking them. We decided to pose five relatively open and broad questions to some of the best philosophers who make formal methods a centerpiece in their work. This book contains their responses to our questions.

———————————— ◆ ————————————

The book is motivated by our curiosity but also by our discontent. Neither of us is content with the prominent histories of analytic philosophy currently on the market and we both believe that the discussion of general methodology of philosophy is in a pretty poor state. One of the most significant faults we see with such recent work is its failure to recognize and tackle the central place of formal methods. Shopworn narratives about the failures of logical positivism, the decline of formal methods in philosophy and the rise of intuitions-based conceptual analysis, are neither entirely true nor particularly helpful. In any case, such talk has been overwhelmed by the ongoing buzz of interesting work from philosophers who look much more like Russell and Carnap than Rorty. We hope that this project can serve as a counterweight to some of the more popular surveys of the philosophical landscape. However, our intention is not to promote the use of formal methods in philosophy. Firstly, it is not necessary for us to do so. Formal philosophy is thriving without any advertising. In our view, rather than promoting this kind of work, we can help to begin a fruitful conversation about the deep and interesting methodological problems that formal work in philosophy presents.

Clearly formal methods by themselves are not a panacea for all that might ail the philosopher, however, it is just as clear that there is something peculiarly fertile in the interplay between formalism and philosophical inquiry. Even those who reject analytic traditions in philosophy recognize that many of the most important developments in philosophy and its broader intellectual environment have arisen out of engagement with mathematics, logic, computer science, decision theory, physics and the other natural sciences. While there are limits to what formal methods can contribute, formal insights have sharpened, radicalized and extended philosophical investigation which would never have seen the light of day without the aid of formal methods.

Of course, it would be foolish to suggest that philosophy is a purely technical enterprise. Clever manipulations of symbols and formal apparata by themselves are not enough to solve or to deepen the understanding of philosophical problems. Philosophers must not only achieve some result, but must also judge that it is relevant to some philosophical problem or line of investigation. It must be determined when the applications of formal methods is appropriate and when something like common-sense, intuition and conceptual analysis legitimately come into play. When one encounters cases where scientific results lead to conclusions that seem to run counter to common-sense, how does one adjudicate? Are there a general set of principles that determine when a given problem can be solved using formal methods? These and related questions arise naturally at the intersection of formal methods and philosophical investigation.

Many of the philosophers we most admire simply avoid taking sides on these methodological questions in their written work. Rather than speaking in broad terms about the nature of the philosophical enterprise, they simply do philosophy. Rather than worrying over the ends or the death of philosophy, they are doing wonderful and important work *in* philosophy. We will not comment on the details of the responses we received to our five questions. Each is self-explanatory and readable and it is not our goal to synthesize one overarching view of the nature of formal work in philosophy. Our purpose in this project is not to articulate any specific agenda or definition but rather to begin to open the discussion of how formal philosophers understand their enterprise. Part of this project involves understanding why these philosophers chose to make formal methods central to their work. Of course, the decision to pursue this kind of work is, at least in part, a matter of taste. However, in and beyond intellectual biography, these responses provide some very illuminating and erudite examples of how philosophers make – formal as well as informal – methodological decisions.

Vincent F. Hendricks & John Symons
Copenhagen and El Paso
December 2005

Acknowledgements

We are indebted to Christopher M. Whalin for proof-reading the manuscript and to our publisher Automatic Press ♦ $\frac{\vee}{|}$P, in particular senior publishing editor V.J. Menshy, for taking on this 'rather unusual academic' project

Vincent F. Hendricks & John Symons
Copenhagen and El Paso
December 2005

1

Johan van Benthem

University Professor and Professor of Philosophy

University of Amsterdam, NL / Stanford University, USA

Why were you initially drawn to formal methods?

My high school education had prepared me for the idea that the Book of Nature is written in the language of mathematics, and as a bachelor's student of physics, I was assiduously trying to read that book. The discovery, made through an accidental encounter with William Stanley Jevons' 19th century textbook *Logic*, that there are also such formal structures in one's own thinking, language, reasoning, and argumentation was an eye-opener to me. Actually, Jevons' book was recommended to me by a humanities student who felt I was always on the losing end in our late-night discussions. I have been hooked on formal methods and methodological issues ever since. My interests have traveled over time across research questions in philosophy, mathematics, linguistics, computer science, and cognitive science, but always with the logician's mind-set.

Discovering new logical or other formal patterns in ordinary activities is still a constant source of surprise to me. They provide a new perspective on, and even an *enhanced experience* of, many things—a bit like the heightened perception of music once you know some structure. Frankly, I hate the term 'formal' here, because it sounds ugly, and makes me think of lifeless pedantry, or even the formaline fluid used for preserving corpses. The following may be the personal idiosyncrasy that predestines people to become logicians, but to me mathematical structures are *beautiful*. They increase enjoyment of whatever one does. So, when I see formulas (within limits), my reaction is the opposite of many formula-haters: I see an enriched version of reality, and even something more. I deeply believe that formal structure also frees us from the shackles of an unreflected reality. It provides the hinges that we can use for *changing* things, devising new languages and new practices of proof, communication, or argumentation. Formal methods to me are inextricably tied up with *creativity* and the historical process of adding new repertoire to human culture.

Of course, this is an idealized picture, and I do encounter lots of applications of 'formal methods' which I find unutterably dreary. The 'enhancement' can also work the other way, just as with drugs: boring people get even more boring when you give them formulas.

What example(s) from your work illustrates the role formal methods can play in philosophy?

My book *The Logic of Time* (1983) used formal methods to analyze temporal arguments from the philosophical literature. But it also used them to construct several *new ontologies* for time, especially interval-based ones outside of the standard mathematical canon, increasing the range of temporal pictures that we can use in imagining and presenting things. Since time is so pervasive in all our activities, any logical insight into its structure and representation immediately percolates across a lot of disciplines. The book is still selling, even though it is not an easy read. From continuing private reactions by readers, sometimes from quite surprising places, it seems to me that it still manages to attract congenial spirits who think like me.

My work on logical syntax and semantics of natural language (*Essays in Logical Semantics* 1986, *Language in Action* 1991) had a similar flavor. I was deeply impressed by the work of Barwise and others around 1980 of stepping away from sterile antagonistic conceptions of 'logical versus linguistic form', and it seemed that every month, beautiful new structures were falling into my lap in quantification, and the general combinatorics of natural language. Moreover, this work led to a new view of the 'natural logic' inside natural language, with elegant calculi of *monotonicity reasoning*, as opposed to just the predicate-logical canon: including a reappraisal of traditional pre-Fregean logic. But again, one should never be a slave to reality. One strand in that work was my use of *semantic automata* as evaluation procedures for quantifiers, which led to an upward hierarchy of complexity that certainly transcends the usual repertoire of natural languages. I notice with interest that some of my work from this phase is being taken up to-day by neuro-scientists in experimental settings.

Finally, my current work is on *dynamic-epistemic logics* of information carrying actions, and more general design of logics for *interaction* (*Exploring Logical Dynamics* 1996, *Logic in Games* 1999). This, too, shows all the above features. I am surprised by seeing logical structures in information flow, communication, and games. I see beauty and regularity in conversations, discussions, and even the wildest argumentative outbursts at department meetings, and other venues where we meet to disagree. Moreover, the dynamic stance making action and interactive processes a core topic for explicit theorizing beyond static propositions and 'meanings' has an interesting synchronicity in philosophy, logic, artificial intelligence, and computer science—and I am sure it will spread still further. My current focus is on the interface between *logic and game theory*, since games seem the interactive model par excellence, and in their restricted compass, they put familiar notions from mathematical and philosophical logic in a clear new light.

Also, in doing this sort of research putting actions at centre stage, I am very much taken with the idea of not only analyzing, but also *designing* new 'social software', in the recently emerging sense. We can enrich our social repertoire of behaviour, and in that way, also become more free as human agents.

One final aspect of formal structure that intrigues me here is its recurrence across disciplines, and hence the potential for *hybrids*. For instance, when Montague stated his famous Thesis that there is no difference in principle between natural and formal languages, he merely made an analytical observation. But once you see the analogy, one can also cross-breed the two kinds of language to form hybrids, and we do, both in science, law, an other practices. Moreover, the same formal structures also occur in a third realm: programming languages and other media in computer science. In a non-analytical but rather activist mode, insights like these drive the current interaction of humans and machines.

What is the proper role of philosophy in relation to other disciplines?

Philosophy should surprise us with illuminating observations from a wider mental space than that of other disciplines. Good examples of that continuing power are most diverse, ranging from analytical philosophy of language to social philosophy. My list of favorites, in addition to philosophical logicians such as Carnap, Prior, Geach, or Hintikka, would contain many general philosophers. In my student years and later on, I learnt to see my familiar world in a different light through encounters with texts such as Kant's *Grundlegung zur Metaphysik der Sitten*, as a model for clear thinking about moral principles to live by, Ryle's *The Concept of Mind*, as a paradigm of analytical thinking about oneself and one's cognitive activities, Habermas' *Theorie der Kommunikativen Kompetenz*, which combined themes from continental and analytical traditions into a new view of what genuine dialogue and debate are about, and the Rawls–Nozick books (*A Theory of Justice*, and *Anarchy, State, and Utopia*) as a show-case of high-quality debate about our society, whose different stances transcend the usual political bickering.

Even so, I do not think that philosophy has any special privileged realm of themes, or even a privileged method of doing business. I think of philosophy as a *spice*, which enhances other fare— not as a sufficient source of intellectual nourishment by itself. It makes discussions about the foundations of the sciences more enlightened, it lifts political discourse to a level beyond opinion-mongering and scoring points, and so on. But, just try to eat the content of a pepper box!

What do you consider the most neglected topics and/or contributions in late 20th century philosophy?

Early 20th century philosophy exposed itself enthusiastically to influences from the most exciting scientific break-throughs of the day: in physics, and the social sciences. By contrast, I feel that modern philosophy has largely ignored similar challenges from what is arguably the contemporary counterpart of these scientific developments: the rise of *informatics* ('computer science', in the unfortunate North-American terminology) and *cognitive science*. Issues of information, computation, complexity, games, or interaction, have hardly affected core philosophy, even though they seem central intellectual notions. I am editing a *Handbook of the Philosophy of Information*, with philosopher, computer scientist, and entrepreneur Pieter Adriaans, which tries to remedy this situation. Likewise, the success of 'anti-psychologism' in philosophy around 1900 erected barriers against open contacts with empirical findings about who we are and what we do, which we are breaking down only to-day with the greatest of efforts. Students of philosophy are often, perversely, even taught to cherish the defining barriers for information flow into the field. It *now* seems time to liberate ourselves from this self-imposed ignorance (did not Someone say this before?), and look at what really happens as reported in cognitive science.

Another thing which I sorely miss is a more general cultural and political avant-garde role of philosophy. The 18th century Enlightenment was driven by endless debate among (often, would-be) 'philosophes' discussing about every subject under the sun without regard for established tradition. Of course, nowadays, we would bar many of these people from our dignified debates, as they have no Ph.D. degrees, let alone tenured jobs. But perhaps as a consequence, I find philosophy conspicuously absent from debate about the genuine burning issues of to-day, including religion, immigration, and so on. And in those cases where philosophers do participate, they seem to represent a somewhat narrow segment of predictable politically correct opinion, rather than iconoclastic irreverence for any kind of entrenched position.

What are the most important open problems in philosophy and what are the prospects for progress?

In line with my answer to 3, I see no special 'philosophical problems' that call for investigation. Philosophers should be found wherever the burning intellectual issues are in contemporary science and society. And they should be radically antagonistic to quiet inward-looking backwaters of so-called 'typical philosophical research programs'. Most philosophical 'reflection' going on there is in the form of mirages.

I am also unsure whether there is progress in philosophy in the same sense as in the sciences. Of course, the repertoire of collective intellectual experience increases, and perhaps, thinking of my own niche, the logical apparatus gets increasingly sophisticated. But in a sense, staying as alert to new issues as the great philosophers that we admire is enough progress to me!

2

Brian F. Chellas

Professor Emeritus of Philosophy

University of Calgary, Canada

I do not know when formal methods first attracted me. My initial awareness of them came in Robert Beard's introductory logic course at Florida State University. But already as a youngster my heart was set on a career as a private detective, and I think my interest in solving mysteries predisposed me to eventual fascination with the logical enterprise.

That is by way of what might be termed a rational account of my beguilement. Years of reflection, and not a little therapy, have persuaded me of an explanation in causal terms. My childhood experience of a broken home and the realization during my teenage years that my mother was an alcoholic engendered a powerful need for order, stability, and predictability. It dominated my thinking until recently, when I left the academy and began playing jazz guitar in earnest. But even in music my enchantment with order and logicality occasionally surfaces. It showed itself early on when, while completing my dissertation, I wrote *Chord Systems for the Guitar* (1968). And in the past few years I have spent a good deal of time looking for a systematic account of the modes of the alt scale. (When I find it I intend to publish the result as "Modal Logic: An Introduction".)

As a graduate student at Stanford University my interests veered toward philosophy of language and, in particular, Donald Davidson's insight that a Tarski-type theory of truth is a paradigm of a theory of meaning. To better understand this idea I spent a year learning as much logic as I could, and ultimately conjoined logic and philosophy of language in my thesis, *The Logical Form of Imperatives* (1969), written under the direction of Dana Scott.

Beginning with the dissertation and an offspring article, "Imperatives" (1971), I directed much of my intellectual effort toward questions in deontic logic. I quickly came to see that the deontic logics of the day were fundamentally wrong (my theory of imperatives being a singular exception!), inasmuch as they were construed as normal modal logics and explicated by means of "all possible worlds" interpretations. (In a normal modal logic, necessity is closed under modus ponens and the necessitation of any validity is itself valid.) I was dissatisfied too with concomitant accounts of conditional obligation, especially as these were deployed in the bewitching Paradox of the Good Samaritan. The principal results of my unease are contained in a paper, "The Story of O" (1973), and the article "Conditional Obligation" (1974). The latter was based on a general account of conditionality that appeared in "Basic Conditional Logic", published a year later (1975). These themes are examined as well in my textbook *Modal Logic: An Introduction* (1980).

Late in my career I returned to the topic of action and to an operator for "seeing to it that" or "bringing it about that" that I had introduced in my dissertation. The chief results were "Time and Modality in the Logic of Agency" (1992) and "On Bringing It About" (1995). It behooves me to say that I do not believe any of the logics of moral obligation proffered to date satisfactorily address the Good Samaritan Paradox. I have faith, nevertheless, that this and other problems in deontic logic and the logic of action will sooner or later succumb to logical analysis.

The other strain in my research has less of a thematic nature and consists mostly of publications on various problems in modal logic. Of these I would single out "The Completeness of Monotonic Modal Logics" (1975, with Audrey McKinney) and "Modal Logics in the Vicinity of S1" (1996, with Krister Segerberg). The paper with McKinney gives the first correct possible worlds completeness proof for a class of weaker-than-normal modal logics; that with Segerberg likewise provides the first correct such proofs for some of the more difficult systems due to C.I. Lewis and others. The conclusions in another paper, "Modalities in Normal Systems Containing the S5 Axiom" (1979), led me to the conviction that Schiller Joe Scroggs's theorem about extensions of the modal logic S5 could be generalized to the case in which the schema expressing that necessity implies truth is not always present. My University of Calgary dissertation student Michael Nagle proved this handily.

On the question of the proper role of philosophy in relation to other disciplines my answer is the one so often given—that philosophy goes hand in hand with inquiry everywhere in the arts and the sciences. Foundational questions are the most obvious area for philosophical exploration. Because I think there is no real demarcation between philosophy and science or art, I ever esteem collaborations between philosophers and thinkers in other disciplines.

When it comes to philosophy in the earlier part of the twentieth century, many contributions are beyond doubt, beginning in 1905 with Bertrand Russell's theory of definite descriptions. Then there are Alfred Tarski's definitions of truth and the theorems of Kurt Gödel, Alonzo Church, Alan Turing, and Paul Cohen. I mention these because they show much about scope and limits in logic and mathematics, and thus much about the potential of formal methods in fields of inquiry such as artificial intelligence.

Beyond the century's midpoint the perspective grows hazy, though here I would mention the efforts of the analytical school with respect to ethical language and concepts, and also the seemingly ever more fruitful connections between philosophy and computing and neuropsychology. And of course there was Edmund Gettier's counterexample to justified-true-belief definitions of knowledge, which entirely reset the agenda for epistemology.

To make judgments about what topics or contributions have been neglected over the past 100 years or so is more difficult for me. In philosophy of language the notions of parataxis and indexicality in connection with analysis of quotation and indirect discourse, for example, have been paid insufficient attention from a logical point of view. More generally, it seems to me that there has not been enough concern for questions of scope and limits in disciplines beyond philosophy. The relative paucity of such efforts may exist moreover within philosophy. It always appears to me that aesthetics offers a dearth of exactitude. The subject seems unruly: perhaps it is simply not amenable to formal methods. If this is so, it would be good to know why.

I connect importance with urgency, so for the most part I do not think some philosophical problems are more important than others, or even more important than problems in areas beyond philosophy. If it is a question of urgency, however, then moral and political questions are preeminent. If nothing more, resolution of such issues might enhance our possibilities for thinking freely and fruitfully about other things, such as logic.

3

Anne Fagot-Largeault

PhD, MD, Professeur

Collège de France, Paris
Chaire de philosophie des sciences biologiques et médicales
Membre de l'Institut (Académie des Sciences)

Why were you initially drawn to formal methods?

I was initially drawn to formal methods because in the nineteen-sixties they were in the spirit of the times. I shall try to say here why I was drawn to a certain kind of formal methods.

In 1966–67 I was recruited to serve as an assistant to Pr. Gilbert Simondon at the university of Paris (Sorbonne). I was supposed to teach philosophy to psychology students. It could mean educating them in the intellectual fashions of the day: psychoanalysis, structuralism, phenomenology[1]. (I did that, too.) However Simondon would not pay much attention to ideologies. I felt a strong need to learn more about real science, and about philosophy of science. I flirted with the beginnings of a degree in medicine. At the end of the year I told my supervisor that I decidedly wanted to spend a year learning mathematical logic at UC Berkeley. Although he commented that he did not understand how a *woman* could be interested in such abstract topics as logic and mathematics, he helped me get a leave of absence from the Sorbonne. I applied to Berkeley. I got a kind letter from Pr. William Craig, saying that he would be on sabbatical: he had told his friend Pr. Patrick Suppes about my request, he recommended that I should apply to

---

[1] Some of the leading books were then: Sigmund Freud's *Metapsychology* (1915, Engl. Standard Ed. 1957, Fr. retransl. 1968); Kurt Goldstein's *Der Aufbau des Organismus* (1934, Fr. tr. 1951); Jean-Paul Sartre's critique of psychoanalysis in *L'être et le néant. Essai d'ontologie phénoménologique* (1943) and *La transcendance de l'Ego* (1936, 1965); Maurice Merleau-Ponty's *Phénoménologie de la perception* (1945) and *La structure du comportement* (1949); Claude Lévi-Strauss's *Anthropologie structurale* (1958).

Stanford. I wrote to Suppes. He answered that he was expecting me. In September, 1967, I began my graduate studies at Stanford, in the special 'Logic and Philosophy of Science' program.

It was a cultural shock. As a student at the Ecole Normale Supérieure in Paris, my training had been in the humanities. There was, however, a traditional link between philosophy and mathematics. After specializing in philosophy, one course in science was required prior to the *agrégation de philosophie*[2] : I had taken mathematics from Pr. Marc Zamansky. Then I had taught philosophy to high school students for five years. I knew Plato, Descartes and Kant far better than even Aristotle's syllogistics. The reference book in logic at the university of Paris had been Goblot's[3]. From Pr. Jules Vuillemin I had heard about Russell and Carnap, but Vuillemin's course had been marginal. I had also tried learning logic by myself, using Dopp's textbook and Tarski's *Introduction to Logic*[4], with very little benefit. In the Fall of 1967 at Stanford, Pat Suppes' course on *Elementary logic* was enlightenment.

Subsequently I learned logic and metamathematics from Gallin, Feferman, Dana Scott, Ehrenfeucht, Kreisel, Hintikka, Dag Prawitz, van Heijenoort, and others. Suppes introduced us to decision theory. I also took courses in statistics and probability in the Mathematics Department. Suppes was my director of studies. After the Stanford 'prelims' I had to choose a dissertation topic. I was interested in the 'logic' of causal explanations, had read Piaget, was tempted by causal (modal) logics. "Don't waste your time with modal logic, advised Suppes, go to probability theory"— maybe the best piece of advice I ever received. I took my PhD in 1971 and went back to France.

I had left France and the (one) Sorbonne before the 1968 students' revolt, on return I found a university of Paris split into thirteen pieces, and a post-revolutionary academic life scattered between strikes and bursts of postmodernism. While teaching philosophy (including mathematical logic) at the university of Paris-12, I became a medical student at the same university, and looked for real cases of causal inquiry. I was curious about etiological diagnosis in the clinic, etiological theories of diseases, and the methodology used by epidemiologists to comfirm or disqualify hypotheses

---

[2] Competitive examination for the recruitement of high school teachers.
[3] Edmond Goblot, *Traité de logique*, 1917 (7th edition 1941).
[4] Joseph Dopp, *Leçons de logique formelle*, Louvain, 3 vols (1950); Alfred Tarski, *Introduction à la logique*, Fr. tr. Paris & Louvain (1960).

involving causal links. I got interested in the way pathologists during post-mortem examinations reasoned about the causes of death. I found out that there had been international lists of causes of death, revised every ten years, and that according to international experts in charge of establishing those lists, old age was *not* a (proper) cause of death. I also discovered that, during the 19th Century, starting with Laplace, a tradition of French mathematicians had written openly (and brilliantly) on the "search for causes through probabilities". I became convinced that, if there was an epistemology of medicine, its formal methodology lied there.

Back in the US one summer, I had the opportunity to discuss the matter with several colleagues. Pat Suppes was particularly enthusiastic about Laplace's causal analyses, initially based on Thomas Bayes's *Essay*[5], further developed into a typology of causes ('absolute' propensity *vs.* conditional probability, constant or 'regular' influences *vs.* 'disruptive' factors)[6]. Wesley Salmon was intrigued by the claim that writing 'old age' as the cause of death on a death certificate was bad standard: he encouraged me to dig further into that. Within Europe I also had an exchange with the British historian of science Alistair Crombie, as he was in the process of writing what would become the section on probabilistic reasoning of his *Styles of Scientific Thinking*[7].

Such exchanges gave me enough momentum to resist the pressure from colleagues who insisted that, were I to persit in doing philosophy of science—while medicine could hardly be taken as science, and in working on causality, I should at least use the analytic tools of causal (modal) logic. Indeed, I gave a course on modal logics to philosophy students, while corresponding with van Heijenoort, who then was at Harvard, working on the semantics of other than classical logics. I had always be skeptical of the possibility to reduce causal relations to classical implication or deductive inference. The covering-law deductive model was clearly unsatisfactory. There are hardly any universal laws in the life sciences, yet there are many good causal claims, and the properties of the claimed causal links are not the properties of ordinary implication. Yet I was well aware of the research on other types of

---

[5] Thomas Bayes, 1763, 'An essay towards solving a problem in the doctrine of chances', *Philosophical Transactions ... London* (1764); Laplace, *Mémoire sur la probabilité des causes par les événements* (1774).

[6] Laplace, *Essai philosophique sur les probabilités* (1819).

[7] Alistair C. Crombie, *Styles of Scientific Thinking in the European Tradition*, 3 vols (published 1994); Part VI: 'Probabilistic and statistical analysis'.

logical implication[8], and also aware of the abundant literature on the counterfactual analysis of causation, from Nelson Goodman to David Lewis and Robert Stalnaker[9]. Any fervent reader of Leibniz can only be seduced by the semantics of possible worlds. I was especially fond of Burks' attempt at catching the 'logic' of causal propositions through the formalism of finite cellular automata[10]. But the logical apparatus needed for approximating probability estimates through modal systems, while presupposing a "set of causal laws governing the universe", looked preposterous with regard to the elegant and sophisticated statistical methods commonly used by researchers working in epidemiology or evolutionary biology, who could identify causal links without having to rely on alleged causal laws.

When applying to study at Berkeley, I had initially assumed that philosophy of science was logic of science, an assumption very much in the tradition of the Vienna circle, relayed by Alfred Tarski and the Berkeley school. I ended up at Stanford, took a probabilistic turn, chose to work in the field of life sciences, and accepted the bet that in the philosophy of life sciences formal methods were to be mathematical methods.

What example(s) from your work illustrates the role formal methods can play in philosophy?

In order to test the conjecture that there was something to the "search for causes through probabilities", I started with a reconstruction of the line of reasoning 19th Century mathematicians had followed in order to find *why*, in the human species, male births outnumbered female births. The fact of the *sex ratio* being unequal at birth was noticed and reported by John Graunt (1661). Arbuthnot (1710) justified it by a controversial teleological argument. Laplace whipped out Arbuthnot's argument, and clarified the research methodology: first, make sure that the observed difference is not an effect of chance (of statistical fluctuations); then,

---

[8] Alan R. Anderson & Nuel D. Belnap, *Entailment. The Logic of Relevance and Necessity*, vol. 1 (1975).

[9] Nelson Goodman, 'The problem of counterfactual conditionals', *Journal of Philosophy* (1947); David K. Lewis, *Counterfactuals* (1973), and his paper on 'Causation' followed by a debate with Bernard Berofsky and Jaegwon Kim in *The Journal of Philosophy* (1973); Robert C. Stalnaker, 'Probability and conditionals', *Philosophy of Science* (1970).

[10] Arthur W. Burks, *Chance, Cause, reason. An Inquiry into the Nature of Scientific Evidence* (1977).

if it can't be, spell out all possible causes of the difference, and pick the most probable cause using Bayes' theorem. After Laplace the case was rehearsed, and the methodology discussed, by Poisson[11], Quételet, Cournot, Bertrand, Poincaré, Borel. For epistemologists there are at least two points of interest in the matters discussed. First, the definition of a cause, as a factor C which raises the probability of an effect E significantly above its *a priori* probability (a C such that $P(E/C) > P(E)$, or a factor which 'makes a difference' for the occurrence of E). Second, the question whether there is a relation between the (epistemic) probability of the causal hypothesis, and the measure of the (objective) strength of the causal influence.

As a trained medical practitioner, I was naturally interested in elucidating the mental process of medical reasoning. Just like the inductive process, or the process of pattern recognition, or the process of finding the class in which some particular sample fits, diagnosis does not go from (general) knowledge to the particular case, it goes reverse, from particular signs and symptoms exhibited by an individual patient to the disease affecting the patient. The art of diagnosis is heuristic, an art of guessing, of perceiving a generality in the particular. Moreover, in medicine, the guess is hypothetical more often than categorical. In the nineteen-seventies, there was a reflection on the diagnostic process, on account of health care institutions wanting to save money, and improve the quality of care, through the development of computer-assisted diagnosis. Several systems were being experimented, such as the one in Leeds (UK) for the diagnosis of acute abdominal syndroms, or the more ambitious 'internist' in Pittsburgh, aimed at modelling the reasoning of a competent general practitioner. Three types of heuristics could be identified: statistical methods (derived from multiple regression techniques), probabilistic (Bayesian) methods, and the methods inspired by 'fuzzy' logic. The merits of the various methods and systems were discussed during a joined British and French symposium at the university of Paris-12 (1979), to which I contributed a paper on Bayesian inference[12]. I contributed several other studies in that area, including one on computer-assisted medical diagnosis[13]. What I want to emphasize here is

---

[11] Denis Poisson, 'Mémoire sur la proportion des naissances des filles et des garçons', *Mémoire de l'Académie ... Paris* (1830).

[12] Fagot, ed., *Médecine et probabilités*, Paris (1982).

[13] 'Le concept de maladie sous-jacent aux tentatives d'informatisation du diagnostic médical', *History and Philosophy of the Life Sciences*, Suppl. Vol.

this. The dream (or nightmare) of typing one's symptoms and getting a competent diagnosis from an oracle-computer has now faded away. The 'logics' of diagnostic inference should certainly be taught to medical students. But from the 1990s on, computer imaging has replaced computer reasoning. It is a major epistemological change, that in neurology, for example, the very fine and delicate art of inferring lesions from observed signs has beeen replaced with visualising the lesions directly on a screen.

Cause of death statistics are published every year by the World Health Organization. That is the modest result of a gigantic and patient international effort which goes back over more than a hundred years, to collect etiological data about each single human death, name and classify all possible causes in a manner homogeneous enough throughout all cultures and languages to allow the data to be treated statistically in a meaningful way, code the data, compute, and come out with a picture from which healh policies can be drawn, aimed at designing (effective, *i.e.* causal) interventions to curb human mortality. A first sketch of the contribution I made to the analysis of that scientific endeavour was presented at the 1978 international Pisa conference on the History and Philosophy of Science[14]. A more detailed study was part of my French Doctorat d'Etat[15], and was published as a book[16]. Several problems in epistemology are considered. The certification of causes of death (at the bedside, or wherever a death occurs) raised the problem of the qualification of the certifier, and of his understanding of the (common) notion of cause; is was partly resolved by the circulation of a standard model of "medical certificate of cause of death", inviting the practitioner to distinguish between the "disease or condition directly leading to death", "antecedent conditions", and "other significant conditions contributing to the death". To clarify the vocabulary, an International Classification

---

10 (1988).

[14]'Probabilities and causes: on life tables, causes of death and etiological diagnoses', in: J. Hintikka, D. Gruender, E. Agazzi, eds., *Probabilistic Thinking, Thermodynamics, and the Interaction of the History and Philosophy of Science*, Proceedings ..., Vol. 2 (1980), Dordrecht : Reidel, Synthese Library n ° 145.

[15]The Doctorat d'Etat was analogous to the German Habilitation: the required degree to become a full Professor at the University.

[16]*Les causes de la mort. Histoire naturelle et facteurs de risque*, Paris: Vrin (1989). (I had a contract for the publication of that book in the *Synthese Library*, but for financial reasons there never was a possibility to have it properly translated into English.)

of Diseases and related Health Problems, published by the WHO in several languages, and periodically revised, serves as the reference for both medical certifiers and statisticians; among the recurrent difficulties is the fact that the classification must change in order to reflect the evolution of medical knowledge, but no changes can be introduced without compromising the comparability of statistics. The task of statisticians is to compile and analyse the data; among their major contributions there has been the notion of a *risk factor*, the investigation of the effects of specific risk factors such as cigarette smoking, occupational exposition to asbestos, poverty, and the designation of "avoidable risks"[17]. How did clinical causal research compare with epidemiological research, that is, was there a way of bridging the clinical approach to etiological diagnosis and treatment, such as Louis' approach when he showed that blood letting made no difference for people with pneumonia, and the probabilistic approach, pioneered by Daniel Bernoulli and E. Duvillard, when they established that inoculation against smallpox was indeed an efficient way to prevent the disease? Another source of perplexity was to identify operational criteria for incriminating a causal factor, in cases where the facts are so rare that no statistics is available; the problem was raised about the detection of rare and toxic adverse reactions to pharmaceuticals, a domain where "algorithms of causal imputation" were proposed. Finally, it seemed that establishing a causal link required a mixture of three ingredients: historical criteria (chronology), statistical criteria (regularities), and judgmental criteria (involving talent, expertise, and decisional capability). That is to say, formal criteria alone do not suffice.

More recently I have been interested in the formalization of causal chains, cycles and cascades, such notions being increasingly popular in biological publications. Of course there are many other areas for formal research. I am aware of genomic science taking advantage of high-performance computing and bioinformatics to increase the throughput of DNA-sequencing, of taxonomists using computerized strategies in their attempts at classifying living beings, and of theoretically oriented biologists (such as the participants in the Los Alamos conferences) or philosophically oriented mathematicians (such as René Thom) trying to model the processes of biological development using sophisticated mathemat-

---

[17] cf. the famous publication by Richard Doll & Richard Peto, *The Causes of Cancer* (1981).

ics or methods of "emergent computation". I myself contributed a paper on the medical approach of causation within complex systems[18], and a chapter on emergence, in which I try to go beyond the mere phenomenological description of emergent evolutionary processes[19]. But I am not clear about the frontier between speculative biology and the use of formal methods to clarify epistemological issues in the life sciences.

What is the proper role of philosophy in relation to other disciplines?

I cannot answer the question in general. On the relations between philosophy and architecture, criminal law, economics, or whatever other disciplines there may be, I have opinions, but no special competence. I do philosophy of *science*. As a philosopher, the professionals I relate to are essentially people working in the fields of *biology* and *medicine*. In concrete terms it means that I have had a long experience of dealing with medical practitioners, while practicing medicine one day a week at the hospital, in the emergency room; that I have been a member of numerous committees for the evaluation of scientific research protocols; that currently, within my institution, I naturally cooperate with biologists, for instance in the conception and organization of interdisciplinary research projects and/or colloquia. That is the background here for my attempt to answer this question. I'll make three points.

First, we philosophers are lucky to live through an epoch in which philosophy is wanted. Many philosophers of science are currently busy trying to meet a *demand* for philosophy, coming from the scientific community and/or from society at large[20]. The first World Conference on Science, jointly organized by the United Nations Educational, Scientific and Cultural Organization (UNESCO) and the International Council for Science (ICSU), met

---

[18] 'Approche médicale de la causalité dans les systèmes complexes', *Archives internationales de physiologie et de biochimie*, Liège (1986).

[19] Chapter 8 in: D. Andler, A. Fagot-Largeault, B. Saint-Sernin, *Philosophie des sciences*, vol. 2., Paris (2002).

[20] Following a request from the French Academy of Sciences, I have just written a chapter on 'epidemiology and causality', to be included in a scientific report on 'epidemiology, how to develop it, and what is the role of mathematics in its development': Académie des sciences, Dir. A.-J. Valleron, *Epidemiologie: conditions de son développement et rôle des mathématiques*, Rapport Science et Technologie, Paris (in press).

in Budapest in 1999. Some 150 countries were represented and agreed on its conclusions. The Declaration adopted by the conference states that "Science curricula should include science ethics, as well as training in the history and philosophy of science and its cultural impact"[21]. Being recognized as useful contributors to the harmonious and responsible progress of scientific research and development (R&D) worldwide is encouraging and gratifying for philosophers. It does not imply that philosophers are scientists, or that scientists are philosophers; it says that they complement each other.

My second point is about a way of telling the story of philosophy's striptease. The relationship between science and philosophy is classically envisaged on the basis of Descartes' famous statement: *"Thus, all Philosophy is like a tree, of which Metaphysics is the root, Physics the trunk, and all the other sciences the branches that grow out of this trunk, which are reduced to three principal, namely, Medicine, Mechanics, and Ethics. By the science of Morals, I understand the highest and most perfect which, presupposing an entire knowledge of the other sciences, is the last degree of wisdom."*[22] There is no doubt that, for Descartes, mechanics and medicine are parts of philosophy, and that, again for Descartes, there is continuity (and no break) from the most fundamental philosophical reflection (as in the *Meditations*) to the most helpful and down-to-earth applications of science, such as the polishing of eyeglasses. Dilthey[23] tried to show how the philosophical tree was stripped off and lost its branches, as *Naturwissenschaften* (such as physics) from the 17th century on, then *Geisteswissenschaften* (such as psychology, in the course of the 19th century), freed themselves and became autonomous, dropping the metaphysical presuppositions inherited, *via* medieval scholastics, from the ancient theory of substantial forms, and catching up with a methodology of causal explanation, to finally endorse a *historical* style. I hold that Dilthey was misinterpreted by those who claim that philosophy, which initially included all sciences, was ripped of its contents and emptied out, as the sciences one by one went away, and who make ironical comments on the vacuity of what remains after the sciences have left the bosom which originally sheltered

---

[21] Unesco, *Declaration on science and the use of scientific knowledge*, Art. 41 (1999).

[22] René Descartes, *Principes de la philosophie*, Lettre-préface (1644).

[23] Wilhelm Dilthey, *Einleitung in die Geisteswissenschaften* (1883) [*Gesammelte Schriften*, Bd. 1].

them. The austerity cure through which science conquerred its *positivity*, namely the extrusion of metaphysical preconceptions (ready-made explanations) did not preclude remaining faithful to the philosophical ambition (inherent in the cartesian program) to both draw a more exact picture of the world, and contribute to building a more hospitable world. Dilthey's argument is quite compatible with such an hypothesis.

This brings me to my third point. Let us accept the hypothesis that the endeavours of scientific research are moved by a philosophical impulse. The Socratic (*maieutic*) role of philosophy may be viewed as the role of a midwife or obstetrician[24]. The role of philosophers is not to be scientifically creative. Scientific researchers have to be creative, they strive to make discoveries and eventually win a Nobel prize, or have some of their inventions patented. They call on philosophers either to ask them questions that may help clarify or disentangle delicate theoretical issues, or to confront the intrinsic normativity of (bio)technologies with other sources of normativity.

What do you consider the most neglected topics and/or contributions in late 20th century philosophy?

I see a cluster of neglected topics at the junction between theoretical and practical philosophy of science and technology. The contributions of Simondon and subsequent philosophers of technology are not sufficiently known.

The results of two modest empirical studies may serve as an introduction to my tentative answer to question 4. In 2001 the French Philosophical Society (SFP) celebrated its centenary. A retrospective survey of all conferences delivered during the SFP meetings evidenced the fact that prior to world war II, scientists and philosophers communicated easily, and many outstanding scientists and/or philosophers of science were invited to address philosophers, while after world war II conferences delivered by scientists, let alone engineers, are scarce[25]. Another piece of evidence comes from a survey in 1999 (in France) of the data files of dissertation topics: a majority of doctoral theses deal with points in history of philosophy, or an author; a minority addresses a philo-

---

[24]Plato, *Theaetetus*, 149 a.

[25]Bernard Bourgeois, in: *Bulletin de la Société française de philosophie*, numéro du centenaire, 2001, Paris (2003).

sophical *problem* directly; among the latter, only a very small minority addresses a problem in philosophy of science and/or technology. The very field in which there is a demand for philosophy is relatively neglected by philosophers, and those philosophers who are attracted to that field oftentimes prefer to engage into *theoretical* rather than *practical* philosophy of science or technology. In the case of life sciences, it appears to be due to a misconception about the nature of contemporary scientific research.

The philosophers' milieu tends to be contemptuous of technology, if not technophobic. Philosophers generally assume that proper (bio)science is speculative (cognitive), having as its outcome the publication of papers in scientific journals such as *Nature*, while the practical aspects of scientific activity are mere applications leading to byproducts, such as genetically modified crops or mice. A dignified theoretical discipline, philosophy of science dissects the mental processes going on in the heads of scientists, and analyses the strategies by which knowledge is acquired (data processing, formulation of hypotheses, design of experimental protocols, validation of results, concept formation, structure of theories). Left for engineers, philosophy of technology is another discipline altogether, dealing with bizarre ontologies, artifacts, cyborgs, dreams of teleportation, and actual environmental hazards. Philosophy of science and philosophy of technology have ignored each other for a long time: one dealt with (noble) ideas, the other dealt with (humble) things.

This is not an accurate representation of contemporary science. Researchers not only produce abstract knowledge, they produce concrete beings. Technology has been integrated into research strategies. A constructed (transgenic, knock-outed) mouse is a living hypothesis, its physiological functioning is a test of hypotheses. It is a real living being, too. That natural science nowadays is *technoscience*, and that the isolation of the philosophies of science from the philosophies of technology is unfortunate—and outdated, is a thesis strongly argued by the Belgian philosopher Gilbert Hottois[26]. It is not a new observation altogether. When Berthelot, the 19th century chemist, launched "synthetic chemistry", he commented that chemistry is not only about analysing the natural properties of substances existing in nature (as Lavoisier said); chemistry is also about synthesizing new substances, that

---

[26] Gilbert Hottois, *Philosophies des sciences, philosophies des techniques*, Paris (2004).

are compatible with the 'laws of nature', but that nature itself did not actualize: "Chemistry creates its object of study"[27]. Chemical science investigates not only existing molecules, but also possible molecules; it opens new ways and creates new entities. Contemporary biology and medicine follow the same path. Not only do they investigate the actual evolution of species on our planet, and the mechanisms of actual diseases affecting human populations, but they ambition to engineer genetically modified drought-resistant maize, and to become able to treat diabetic patients with transplants of human cells obtained by the technique of nuclear transfer. The claims of what is already called "synthetic biology" to "make never-before-seen living things", to confound the taxonomists' systems of classifying species, and to blur the philosophers' distinction between the natural and the artificial[28], may be exaggerated, nay quixotic. But the fact is there: science today is hardly dissociable from technology, and the engineering of human cells is as much a tool for fundamental research as it is a hope for curative medicine.

Claude Debru[29] has reflected that the territory explored by (bio)sciences extends between two frontiers, which should attract the philosopher's curiosity: one one side, the frontier of the impossible (that which the 'laws of nature' prohibit), on the other side the frontier of the undesirable (that which, although feasible, we would prefer not to introduce into our world). Theoretically-oriented biologists and epistemologists will be interested in exploring the first frontier, and center their inquiry around the question: what are the intrinsic 'logics' (if any) of natural processes, for example, of biological evolution on earth?[30] Practically-oriented biologists and philosophers will worry about the objectives and justification of research programmes, consequences of research practices, the uses made of scientific inventions or discoveries, and the destiny of technical objects once incorporated into natural and/or social environments. On either side formal methods may be of help: for instance, computer-assisted modelling of evolutionary processes in theoretical philosophy of science, and the theories of rational choice in practical philosophy of science. On neither side

---

[27]Marcelin Berthelot, *La synthèse chimique*, Paris (1860).

[28]See *online* a paper by Paul Elias, last updated August 2005, and other articles on the Internet under the headline "synthetic biology".

[29]Claude Debru, *Le possible et les biotechnologies*, Paris (2003).

[30]See for example: Michael Ghiselin, *Metaphysics and the Origin of Species*, Albany: State Univ of New York (1997).

formal methods will be sufficient. About such topics, as far as I know, the most decisive, and insufficiently known contribution is that of Simondon[31]. He raised the problems of technology transfer and capacity building, of scientific and technological education as a condition of development, of the responsibility of philosophers in helping integrate technological culture into general culture, of the relative autonomy (and potential universality) of scientific and technological normativity with respect to the variability of cultural norms.

What are the most important open problems in philosophy and what are the prospects for progress?

Just as Hilbert did in 1900, in Paris, on the occasion of the 2nd international mathematical congress, distinguished philosophers have recently attempted to list a series of problems as a program for (formal or other) philosophers at the turn of the 21st century. I feel embarrassed by the exercice. What I propose is only tentative and stamped with perplexity. Three problems will be pointed out (respectively in ontology, epistemology, and practical philosophy). I shall not hazard a guess about the prospects for progress. I tend to assume that philosophical questions are more apt to mature than to be resolved.

In recent years we have been plagued by a battle between simplistic Darwinian conformism on one side, and creationism or its substitutes (intelligent design) on the other side. We urgently need to elaborate an ontology of becoming, independent of prefabricated ideologies. This is an old philosophical problem. It can be traced from Aristotle to Bergson and Whitehead. The lessons we learn nowadays from astrophysics, evolutionary biology, the biology of development, the psychology of learning, are a rich material for a renewal of the reflection on becoming. They have inspired vast syntheses[32], perhaps a bit too systematic or far-flung. The literature, in science and philosophy, abounds with descriptions of evolutionary processes. The problem is to find out whether it is possible to go beyond phenomenological accounts and/or historical narratives. Formal methods designed to engender or

---

[31] Gilbert Simondon, *Du mode d'existence des objets techniques*, Paris (1958).
[32] Eric Chaisson, *Cosmic evolution. The Rise of Complexity in Nature*, Harvard (2001).

mimic processes analogous to morphogenetic development, epige-
netic acquisitions, or partially unpredictable phenomena such as
the spread of epidemics, can be of help. The field is open. One does
not know whether the research program initiated around 1950 by
von Neumann and his theory of self-reproducing automata will
culminate in a naturalization of the ontology of life, or whether it
will leave us rich with mathematical tools for the analysis of complex systems, while the deeper problems of biological ontology and
the drift of time remain unresolved.

The epistemological (and anthropological) problem of the status of rationality has been elaborated by Bertrand Saint-Sernin[33].
It used to be that reason was assumed equally distributed among
human subjects, and that individuals were presumed able to assimilate and comprehend the whole of scientific knowledge, if only
they had time to learn. That is no longer the case. No human mind
today can possibly encompass even the totality of one scientific
domain, scientific research has irreversibly become a collective endeavour, and within large scientific programs (as were the Manhat-
tan project, or the Human Genome project), scientific rationality
appears to be distributed among a great many individuals, each of
whom contributes to the achievement and knowledge acquisition,
none of whom possesses a complete intellectual mastery of all aspects of the task. Consequently, intersubjectivity plays a role in
the construction of scientific objectivity; collective rational agents
are interactive. How does interactive rationality function (or dys-
function)? The formal methodology available for the analysis of
collective rationality may be found in the theory of games, or the
theories of rational decision making. Here again, formal methods
will hardly suffice. The questions of scientific controversies, of scientific fraud, will have to be met. One may also ask whether (and
how) philosophical research could, or should, become a collective
rational undertaking.

A possibly minor open problem, however pressing, and linked
with the previous one just mentioned, is: should we all formulate
our philosophical thoughts and arguments in (currently) the English language, and attempt at *thinking* philosophy in English, or is
philosophical reasoning sensitive enough to the language in which
it is expressed, that losing the variety of languages would imply

---

[33] Bertrand Saint-Sernin, *La raison*, Paris (2003); and 'Problèmes ouverts',
in: *Bulletin de la Société française de philosophie*, numéro du centenaire,
2001, Paris (2003).

impoverishment and/or conformity. Formal methods are part of the answer, to the extent that they are meant to be independent of particular languages and cultures. Formal methods, however, are devised to clarify, resolve and *close* some of the questioning (which is *progress*, in one way). The discussion about what formal method is appropriate in a given case, or what aspects of the problem remain open, is carried in ordinary language. The *opening* of a problem may be deemed *progress*, in another way, and it might be language-dependent, at least for a part. When Lalande, in 1905, launched his project of publishing a *Vocabulary of philosophy*, he made it clear that his (modest) ambition was to establish and stabilize the current meaning of philosophical words in order to facilitate communication, and help the philosophical language develop towards "increasing universality". Bergson objected that philosophizing does not consist in choosing with exactitude between old concepts, but in creating new ones. The *Vocabulary* was a success, but it also showed how extremely difficult it is for philosophers to engage in a collective rational undertaking, and bring it to completion—always a provisional completion, open to revision and subject to the erosion of time.

4

Melvin Fitting

Professor

Lehman College and the Graduate Center, CUNY, NY, USA

Why were you initially drawn to formal methods?

Formal methods are a hope for certainty in an uncertain profession.

My undergraduate education was at an engineering college, where I was a mathematics major. While there I took some philosophy courses, and one of them was on symbolic logic. It was very tedious and detailed, but near the end of it there was a brief presentation of modal logic, done in the historic style of C.I. Lewis. It was at this point that I realized I liked manipulating the symbols. This sounds a bit facile, but I think something deeper was going on. My calculus courses, for instance, were vast in scope, involving the nature of the real number system, limits, sequences, differential equations, applications to physics, to three dimensional geometry, and so on. Such an array of concepts historically took hundreds of years to develop and sort out. And at that point in my education, calculus applications necessarily involved the intuitive use of fuzzily understood techniques. It was all impressively powerful, yet disquieting in its mixture of vagueness and proved certainty. Modal logic was something quite different. Its scope was narrow and precisely delineated. Within that scope the rules were sharp and clear. The problem it set out to address, the distinction between necessary truth and truth, was of significant philosophical interest and much might be said about it, but the Lewis approach involved little discussion. More or less, it just said: here are formal statements involving necessity; you might argue which are correct, but if you accept these, you are committed to these others. This provided a sharp analysis that, while not solving the problem, made important aspects of the problem unmistakably clear in a way that endless discussion would not. I think this is what I mean by saying I liked manipulating the symbols.

I think that when formal methods have been most successful they have dealt with small, compact, and isolatable problems. Bertrand Russell's "On Denoting" is a good example. One might describe it as an examination of the logic of the word "the." (It's rather broader than this, but what I wrote is near enough for this discussion.) The "the" problem is complex enough to be of interest to generation after generation, yet sharp enough to be addressed using a mathematically precise methodology whose outlines are intuitively clear to us. By contrast, Montague's formal semantics of natural language is not widely popular despite its genuine successes—its scope is too broad for that. A formalization of natural language may be needed someday if we are to talk with computers, but in its entirety it would be rather overwhelming and under-enlightening. There is a nice illustration of this point by Lewis Carroll, in his relatively unknown book *Sylvie and Bruno*, from which I quote.

> "That's another thing we've learned from *your* Nation," said Mein Herr, "map-making. But we've carried it much further than you. What do you consider the largest map that would be really useful?"
>
> "About six inches to the mile."
>
> "Only *six inches*!" exclaimed Mein Herr. "We very soon got to six yards to the mile. Then we tried a hundred yards to the mile. And then came the grandest idea of all! We actually made a map of the country, on the scale of a mile to the mile!"
>
> "Have you used it much?" I enquired.
>
> "It has never been spread out, yet," said Mein Herr: "the farmers objected; they said it would cover the whole country, and shut out the sunlight! So we now use the country itself, as its own map, and I assure you it does nearly as well." [1]

At the heart of formal methods are formal metaphors.

Even when successful, formal methods do not end discussion. There remains the issue of how well a particular formal method

---

[1] *Sylvie and Bruno Concluded*, Chapter XI, The Man in the Moon, Lewis Carroll.

captures the essential features of a problem. Eubulides of Mile-tus prompted centuries of discussion with his liar paradox, and not surprisingly solutions have been given using formal methods. But there are several solutions, and they are largely incompatible. Following Tarski, one might conclude that natural language is not formal in the technical sense, because it contains its own truth predicate and formal languages cannot do this. Following Kripke, not all sentences of natural language involving the truth predicate have truth values. Following the fuzzy logicians, perhaps the liar sentence is a bit true and a bit not. Following the paraconsistent logicians, perhaps the liar sentence is both true and false, and so what? In each case the formal methods are meticuously developed. The conclusions vary because the premises vary. Formal methods make it clear what we get with the purchase of a philosophical position; they cannot of themselves tell us which position to buy.

Applications of formal methods that are considered successful have a common feature that, perhaps, we might not like to admit: they make us believe we understand the problem being addressed better than we did before. This is not an essential characteristic of formal methods—basically they just say "you are committed to this if you accept these principles." Belief that our understanding has been improved is a different thing. For example, modal log-ics have both algebraic and relational (possible world, Kripke) se-mantics. Algebraic semantics is older, and provides suitable math-ematical machinery for proving things about modal logics, yet the introduction of relational semantics revolutionized the subject. Why? Because people believed that relational semantics provided insights into the way modal operators "really" worked—possible worlds were more than a metaphor, instead they formalized what we were actually doing on some level. It's hard for Boolean alge-bras with operators to compete with that. An analogous treatment of relevance logic, using a ternary relation, did not have anything like the same impact, probably because people did not feel it en-lightened, and not because of its lack of mathematical utility. It is a matter of aesthetics, but something more is involved. Some things just resonate more than others. Still it's probably worth asking, from time to time, whether the enlightenment provided by some particular formal methodology is real or spurious. One should not ask such a question too soon, of course. One should enjoy the heady days, the rush, the excitement. But when the tu-mult and shouting has died, it's appropriate for nagging doubts to surface. All applications of formal methods have a philosophical story at their heart—they are philosophical metaphors, and that should not be forgotten.

What example(s) from your work illustrates the role formal methods can play in philosophy?

I believe I made it clear above that I am a bit of an agnostic about formal methods. I do not believe they settle problems. But, by showing that a certain position has a formal model of some kind, one provides a degree of respectability to that position. At one time there seemed to be a belief that if you couldn't say something in first-order classical logic, you shouldn't say it. That has gone, if it ever existed in the extreme form I just said it. Now more general logics are allowed, and it is easier to establish coherency for a position. One might think that coherency should not be enough—undesirable consequences should be sufficient cause for the rejection of a philosophical position. But undesirability is a matter of taste, it seems. I remind the reader that there are those who believe contradictions exist in the real world. So coherency, the existence of some formal treatment, establishes a degree of respectability. It's hard to see what the crusher argument that convinces all might be like, no matter what the subject. I try to make sense of small things, no more.

Since most of my work in philosophical logic has involved modal logic, I'll start with that. And I'll skip over propositional modal logics, since much of my contribution there has been to proof methods, and not to philosophical issues.

In first-order modal logic I've devoted some effort to studying non-rigid designators. As Carnap noted, these can formally model intensions. But Thomason and Stalnaker emphasized that if used naively in modal formulas, non-rigid terms lead to syntactic ambiguity. Similar problems arise with non-designating terms, as Russell observed. Does "the King of France is not bald," mean "the King of France is non-bald," which is false under Russell's treatment of definite descriptions, or does it mean "it is not the case that the King of France is bald," which is true? Using a device of Thomason and Stalnaker, which has come to be called "predicate abstraction," this ambiguity can be eliminated at the cost of complicating the language. Further, it is natural to combine non-rigidity with the possibility of non-designation, as in the "King of France" example. This does not complicate matters—it simplifies them.

Allowing non-rigidity, and providing predicate abstraction, makes it possible to formally treat several so-called philosophical puzzles. One can represent the contingent identity of the number of the planets and the number 9 (or whatever the latest integer candidate is), without automatically being committed to synonymy. Similarly for the morning star and the evening star, and other such examples, including one nicely presented by Lewis Carroll, again.

> The Other Professor looked thoroughly puzzled. "Well, well!" he said. "Try some cowslip wine!" And he filled a glass and handed it to Bruno. "Drink this, my dear, and you'll be quite another man!"
>
> "Who shall I be?" said Bruno, pausing in the act of putting it to his lips.[2]

The possibility of having a formal setting in which such distinctions are simply and naturally made should free us from the tyrany of classical first-order logic. (At least, those of us who are still tyrranized in this fashion.) There are also more technical spill-overs. For instance, Skolemization in modal formulas becomes possible—in a Kripke model the instantiation of an existentially quantified formula might be different at different possible worlds, and so a non-rigid designator is a natural tool, which in turn requires predicate abstraction to avoid ambiguities.

Over the years I've worked at finding the simplest, most natural formulation of first-order modal logic allowing non-rigid, non-designating terms. I have produced several alternatives, which have some formal differences from each other, but which agree on basic principles. The one I seem to be settling on is FOIL (first-order intensional logic). This probably has more machinery than people would like, though different people will probably dislike different parts. It makes both objects and intensions into first-class citizens, allows quantification over both, and provides predicate abstraction for intensions, and equality for objects. Many of its sublogics are natural and expressive. And in it one can formally represent and disambiguate the kind of designation problems mentioned above.

Lately I have been particularly interested in the technical aspects of FOIL. There is a Kripke-style semantics, and tableau

---

[2] *Sylvie and Bruno Concluded*, Chapter XXIII, The Pig-Tale, Lewis Carroll.

systems corresponding to it. Recently axiomatizations of some interest have been developed. There is also the curious fact that even if quantifiers are dropped, and only predicate abstraction, modal operators, and propositional connectives are left, one still might have undecidability (depending on the underlying modal assumptions). This is a bit surprising, and somewhat lessens the significance of the Skolemization possibilities mentioned above. All this is still work in progress, however.

Gödel concocted a particularly sophisticated ontological argument which, fairly recently, has become better-known than it once was, because of the publication of his collected papers. I got interested in that, and similar, arguments, not for their own sakes but as a testing ground for modal techniques. In order to analyize them, I devised a variation on the higher-type intensional logic of Montague and Gallin, and equipped it with a tableau system. This is a good example of my earlier point that the use of formal methods does not, by itself, determine truth; it determines what is true based on what premises you accept. Gödel's premises are debatable, certainly. Moreover, in the case of Gödel's ontological argument, Sobel had shown that the premises are too strong—truth and necessary truth coincide. I was able to show that this does, or does not, happen depending on whether 'positive' properties are thought of as extensional or intensional. I have no idea which way one might want to take them. For me this is an exercise in pure formal methods, with no ontological commitment, so to speak.

Modal logic can provide an enlightening setting for the presentation of the technical details of forcing arguments in set theory. At some point I realized that what was going on was a kind of *intensional* approach to set theory, with the generic reals introduced to falsify the continuum hypothesis being non-rigid sets. This is an idea I hope to pursue further at some point, or perhaps someone else will.

As to formal methods that don't involve modal logic, I have been interested in the applications of *bilattices* to the fixpoint theory of truth. Bilattices are a family of multi-valued logics that generalize a particular logic introduced by Belnap. It turns out that they have exactly the structure appropriate for the presentation of an extremely smooth version of the Kripke approach to the theory of truth. One of the advantages of this rather abstract approach is that one can then see similarities between the Kripke theory and work on the semantics of logic programs. In particular, I was able to apply ideas from Kripke's work to logic programming, and from the stable model semantics for logic programming to the theory of truth. One of the outcomes was a natural class of fixpoints for Kripke's operator that nobody seems to have considered before. I can't resist one more quote from Lewis Carroll, but this time because I think he, or his character, is wrong. Seeing similarities across disciplines is often a key to progress.

> "Well, this is one of them," said the Professor. "When a man's tipsy (that's one extreme, you know), he sees one thing as two. But, when he's extremely sober (that's the other extreme), he sees two things as one. It's equally inconvenient, whichever happens."[3]

What is the proper role of philosophy in relation to other disciplines?

I remember once hearing a talk by a well-known mathematical logician, who shall remain nameless, addressed to non-logician mathematicians. What he more-or-less explicitly said was, "You thought you were doing thus-and-so. Now I'm going to tell you what you were really doing." Of course, this was not a good way to win over an audience, or even to convince it to listen attentively. I think the proper role of philosophy in relation to other disciplines is to keep them honest, without suggesting the possibility that they might not be. Currently, artificial intelligence and consciousness seems to be a good testing ground.

---

[3] *Sylvie and Bruno*, Chapter X, The Other Professor, Lewis Carroll.

5

Dagfinn Føllesdal

C.I. Lewis Professor of Philosophy

Stanford University, CA, USA[1]

Why were you initially drawn to formal methods?

I was initially drawn to mathematics, and not in particular to formal methods. One cannot do mathematics without formal methods. However, what drew me to mathematics was definitely not its formal methods, but, I think, the structures that are studied in mathematics. I found these structures highly interesting, and I experienced the study of them as exploration and discovery. Originally, my plan was to study mathematics in order to use it in science, primarily physics. I studied mathematics for two years, and then went on to study science, concentrating on mechanics and astronomy. I later had a full time job for two years on a project devoted to study of the polar aurora.

However, mathematics engaged me more and more strongly, and instead of continuing in the sciences, as was my original plan, I continued in mathematics. I went to Göttingen to study with Carl Ludwig Siegel, and then came back to Norway to study with Skolem. Philosophy was a side interest, and I could not imagine having philosophy as a profession. However, I then discovered Quine's writings and they made me decide to go full time into philosophy. I applied for a fellowship in order to study with him, and since then I have been a philosopher.

My background in mathematics has been of great help to my work in philosophy. How? Not because I use mathematics in philosophy, I have worked very little in the philosophy of mathematics and philosophy of science. Not because mathematics is of help in economics, decision theory and many other fields that are pertinent to philosophy; I have not gone into these fields, although

[1] I am grateful to Alistair Isaac for helpful suggestions.

I find them very interesting. The main reason why the study of mathematics has been of help to me is that it has trained me in dealing with structures. Mathematics gives one a large repertoire of many different kinds of structures and training in how to deal with them. One sees possibilities that one might not otherwise think of, and one sees more quickly what they may lead to and how they fit in with other possibilities.

Philosophy is, like mathematics and many other intellectual fields, concerned with structures. One reason for this is that philosophy, at least the way I conceive of it, is very holistic. One is concerned with how one's view on one issue fits in with one's view on other issues, and how apparently small modifications on one point may have far-reaching repercussions elsewhere.

Formal methods are a good tool for studying such structures, in philosophy as in mathematics. However, I look upon formal methods as instruments on a par with telescopes and microscopes. Our eye is a very good all-round instrument which enables us to get the general picture and note what is worthy of our attention. However, when we start attending to matters that we regard as important, we may wish to examine them more closely by disregarding features that seem irrelevant. This is just what we do when we use formal methods.

> *Formal methods are not well characterized by saying that they make use of formalism. What distinguishes them is in my opinion that that they focus on some features of the situation in abstraction from others, and thereby help us see and explore features that we regard as particularly pertinent to the issues we are engaged by.*

Often, formalism makes these features come out in a more perspicuous way. Who would do mathematics without using formalism? And who would write or play music without using musical notation? However, while I think that philosophy cannot be done without formal methods in the above sense, I have two warnings concerning formalism. First:

> *Formalism may be overused. It is sometimes used to present reasoning or results that can just as easily be presented without the formalism. In such cases one must consider who the readers are likely to be and whether they will be helped or hampered by the use of the formalism.*

Second:

> *Remember that when one uses formal methods, one fo-*
> *cuses on some features of the situation and disregards*
> *others. Take heed not to disregard features that may be*
> *pertinent to the issue at hand and to the concerns that*
> *moved one to examine it.*

After these words of warning, I will now turn to an example from my own work that, I hope, does not flout these warnings.

What example(s) from your work illustrates the role formal methods can play in philosophy?

An example from my own work that illustrates several aspects of the role formal methods can play in philosophy, is my dissertation, *Referential Opacity and Modal Logic*, which I wrote with Quine as my advisor in 1961.[2] On the face of it a treatise on logic, with formulae, proofs and theorems. However, its main concern is to propose a new semantics for names and other singular terms, and to show why such a different semantics is needed.

I will first use it to discuss some uses of argument analysis in philosophy and thereafter use it to discuss the relation between formal methods and traditional metaphysics, which are often regarded as opposites.

Uses of argument analysis in philosophy

The first point to note is the following:

> *Problems that arise in our ordinary use of natural lan-*
> *guages can be elucidated by discussing them in the con-*
> *text of a regimented logical formalism. It is then often*
> *easier to see what the problems are, how they arise and*
> *how they can be solved.*

The fact that in my thesis I discuss the problems of referential opacity by help of formal systems of modal logic, is not primarily due to an interest in formal systems; the issues I discuss arise

---

[2] *Referential Opacity and Modal Logic.* My doctoral dissertation (1961), with an Introduction and Addenda, published in the series *Dissertations in Philosophy*, edited by Robert Nozick. London: Routledge, 2004. ISBN 0415938511.

in our ordinary use of language, and the solutions I propose are supposed to apply to ordinary language. The formalization is only meant as an aid to seeing the problems more clearly, and to expressing my solutions to them more precisely and concisely.

My plan for my dissertation was to write on reference. When Quine's *Word and Object* came out in 1960, there was, in particular, one issue that struck me as problematic: Quine presented an argument to the effect that when one quantifies into modal contexts modal distinctions collapse. This argument represented the apparently conclusive culmination of a series of objections Quine had raised against the modalities from 1941 on. His earliest criticism merely demonstrated the obscurity of the modal notions. This new criticism was a step-by-step argument to the effect that the interpretation of the quantifiers and other singular terms forced the modal distinctions to collapse.

I was disturbed by this argument. Not because I cherished the modalities—I did not—but because an inspection of the argument showed that it was independent of the modalities and applied to any attempt to single out by help of an operator a proper subclass of the true sentences. Any such attempt would fail; the subclass would coincide with the whole class. Take as an example "knows that." Sentences like "There is something that I know to be a book" would, within a full semantics with names and other definite singular terms, lead to a collapse of epistemic distinctions. Not only would everything that is known be true, which is what we want, but also everything that is true would be known to be true. Quine's argument could be repeated for belief, causality, counterfactuals, probability, and the operators in ethics, such as "it is obligatory that," "it is permitted that." They would all collapse. The argument was simply too disastrous to be correct. This observation, that Quine's argument generalized in this catastrophic way, is a matter of focusing on its formal structure. We here have a second use of formal methods:

> *The validity of an argument depends on its formal structure, and attending to its structure can make one notice that other particularities of the argument do not matter.*

The problem was then: what is wrong with the argument? This is again a place where formalization comes in. In order to find out what was wrong, I formalized the argument, so that it was turned into a pure deductive argument.

*Formalization of an argument makes explicit its tacit
assumptions. In some cases, one or more of these are
clearly false, and one sees immediately what is wrong
with the argument. In other cases, when the conclusion
of the argument is unacceptable, one is forced to think
through the premisses of the argument, and one may
discover that what was generally taken for granted may
not be true.*

In this case, none of the assumptions of the arguments seemed to
be false. One would not expect that Quine would have overlooked
any dubious assumptions, one of his many virtues as a philosopher
was his awareness of assumptions and difficulties that others did
not notice. Once the argument was formalized, it was easy to see
that all the assumptions he used in his argument were generally
accepted at that time. However, something had to be wrong.

The only assumption I could think of questioning, was a transition that is made in the argument between *singular terms* and
general terms. This is based on a presumption that had gone un-
questioned until then, namely that singular and general terms
have the same kind of semantics: they have a sense—a descriptive
content—and their reference or extension is determined by this
sense. This had been taken for granted by all the main figures in
the development of semantics, the few indications to the contrary,
such as Mill's "Dartmouth," had been forgotten. Frege treated
all expressions, singular terms, general terms and sentences, on a
par, and he took this unification as an argument in favor of his
semantics.

All twentieth-century semanticists had followed him in this,
with the exception of Russell, Arthur Smullyan, and a few others
who regarded names as a spurious kind of expression that should
be eliminated by help of definite descriptions. By not recognizing any names—expressions that refer and are subject to rules
of inference such as substitutivity of identity, existential generalization and universal instantiation—Russell and Smullyan evaded
the issues of interpretation that concerned me in the dissertation.
However, these issues remain challenges if one wants to understand how reference works. I believe this is what underlies Gödel's
remark in his article on Russell in 1944, to which I shall return
below: "I cannot help feeling that the problem raised by Frege's
puzzling conclusion has only been evaded by Russell's theory of
descriptions and that there is something behind it which is not

yet completely understood."[3]

When Quine set forth his criticism, nobody had proposed a system of quantified modal logic that contained names, and the belief that all problems connected with reference were adequately dealt with by Russell's theory of descriptions does a lot to account for the fact that modal logicians were not as troubled by Quine's arguments as I was.

Inspection of Quine's argument showed that there was hardly any other way out: one had to give up Frege's and Carnap's neat one-sorted semantics in favor of a two-sorted one, where singular terms behave radically differently from general terms and sentences. The solution could hence only be that names preserve their reference. As I put it in the dissertation "This solution leads us to regard a word as a proper name of an object only if it refers to this one and the same object in all possible worlds."[4]

Not all expressions that traditionally have been regarded as singular terms relate in this way to their object. For example, definite descriptions in most of their uses do not. Those expressions that do, I called *"genuine singular terms"*, they are defined in exactly the same way as Kripke nine years later defined '*rigid designators*', a very apt phrase for this kind of unswerving expressions.[5] Definite descriptions and other expressions that have traditionally been classified as singular terms, but exhibit philandering behavior, I classified semantically together with general terms. They should be regarded as general terms that just happen to be true of a unique object; they should not be regarded as *referring* to it.

The variables of quantification are the archetypical kinds of gen-

---

[3] Kurt Gödel, "Russell's Mathematical Logic." In P.A. Schilpp, ed., *The Philosophy of Bertrand Russell.* Evanston, Ill.: Northwestern University, 1944, pp. 125–53, esp. pp. 128–131 (= pp. 122–124 of the reprint in Solomon Feferman et al., eds., *Kurt Gödel, Collected Works.* Volume II, Oxford: Oxford University Press, 1990, pp. 119–141).

[4] *Op. cit.* Section 17, page 75.

[5] Kripke presented these ideas in three lectures on reference in Princeton in January 1970, and also in an article, "Identity and Necessity," in Milton Munitz, ed., *Identity and Individuation* (New York: New York University Press, 1971, pp. 135–164). The Princeton lectures were published under the title "Naming and Necessity" in Donald Davidson and Gilbert Harman, eds., *The Semantics of Natural Language* (Dordrecht: Reidel, 1972, pp. 253–355) and later expanded into a book: *Naming and Necessity* (Cambridge, MA: Harvard University Press, 1980). Kripke's discussion contains an admirable analysis of the behavior of names in ordinary language. Kripke also proposes an interesting and widely discussed "historical chain" view on the relation between names and their objects.

uine singular terms. The whole point of a variable, as of a pronoun, is to refer to an object and keep on referring to that same object, in all possible worlds, through all changes, etc. This is how they were interpreted in the dissertation. One main aim of the dissertation was to show that names behave the same way (although they differ from pronouns and variables in other ways, for example in the way they become attached to an object and how long they keep that attachment).

This view on proper names was hence supported by two kinds of arguments: It blocked Quine's collapse argument, and it resulted from a semantic analysis of how reference works. The view on reference and names that was proposed in the dissertation was hence not an *ad hoc* obstruction for Quine's argument, but it provided a coherent semantics which made clear how reference works and why the traditional Fregean view on reference leads to difficulties.

The "Slingshot": Gödel's suspicions

Quine's argument for the collapse of modal distinctions is similar to arguments that have been used by Church and Gödel for the collapse of various other distinctions. Church[6] used an argument of this kind to argue for his Fregean semantics. Gödel[7] proposed an even simpler argument and showed that "leads almost inevitably to the conclusion that the true sentences have the same significacion (as well as false ones). (pp-129–130). He noted that "Frege actually drew this conclusion; and he meant it in an almost metaphysical sense, reminding one somewhat of the Eleatic doctrines of the 'One'." (p. 129) Gödel presented the argument in a discussion of Russell's philosophy, and he observed that Russell's contextual elimination of definite descriptions blocks the argument. However, Gödel noticed that the argument raised serious problems for the traditional Fregean view on names and reference. He concluded that "I cannot help feeling that the problem raised by Frege's puzzling conclusion has only been evaded by Russell's theory of descriptions and that there is something behind it which is not yet completely understood." (p. 130)

---

[6] Alonzo Church, Review of Carnap's *Introduction to Semantics*. *Philosophical Review* 52 (1943), pp. 298–304, esp. pp. 299–300.

[7] Kurt Gödel, *op.cit*, pp. 125–53, esp. pp. 128–131 (= pp. 122–124 of the reprint in Solomon Feferman et al., eds., *Kurt Gödel, Collected Works*. Volume II, Oxford: Oxford University Press, 1990, pp. 119–141). The page numbers in the text refer to the original text.

A hint of what Gödel had in mind here, comes a little bit later, where he writes: "Closer examination, however, shows that this advantage of Russell's theory over Frege's subsists only as long as one interprets definitions as mere typographic abbreviations, not as introducing names for objects described by the definitions, a feature which is common to Frege and Russell." (p. 131) So what Gödel was missing, was a semantics for names that gets around his argument. In the dissertation, I proposed such a way of handling names: names do not philander from object to object the way definite descriptions do; they stick to the same object in all possible worlds. This solution works not only in formal languages, but it also seems to reflect a crucial feature of the behavior of names in ordinary language: Names do not behave like disguised descriptions.

My diagnosis of what goes wrong in Quine's slingshot argument is, as mentioned, that in the argument one slides too easily between general terms and singular terms. The proposed two-sorted semantics prevents such a slide and does justice to the behavior of names in natural languages.

In the years that have followed, a large number of articles and books have been devoted to the argument that was used by Frege, Gödel, Church and Quine. A notable contribution was made by Barwise and Perry in 1981.[8] The very apt name "slingshot" is due to them.

Substitutivity of identity and necessity of identity

During the twenty years before the publication of *Word and Object* Quine had directed a number of other arguments against the modalities. Many of these survive after one has introduced a two-sorted semantics. However, when analyzed against the background of this new semantics, they turn out to be innocent. Rather than being objections they give insight into how the two-sorted semantics works. This holds for Quine's claim that identities are universally substitutive and necessary, and also for his contention that

---

[8] Jon Barwise and John Perry, "Semantic Innocence and Uncompromising Situations." *Midwest Studies in Philosophy* 6 (1981), pp. 387–404. See also John Perry, "Evading the Slingshot." In A. Clark, et al., eds., *Philosophy and Cognitive Science.* Dordrecht: Kluwer, 1996, pp. 95–114. Reprinted in John Perry, *The Problem of the Essential Indexical and Other Essays.* Expanded Edition, Stanford: CSLI Publications, 2000, pp. 287–301. See also Stephen Neale, *Facing Facts.* Oxford: Oxford University Press, 2001, and the literature referred to there.

quantified modal logic commits one to "Aristotelian" essentialism.

Let us consider identity first. In the dissertation I argued that identities are necessary, while non-identity, or distinctness, is not necessary.

In particular, the substitutivity of identity has disturbed many. Already in his first criticism of the modalities, his contribution to the Whitehead volume in the *Library of Living Philosophers* in 1941,[9] Quine observed that the principle of substitutivity of identity seems to break down in modal contexts: If in '(the number of planets < 7)' which is presumably true, we substitute for '9' 'the number of planets', we get '(9 < 7)', which is false. So what, then, is meant by the identity statement 'the number of planets = 9'?

This objection was utterly distressing within traditional one-sorted semantics, à la Frege and Carnap. Some modal logicians tried to get around it by contending that names and variables in modal contexts refer to intensions rather than to regular objects. However, I argued in the thesis that restricting the universe to intensions is the wrong way to go. The trouble lies with the referring expressions and their semantics, not with the objects: the variables and quantifiers alone do not require us to individuate our entities finer than they are individuated in extensional logic. The trouble comes in with our singular terms. Others, for example Ruth Marcus, have suggested substitutional interpretations of quantifiers and names.[10] However, this is a radical deviation from normal quantification and reference, and it throws no light on the relation between language and the world.

Others again have introduced restrictions on substitutivity and have maintained that not all singular terms can be substituted for one another in modal contexts. However, no argument has ever been given for such a restriction, except that it saves one from undesirable results such as those pointed out by Quine. Giving up the old Frege-Carnap view on reference in favor of a new view on reference, where names and other "genuine singular terms" refer, while other expressions that have traditionally been regarded as singular terms, including definite descriptions in most of their uses, are

[9] "Whitehead and the rise of modern logic." In Paul Arthur Schilpp, ed., *The Philosophy of Alfred North Whitehead* (Library of Living Philosophers). Evanston, IL: Northwestern University, 1941. 2.ed. New York: Tudor, 1951, pp. 125–163, esp. pp. 141–142, n. 26, and p. 148.

[10] For example in "Modal Logics I: Modalities and Intensional Languages." *Synthese* 13 (1961), pp. 303–322.

classified semantically together with general terms and sentences, as having a sense that determines their extension, solves the problem. Given this semantics, statements like Quine's 'the number of planets = 9' are not regarded as proper identity statements, the description on the left side is not a referring expression, but is a general term that in the actual world happens to be true of the number 9.

Two-sorted semantics

Such a two-sorted semantics, where general terms and sentences behave as in standard Fregean semantics, while singular terms keep their reference "in all possible worlds," undermines Quine's argument. There is no collapse of modal distinctions, and quantification into modal contexts makes sense. This is due to the fact that two-sorted semantics makes it possible to have contexts that are referentially transparent, so that quantification into them makes sense, and extensionally opaque, so that modal distinctions do not collapse.

As a small aside, which illustrates another application of logic in my thesis, I might mention that not all combinations of referential transparency and extensional opacity are permissible. Thus, for example, one may prove that:

> *Every extensional construction on sentences and general terms is referential*

and likewise that:

> *Every referential construction on singular terms is extensional*

However, luckily for quantification into non-extensional contexts:

> *Referential constructions on sentences and general terms can be non-extensional*

The constructions that are needed to overcome Quine's argument are just such constructions. They are constructions where the operators 'necessarily', 'possibly', 'knows that', 'believes that', 'it is probable that', 'it is obligatory that', etc, apply to sentences or general terms.

Formalism: validity versus provability

A danger when one uses formal methods is that one constructs a formal system with axioms and rules of inference and then explores what it is possible to prove within the system, without investigating whether or not the system is semantically complete. Systems can be incomplete in the sense that formulae that are true under all interpretations of the system are not provable in the system. It may then happen that some important formulae is semantically valid, but not provable. In such cases one should be aware of the following:

> *What matters for the philosophical application of a formal system is not only what is provable in the system, but also what is valid in the system, what is required for the interpretation of the system.*

The dissertation contains one example that illustrates this point. The first systems of quantified modal logic that were proposed had no singular terms other than variables. Since variables keep their reference from one possible world to another, the collapse discussed by Quine was not brought to the fore until one got systems of quantified logic that included singular terms other than variables. The only such system by 1961, when the dissertation was written, was Carnap's system S_2 in *Meaning and Necessity*. It contained definite descriptions, but no names.

In the discussion of definite descriptions in section 16 of the dissertation it is proved, on pages 73–74, that: S_2 is saved from a collapse of modal distinctions by the circumstance that its theory of descriptions is not a standard one. [Carnap states on page 184 of *Meaning and Necessity* that "in order to avoid certain complications, which cannot be explained here, it seems advisable to admit in S_2 only descriptions which do not contain '$\Box$'.] So, although the interpretation of S_2 requires the modalities to collapse, the collapse, that is the formula '$p \supset \Box p$', is not provable in S_2. Carnap never tells us what the complications are that he is aware of. He is not likely to have seen that his system collapses when the restriction is revoked. However, as long as we do not know his reasons, the restriction seems *ad hoc*.[11]

---

[11] A thoughtful attempt to rescue Carnap has been made by Genoveva Marti in "Do Modal Distinctions Collapse in Carnap's System?" *Journal of Philosophical Logic* 23 (1994), pp. 575–594. I think Marti is right in her most

Formal methods and traditional metaphysics. An example: "Aristotelian" essentialism

Carnap and many others held that if one makes one's philosophical position and one's arguments clear by using logic and formal methods one could avoid falling into old metaphysical nonsense, such as the old Aristotelian doctrine that necessity resides in things and not in the words we use to talk about things. In lieu of this Carnap proposed a linguistic doctrine of necessity: necessity is a matter of our language, of how we describe things.

One of Quine's many arguments against the modalities is specifically directed against Carnap and his linguistic doctrine of necessity. Quine contended that quantified modal logic presupposes "Aristotelian" essentialism. This is the doctrine that some of the attributes of a thing are essential to it, necessary of the thing *regardless of the way in which we refer to it*, while other attributes are accidental to it. I shall not discuss here whether this view is found in Aristotle. What matters for our discussion is that Quine is right: "Aristotelian" essentialism as defined by Quine is indispensable in quantified modal logic. However, while Quine's objection was originally intended as a *reductio* of modal logic, it is concluded in the dissertation

> that if the modal operator '□' itself makes sense, then
> ... open sentences with a '□' prefixed make sense too if
> we restrict our stock of singular terms appropriately.

> To make sense of Aristotelian essentialism and to
> make sense of open sentences with a '□' prefixed are
> one and the same problem, and a solution to the one
> is a solution to the other. (page 92)

The combination of extensional opacity and referential transparency which is made possible by two-sorted semantics is just what "Aristotelian" essentialism amounts to:

> We distinguish between necessary and contingent attributes (*extensional opacity*), and the objects over

---

interesting analysis of Carnap's motivation for his seemingly so *ad hoc* prohibition of modal operators within definite descriptions. However, her attempt to block my argument for the collapse turns in my opinion too strongly on the unclarities in Carnap's double interpretation of variables, which I criticize in this dissertation.

which we quantify have these attributes regardless of
the way in which the object is referred to (*referential
transparency*).

Carnap and other advocates of modal logic who explained modality by help of analyticity and who rejected Aristotelian essentialism as metaphysical nonsense might find this result hard to
swallow. However, Quine himself changed his attitude to "Aristotelian" essentialism. On February 8, 1962, in a discussion following a lecture by Ruth Marcus, he said: "I think essentialism,
from the point of view of the modal logician, is something that
ought to be welcome. I don't take this as being a *reductio ad
absurdum.*"[12]

It might be helpful to distinguish three different notions of essentialism. The first, weakest notion was developed by Quine in
response to Carnap, Lewis, and others, who championed quantified modal logic while at the same time rejecting as metaphysical
nonsense the traditional Aristotelian view that necessity inheres
in things and not in language. In *From a Logical Point of View*
Quine says that quantification into modal contexts requires Aristotelian essentialism, in the following sense:

> An object, *of itself and by whatever name or none,*
> must be seen as having some of its traits necessarily
> and others contingently, despite the fact that *the lat-
> ter traits follow just as analytically from some ways of
> specifying the object as the former traits do from other
> ways of specifying it* ...
>
> ...
>
> [This kind of] essentialism is abruptly at variance
> with the idea, favored by Carnap, Lewis, and others,
> of explaining necessity by analyticity.[13]

Quine saw that Carnap and Lewis's linguistic conception of necessity was untenable if one wants to quantify into modal contexts,
and that their position therefore was incoherent.

---

[12] "Discussion after Ruth Barcan Marcus's lecture February 8, 1962." In
Max Wartofsky, ed., *Boston Studies in the Philosophy of Science*. Dordrecht:
Reidel, 1963, pp. 105–116. The quoted passage occurs on page 110.

[13] *From a Logical Point of View*. Cambridge, MA: Harvard University Press,
2. ed. 1961, p. 155. The italics are mine. The passage does not occur in the
first edition.

A second notion of essentialism is the view that for each kind of object there is some essence that all things of that kind have. This is a fairly widespread notion of essentialism in philosophy, but it is not required in order to provide a satisfactory semantics for the modalities. And it is not what Quine means by 'essentialism'.

The third, very strong, notion of essentialism is evoked by a new historical situation very different from the one Quine discusses in his writings in the 1950s. While the earlier situation was focused on Aristotelian essentialism, the new situation arose from the discussion amongst modal logicians in the seventies concerning how one should identify objects from one possible world to another, how one should draw what David Kaplan oppositely dubbed "trans-world heir lines." One proposal that sometimes was made was that each object has an individual essence, a set of properties that it has by necessity and that no other object has. Much of the later discussion of essentialism is marred by confusion of these three different notions of essentialism.[14]

What is the proper role of philosophy in relation to other disciplines?

After having discussed the role formal methods can play in philosophy I will now turn to the role philosophy can play in relation to other disciplines.

One classic view is that philosophy is a metadiscipline different from all other disciplines. It is supposed to provide *a priori* foundations for the other disciplines, or to tell us what is the task and nature of these other disciplines. Another traditional view is that philosophy is a quite different enterprise that has nothing to do with other disciplines.

My own view is that philosophy can play a role in all other disciplines. But which role?

General problems

Philosophy is a reflection on all aspects of us humans and the world in which we live. The various disciplines tend to concentrate on one particular sphere or one particular issue, while philosophy

---

[14] For a fuller discussion of this, see my "Essentialism and reference." In Lewis E. Hahn and Paul Arthur Schilpp, eds., *The Philosophy of W.V. Quine* (The Library of Living Philosophers). La Salle, IL: Open Court, 1986, pp. 97–113. (Reply by Quine: pp. 114–115).

takes up very broad and general problems, problems that are not covered in one particular discipline. Often philosophy will seek to clarify notions that play a role in other disciplines but are not themselves objects of study in that discipline. Examples are notions of causality, explanation and justification.

Problem awareness

Another kind of contribution that philosophy can make to other disciplines is to make them aware of fundamental problems that are overlooked. A good example of this is the notion of time. Time is studied and used in very many disciplines. Time is used as a parameter, and in many disciplines one reflects on it, how it should be measured, etc. It is hence an example of the kind of general notions that we just mentioned. However, time also illustrates another distinctive feature of many applications of philosophy in other disciplines. Saint Augustine expressed it very well when he wrote: "What then is time? If no one asks me, I know; if I wish to explain it to one who asks, I know not." This is typical of the kind of questions that engage philosophers. Philosophers will tend to ask questions when others do not ask them. They will make us aware that there are obscurities and problems where we thought that everything was well. In fact, what characterizes the good philosopher is *problem awareness*. It is good that a philosopher has imagination and creativity and can communicate clearly and well. However, problem awareness is a *sine qua non* for a philosopher.

Of course many people from other disciplines take up such issues and reflect on them. They are then doing philosophy, I would say. There is no clear line to be drawn here, and I do not regard it as important where we draw the line, or even whether we draw one.

Clarity

Another important goal of philosophy is to help to clarify issues. A large amount of intellectual activity aims at clarification, but philosophers have a special responsibility here. Our contribution does not consist in collecting empirical material or making experiments, but in dealing with abstract and complicated issues. What I enjoy the most are philosophers who address issues that are important and complicated, so-called "deep" issues, and who do it in such a clear way that they provide insight. I do not regard obscurity as evidence of depth. Obscurity is enough to turn me off. However, clarity by itself is not enough to turn me on. It is easy to be clear about simple issues. What I enjoy the most are clear discussions of "deep" issues. Our main challenge is to think about these issues in such a way that we come to understand them better. And I agree with Nicolas Boileau that "What one understands well, one expresses clearly."

Clarity is so important in philosophy that philosophers should regard it as part of their calling to help clarify issues that are of importance for the society in which they live. And the training of philosophers should reflect this. I become highly suspicious of philosophers who when they write on simple issues are not able to express themselves clearly. How shall they be able to think clearly about the difficult and complicated issues one deals with in philosophy?

What do you consider the most neglected topics and/or contributions in late 20th century philosophy?

Among the neglected contributions in late 20th century philosophy I would like to mention the late Stig Kanger's work on the interpretation of modal logic, decision theory and other fields. These contributions are now becoming more accessible and better known, through the publication of Kanger's *Collected Papers*[15] and through discussions of his work, such as Edgar Morscher's recent article "Stig Kanger—Ein Bekannter Unbekannter Oder Ein Unbekannter Bekannter?" *Grazer Philosophische Studien* 68 (2005), pp. 175–200.

Kanger's contributions were neglected mostly because they appeared in unpretentious mimeographs or were written in a very compressed style. Other philosophers are neglected because of the compartmentalization of philosophy and of intellectual fields in general. They have important new ideas that are highly relevant within many areas of philosophy and also outside philosophy, but these ideas are virtually unknown outside their own field. Many ideas and names come to my mind. However, rather than making a list that would be biased and soon outdated, I will emphasize how important it is for philosophers to have a broad knowledge of their field. Philosophy, more than any other subject that I know, is a subject where all the different subfields are relevant to one another.

As for the relevance of philosophical ideas outside the field of

---

[15] *Collected Papers of Stig Kanger with Essays on His Life And Work.* Ghita Holmstrom-Hintikka, Sten Lindstrom and Rysiek Sliwinski, eds. Dordrecht, Kluwer, 2001.Paperback. Kluwer Academic Publishers 2001.

philosophy, there is clearly a need for philosophers to communicate more with people from other fields and to present important philosophical contributions in a setting and in a language comprehensible to non-specialists. Too many popular writers on philosophy are down on what they are not up on, and this often disserves the technical and more formal contributions. The non-philosopher should learn to be skeptical about all attempts to denigrate whole fields of philosophy or groups of philosophers. Philosophy is such a rich and complicated field that such wholesale criticism is bound to overlook important differences.

Criticism that is not aimed at a particular position or argument is often directed against a scapegoat, a position that nobody holds. It often makes use of broad characteristics or labels, such as various kinds of "-isms." It is psychologically understandable that one may be happy to learn that there are large chunks of philosophical literature that one need not bother to read. But it is unfortunate that such wholesale rejection of philosophical positions and contributions closes people's minds. The best defense against it is to neglect it and do one's best to communicate not only with philosophy colleagues, but also with colleagues from other fields and with the general public.

What are the most important open problems in philosophy and what are the prospects for progress?

One of the most important problems in philosophy is the mind / body problem. It is universally regarded as a very important problem, central to our understanding of ourselves and our situation in cosmos. It has resisted more than 2000 years of intensive efforts by the greatest philosophical minds. This makes the prospects for major progress small. However, many discussions of the problem, both ancient and contemporary, have given me some illumination, and I am hoping for more to come.

6

Haim Gaifman

Professor of Philosophy

Columbia University, NY, USA

Why were you initially drawn to formal methods?

As an undergraduate I specialized in mathematics, philosophy and physics. My first result (the equivalence of context–free and categorial grammars) was a mathematical answer to a linguistically motivated question. After graduation I planned to write a thesis in the foundations of probability, sponsored by Abraham Robinson, while being Carnap's research assistant—a situation that reflected well my dual interests. My eventual dissertation under Tarski was however on different, purely mathematical subjects (not even, properly speaking, in mathematical logic), and in most of my academic career I was based in the mathematics department of the Hebrew University. I researched at the same time, and wrote occasionally on philosophical subjects, holding various visiting positions in philosophy and computer science. Given this spectrum of interests, the use of formal methods in philosophy seemed a natural choice. It was not ideologically motivated; when I was a student Spinoza was my favorite philosopher and Nietzsche was a looming figure. The choice was dictated by the necessity to work on subjects in different fields that formed somehow a continuous group. There are so many things that one can do.

What example(s) from your work illustrates the role formal methods can play in philosophy?

Strictly speaking, the use of formal methods means that some formal (or mathematical, or semi–formal) setup is offered in order to model, or analyze a given subject. More broadly, it can mean the inclusion of a sufficient amount of formal or mathematical items, which cannot be avoided if the subject requires it. Thus, a philosophical analysis of Gödel's result (exemplified in my "What Gödel's Incompleteness Result Shows and Does Not Show", *Journal of Philosophy*, 2000) must address some technical aspects, but does not amount to "use of formal methods". My paper on Dummett ("Is the "Bottom-Up" Approach from the Theory of Meaning to Metaphysics Possible?", *The Journal of Philosophy*, 1996) certainly does not, nor do my recent published works (also on my website) in the philosophy of mathematics. Among more recent works, the role of formal methods in the strict sense, is exemplified in:

- "Pointers to truth" (*Journal of Philosophy*, 1992).

- "Pointers to propositions" in *Circularity, Definition and Truth* (ed. Chapuis and Gupta), 2000.

- "Vagueness, Tolerance and Contextual Logic" (Since 2002 on my website http://www.columbia.edu/~hg17. I still have to get down to publish it.).

- "Reasoning with Bounded Resources and Assigning Probabilities to Arithmetical Statements" (*Synthese*, 2004).

I should clarify that, in general, formal modeling are not offered as realistic pictures of actual reasoning. It is not claimed, in my probabilistic modeling (in earlier works), that human beings actually compute Bayesian probabilities. Neither is it claimed that the pointer-evaluation algorithms is how in fact we judge truth and falsity in complicated situations. The point of the model is to uncover certain basic mechanisms that, in principle, are operative in our thinking. This applies across the board, the prime examples being the modeling of logical reasoning in Boole and Frege. Of course, the model can evolve a life of its own: in practical applications (e.g., the use of Boolean algebras in computer science), or in the service of a metaphysical program (e.g., *Principia Mathematica*).

What is the proper role of philosophy in relation to other disciplines?

I take it that we should view this from the point of view of analytic philosophy. But since the phrased question is about philosophy *tout court* let me first take the philosophical license of considering the question itself. 'Philosophy' is now applied to a congeries of writings and discussions, for which the question of role cannot be answered except in vague generalities. What ball park are we in? This is up for grabs; we have "philosophy of friendship", "philosophy of sport" and what not. Some of it is done by clever writers, a sort of intelligent journalism, which can make interesting reading on a plane. Adhering to a more traditional framework, the spectrum is still extremely broad, from Frege to Heidegger (not to mention trendy concoctions by Lacan and Zizek). The beginning of this story, in Greece, may therefore be used to give us orientation. Originally, philosophy was a total enterprise, a "theory of everything". (It was also, for some groups, a practical way of life—an aspect I shall, for obvious reasons, ignore here.) It aimed, naively and profoundly, at a picture of the world. When Hamlet says "there are more things in heaven and earth, Horatio, then are dreamt of in your philosophy" he means by 'philosophy' a general frame of knowledge; 'natural philosophy' is another surviving testimony to the original philosophical ambition. What distinguished it from verbal art was the use of the thinking faculty as the major tool in constructing the picture. This overall conception involved, as it must have, systematic use of metaphor (analogical thinking). Nietzsche claimed that that type of knowledge is based on worn out metaphors and is therefore doomed to error. Large scale metaphor is indeed essential to science, which constructs the unfamiliar from familiar materials. But in science, systematic repetitive use, the very thing that kills metaphors in art, gives them life. Their survival, moreover, depends on their passing the repeated severe test of success; metaphors are refined and modified in a continuous feedback; as new forms become familiar to the professional, they serve as a basis for newer more abstract ones. (Mathematics requires a different analysis, the fundamental role there is played not by metaphors, but by structures, or basic modes of organization; I cannot however enter into it here.) It has been often observed that scientific disciplines, at least some of them, have their roots in philosophy. One can say that philosophy, properly speaking, is the enterprise that, avoiding the sacrifice involved in narrow specification and the methodology of experimental success, remains faithful to the goal of "true picture", or "basic account". This still leaves open the kind of building blocks and the kind of tools employed in giving the account. One major divide is between those who place human experience and interests at the center, most notably phenomenological philosophy (exemplified by Husserl and Heidegger) and those who make place for brute scientific facts, as an independent ingredient in the picture. To put it bluntly and somewhat naively, whatever the insights in Heidegger's account, whatever its truths, it is highly probable that 10 million years ago there was no *Dasein*, i.e., no basic structures of the existential *human*, and no Being of entities (unless the dinosaurs, or some extraterrestrials, were the source of some such structures); and it is highly probable that *Dasein* and Being will not subsist two hundred million years from now (unless, again, humans migrate to other planets, or there are extraterrestrials, etc.). But there were and will be stars and galaxies, and the truth of '$2^{25964951} - 1$ is a prime number' will not be affected (the truth of certain English statements does not require that English, or any language, exist at the time in question). Heidegger may regard this naïve claim as fundamentally misguided, since the entities of physical science are derivative: the outcome of the "objectifying" processes in the *Dasein*; or he might regard it as philosophically uninteresting. But I cannot help being dogmatically impressed by such objective facts and by science's claims (at least some of them) to reveal non–trivial truths. This does not mean that I endorse "scientism"—a reduction of "everything" to science. *Meaning* is basic; but whatever the picture, it will have to accommodate some scientific truths as self-standing elements, not merely as human constructs.

The science-friendly (and mathematics-friendly) attitude inclines one naturally to emphasize clarity and precision in the choice of tools. The prime example is Frege, whose analysis of logical structure, in thought and language, was achieved by setting up, in his words: "a formula language, modeled upon that of arithmetic, for pure thought". This does not obviate the use of metaphors, of which Frege availed himself freely, e.g., the distinction between *saturated* and *unsaturated* entities, which marks the essential difference between objects and concepts (or, more generally, functions). His proposed analogy between *moon, moon's projection in the telescope, moon's projection on one's retina*, on one hand, and *reference, sense, subjective associated idea*, on the other, is a rather crude didactic aid, which is dispensable. Not so the subtle metaphor that underlies his characterization of the sense of an expression as "the mode of presentation", or "the way the reference is given to us". (This metaphor, I think, is often misunderstood.)

To come back to the question, the proper role of philosophy derives from what remains of its initial ambitions, given the accumulated intellectual history of the human race, including of course science. It is *au fond* a way of knowing, of apprehending, of "getting it". What can this way do for us now? Wittgenstein, in the *Tractatus*, boils it down to "elucidations", which "... make clear and delimit sharply the thoughts which otherwise are, as it were, opaque and blurred." In his later period he seems, in some pronouncements, to restrict it further to a therapeutic activity that cures philosophers by dissolving their confused questions. I think that "elucidations" is nearer to the mark, provided that we interpret the term broadly, unencumbered by the Tractarian framework. Elucidation can be a great creative project, like the elucidation of logical categories and logical structure, by Boole, Frege, Peirce and others; or the elucidation of what *algorithm* means, proposed by Church and Turing. Naturally, I give examples that are nearer to my professional interests, but the principle is wide. Conceptual clarification, an analysis of plausible approaches and how they are related, of what is implied by this or that view, can be invaluable in ethics as it is in probability or foundational physics. Philosophy has moreover a similar task with regards to its own history; it rediscovers, reflects on, and critically reconstructs its past. It goes without saying that nothing is implied here concerning formal tools, whose justification depends on how and where they are used.

The answer, given from the perspective of analytic philosophy, makes no claim of exclusivity. In a more general perspective, any "systematic" thinking that shows us something significant, worth getting, through the use of intellectual metaphors can qualify as fulfilling the task. It may use a specially designed, dense vocabulary (the reader can judge at the end whether his or her effort was worth it). And it can be "systematic" in being non-systematic, like Wittgenstein's *Philosophical Investigations*, which tries to deliver the picture by an assortment of observations, thought experiments and little fables.

What do you consider the most neglected topics and/or contributions in late 20th century philosophy?

I must qualify my answer in two respects: "Most neglected ... in late 20th century philosophy" is too dramatic and sweeping for my present mood. Naturally, my views relate to philosophy that treats of logic, language, mathematics, epistemology and metaphysics; that is: not ethics (except that I take understanding and aiming at truth as basic values), not political philosophy, and not aesthetics.

In areas related to my own activities, the abundance of published (and e-published) material is such that one always risks missing relevant works. The following is a list of important topics that deserve more philosophical effort than they got.

Waismann's work on open texture merits a follow up and a more systematic analysis that relates it to the analysis of vagueness. The borderline between the two is itself vague, yet paradigmatic examples clarify the distinction. Whether the same sort of fine-grained analysis (not to speak of formal modeling), which has been applied to vagueness, is feasible here remains to be seen. Open texture can make for a better understanding of the analytic/synthetic distinction than Quine's form of behaviorism. In fact, Waismann anticipated Putnam's observations about the splitting of concepts under the impact of new discoveries.

Related to this is the wide subject of analogical thinking, in empirical science and mathematics. In empirical science (perhaps also in certain aspects of mathematical thinking) we have also metaphors. This, to be sure, is a difficult subject, but at least we have a lot of examples to go on; even a preliminary sorting of basic parameters should be of great value. Works on mathematical heuristics have been written by mathematicians, but the philosophical task remains. I should note that analogies, which are often marked by "similarly", "by the same token", "in the same way" and their like, can be quite precise; yet, their recognition often amounts to having major insights. Formal logic results, in fact, from recognizing and simulating patterns of reasoning; the back-and-forth moving between different levels of language, "from within" and "from without", is a common technique in mathematical logic. The proofs of Gödel's incompleteness results, as well as the results concerning $V = L$, are based on these insights. The difficulty of simulating some of these proofs in a powerful automated theorem prover such as *Isabelle* indicates how deep these human insights are.

In mathematics, the subject connects naturally with that of mathematical intuition, including in particular, geometric intuition; it also includes the use of paradigmatic examples. Here is a simple illustration. An interval (by which I mean a *closed* interval) consists of two points and all the points between them (in the strict sense of 'between'). If between every two points there is a point, then the union of two disjoint intervals is not an interval. These concepts are easily accessible, and the claim is immediately recognized as true by anyone (say, a seven-grader) who considers the drawing: A——B - - - - C——D; using another drawing, he or she will also see that the union of two intersecting intervals *is* an interval. We can logically derive the claim from the axioms of linear order, $<$, and the definition: X is between A and B iff $A<X<B$ or $B<X<A$. The proof—and I am not speaking of a formalized proof—is easy, but requires going through various cases and using repeatedly the properties of $<$. I noted that, without sufficient mathematical training, highly intelligent college students find the construction of the proof quite difficult. Now, in mathematical practice, some "seeing" of this kind is applied to highly abstract structures; proofs are then written as a check against error and for purposes of communication.

This brings me to the more general topic of *understanding*. Great philosophical efforts were centered around belief and knowledge, not so around understanding. More recently, there have been attempts, mostly in the AI community, to treat is as competence to perform various derivations, pertaining to syntax and semantics, which can be simulated in certain computational networks. But what I mean here is a subject that tries to address questions such as: What does it mean to understand a mathematical proof? (It certainly does not mean that one has gone over a formalized version and checked every step). The point is to investigate understanding without being bogged down by questions about consciousness. I do not know how much a philosophical analysis can accomplish, but it is worth trying.

The general notion of *proof* is another highly deserving topic. Roughly, and in all generality, a proof is an object whose presence in a given context serves as justifiable grounds for belief in a certain statement (where "justifiable" may include probabilistic estimates). Developments in theoretical computer science provide new interesting angles on this. One is the concept of zero-knowledge proofs. Here, the setup consists of two parties, the prover and the verifier; the prover aims to convince the verifier of the existence of a mathematical object satisfying certain constraints (e.g., a proof of a given theorem, or a solution of some equation), without revealing anything else about the object (this can be given precise probabilistic meaning). Both parties follow a certain protocol of exchanging messages, in which the verifier can use random numbers. If the prover has performs successfully to the end, the verifier concludes that the object exists with very high probability, which can be as near to 1 as wished by increasing the number of steps in the exchange. Another, more recent development gives rise to

PCP (probabilistic checkable proofs); it establishes the possibility of encoding candidates for proofs in such a way that their correctness can be verified in very short time by methods of statistical sampling (with probabilities as near 1 as wished).

There is place for philosophical work on the concept of *algorithm*. Some work has been done on the Church-Turing thesis, but I think that more is required, including, in particular, evaluations of Gurevich's *Abstract State Machines* and of Moschovakis' *recursors*.

In the foundations of probability, the question: what is a good Bayesian prior? deserves more philosophical attention than given to it. An argument first made by Putnam and further developed in my work with Snir ("Probabilities over rich languages, testing and randomness" 1982, *JSL*), suggest that priors that enable us to learn more from experience involve an inevitable price in complexity. This shows that there must be a limit to the use of Bayesian methods. At some junctures we must jump to conclusions not via conditionalization. There are theorems to be found, which establish more down-to-earth estimates of the complexity cost for being non-dogmatic. Philosophically, the significance of in principle limits on deductive capacity and the value of *ignoring* information, have been largely underappreciated. Within the framework of probability theory there have been proposals by Hacking, Garber, and lately by myself (in my paper in *Synthese*) for incorporating bounds on resources in the general probabilistic picture. Much more needs to be done, both technically and non-technically.

We still need more comprehensive accounts of the relations between various conceptions of probabilities (subjective, objective, dispositions, frequentists, von Mises's collectives), accounts that will also do justice to the fact that in practice we do not have infinite sequences and we decide via methodologies of significance levels and confidence intervals. In my paper "Towards a unified concept of probability" (*Proceedings of the 1983 Congress for Logic Methodology and Philosophy of Science*), I have sketched a way of "deriving" objective probabilities from subjective ones. Whether this is accepted or not, more needs to be done.

In the philosophy of mathematics we need accounts that reflect more the actual ways in which mathematics has been practiced. The general items discussed already have direct bearing on this, but let me specify more. The point is not to give an entertaining account of mathematics as a social cultural phenomenon, or of "the mathematical experience", laced with interesting stories, but to do real philosophical work. The fact that there were many mathematical errors and that mathematical history contains significant shifts should be addressed, but at greater depth than the shallow conclusion that mathematical beliefs, like all other human beliefs, are "eternally corrigible". And I do not think that mere history can lead to insights, unless it is guided by a philosophy based on an internal grasp of the subject. Here are some other directions that are important in my view.

It appears that the classical debates between the various brands of constructivism and realism (or Platonism) have come to an impasse. By far and large, mathematics, contrary to the initial expectations of intuitionists and constructivists, uses classical logic and has no qualms about infinities. The reason is that adopting a realistic stance within a classical framework, and accepting various infinities as is needed, is so much more convenient, hence more efficient. The foundational questions remain however. Many philosophers shy away "on principle" from a critical evaluation of mathematical practice, contending themselves with giving some plausible philosophical picture of whatever is accepted by the majority of mathematicians. The worth of this picture, which depends on the presupposed philosophical vocabulary, varies. But in the long run , this tendency is likely to produce a self-contained industry, which settles its internal debates by superficial reliance on what mathematicians do. A philosopher can however, without settling foundational questions, map what he or she considers feasible positions, and what they imply; and here one *does* adopt a critical stance based on a good grasp of the subject. In this direction I would like to mention two projects.

In the foundations of set theory we are in dire need of a good account that explains recent developments and their philosophical significance. Addressed to the non-expert who knows some set theory, this, by itself, would amount to a major philosophical enterprise. In the last forty years set theory has grown in technical sophistication to such an extent that mathematical logicians, who are not among the small number engaged in cutting edge research, find it extremely difficult. At the same time the subject is of high philosophical interest, and there are clear philosophical motivation driving some major technical works. A good in depth explanation is needed also because some published philosophical papers—which try to use recent set theory in support of philosophical claims—are of embarrassing quality, displaying technical errors, as well as a miscomprehension of the role of quantification over classes in set theory. (There is also a wide spread philosophical misconception of second order quantification in general, but this is a somewhat different matter.)

The second topic is strict finitism, the view that certain numeric terms, e.g., $2 \uparrow 5$ (which is 2 with four 2's stacked on top, it comes to 2^{65536}; the definition is:

$$2 \uparrow 1 = 2, \qquad 2 \uparrow (n+1) = 2^{2\uparrow n}),$$

fail to denote existing numbers. Is such a view feasible, and if so what does it imply? In his impressive *Predicative Arithmetic*, Nelson has proposed a framework based on this view, motivated by nominalism: the scarcity of physical objects that can underpin extremely large segments of natural numbers (the predicativity constraint is related, but does not, in itself, imply strict finitism; it only implies inability to prove, on the basis of addition and multiplication, closure under exponentiation). The work is related to other technical works by logicians and computer scientists. Nelson suggested a modified Hilbert program, whose goal is a demonstration of the system's consistency, which does not transgress its basic principles. In an *Erkenntnis* paper from 2000, Iwan uses previous results in mathematical logic to argue convincingly that *that* goal is unachievable. Questions concerning the feasibility of strict finitism and its philosophical implications remain however. I think that strict finitism should make its claim explicit by incorporating in the system statements of the form "t exists" and their negations, where t is a numerical term (this calls for some version of free logic). It should moreover include closure principles of form: "for all n, $f(n)$ exists" (which means: for all existing n, $f(n)$ exists), where $f(n)$ is a sufficiently slow-growing function; e.g., for all n, $n+1$ exists, or, for all n, n^2 exists. For an appropriate term t, this can be compatible with "t does not exist", since the derivation of t's existence from the closure principles is so long that it is non-existent. This line of thought can be combined with Yessenin Volpin's suggestion of treating the natural numbers as a bounded vague totality; it is obviously related to the Sorites. The idea was considered by Dummett in his paper "Wang's Paradox"; instead of 'existing number' he used the predicate 'small number'. He argued that this still leads to paradox; but in fact it does not (his argument rests on an interesting oversight). While $2 \uparrow 5$ is "too small" for a non-existence claim (since it can be reached in $2 \uparrow 4$ steps of repeated-squaring), arguments given by Nelson suggest that $2 \uparrow (2 \uparrow 5)$ might be a good candidate (perhaps we will have to go higher). I believe that even a strict finitist is committed to some form of realism, that is, to evidence-transcendent truth. The subject merits both technical and philosophical effort.

I believe that questions in the foundations of mathematics are metaphysical; they touch on ultimate aspects of reality. I hesitate to use 'metaphysical' since nowadays it may serve as a rubber stamp, intended to confer gravity on any kind of enquiry. The positivists tried to rule out metaphysical questions as confusions due to misuse of language. They were wrong, but their demise opened the floodgates, and a lot of what passes under "metaphysics" is the result of pushing forms and metaphors from everyday language, beyond their domain of significance. Historically such theorizing can be very fruitful, e.g., ancient atomism. But we are not in ancient Greece and elementary particles are essentially different entities, though many philosophers do not appreciate this. An attempt to systematize everyday conceptions can be interesting and rewarding. But reading metaphysical debates in mereology whether there is a possible world containing only gunk (atomless stuff), I know that something wrong has happened to "metaphysics".

What are the most important open problems in philosophy and what are the prospects for progress?

I shall point out one: the mind-body problem. I do not think we will ever give it a satisfactory answer. And I shall make one observation about reductionism.

When we reduce physical heat to molecular velocities, we are working within the same framework, and this enables us to derive physical heat from velocity-distribution. We can predict from the distribution what the heat will be, even in situations not encountered before. In other examples, the derivations are not practical, due to complexity. The output (or "move") of a complicated computational interactive system is derivable from its basic state at that moment , which boils down to an assignment of binary values to all memory locations. The enormity of the setup blocks any attempt to specify, even approximately, this state. Yet we know that this is all there is to it, states succeeding states according to the inputs and the system's program. We know how it works, because we have built it. When it comes to human beings, we have no such in–principle derivation. I cannot see any way how something like a succession of enormous array s of 0's and 1's, translates into color sensations or pains. Experimental research might help to set up empirical correlations: such and such a sequence of neuron firings is associated with such and such a sensation. These will make up a list of brute facts. There will be no theory of the kind that derives heat from velocities, or the computer's behavior from its state.

I think there is scope for progress in sharpening the concept of supervenience and clarifying more what is implied by it. We might see more clearly how, in certain respects, supervening entities are different from the ones on which they supervene, or from disjunctions of the latter.

I prefer to stop here, rather than extend my portion of answers, which is too long already.

I wish to express my appreciation of your project and my thanks for the unique opportunity of thinking and expressing my views on such a wide range of subjects.

7

Clark Nøren Glymour

Alumni University Professor

Carnegie Mellon University, PA, USA

Why were you initially drawn to formal methods?

A bit of biography then.

My family history is a story of educational mobility: my grand-father went to school with Einstein, I went to school with Evel Knievel. I spent my high school years in Butte, Montana, then a hard but joyful mining town high in the Rocky Mountains, since laid desolate by corporate America and not long from now to be uninhabitable from the same cause. There were few books of interest—the city library owned only one "philosophical" book, Schopenhauer's *Essays,* and I swear there was no work of logic in the entire county—yet my father kept a small but serious library, including Darwin's *Origin of Species*, and Spinoza's *Ethics* which was, I suppose the first source of my interest in formal methods in philosophy.

The summer of my 15th year, still suffering from adolescent reli-gious angst and fascinated with the prospect of *proofs* about God, I decided to work through *The Ethics*, lemma by lemma. Pencil in hand and pad in lap, I spent summer days under a tree over-looking the tracks of the Butte, Anaconda and Pacific Railroad, which carried copper ore from Butte's mines past my house to the smelter in Anaconda, 28 miles away, while I tried to reconstruct demonstrations about the Deity's lack of parts. I could make no sense of Spinoza's purported deductions; the meaning of each term seemed to morph and meander in the course of each argument. I had completed a year of plane geometry taught more or less from Euclid, and since the *Ethics* was obviously an imitation, I hit upon the following strategy: for each of Spinoza's terms, I would try substituting a geometrical term, and see if Spinoza's purported deductions became valid proofs in geometry. Faint hope, which I soon gave up for another task. Since Spinoza's terminology seemed to me so slippery, I would substitute throughout a letter for each occurrence of a term, distinct letters for distinct terms, and see if the resulting reasoning seemed sound. It never did. I gave it up, and for the next 25 years I thought the experience showed a defect of my intellect, until I read George Boole's attempt, in *The Laws of Thought*, to provide logical reconstructions of the same arguments, with results similar to my own. The following summer break from Butte Public High School I read Darwin, who made me an atheist ever after, and removed any motivation for trying further with Spinoza.

I was never good at mathematics in school, and not much interested in it. I matriculated at the University of Montana in 1960, where I immediately (and secretly, since my father opposed it) began studying philosophy, almost exclusively, even withdrawing from an introductory mathematics course in my first year. My private concern was with a single question – what are the limits of knowledge – but I enjoyed courses on every topic except Sartre, whom I thought was cute rather than profound, and Heidegger, whose work was badly taught by a Polish disciple, Zygmunt Adam-czewski, as a scripture rather than a hypothesis. (Adamczewski had avoided execution in the Katyn Forest only because he was too young to have the officer's pins he, as a Polish aristocrat, would have received at age 18. Nonetheless, he literally worshiped Heidegger, the man who sought to be Hitler's Minister of Education, and was deeply wounded when Heidegger broke a promise to let Adamczewski publish his English translation of *Sein und Zeit*.)

The result was that within two years I had completed all of the requirements of a major in philosophy except a course in logic. At the end of my second year, the University dismissed me because I refused to take part in military exercises, which were then required in many American colleges and universities. At the University of New Mexico, to which I transferred with the intention of continuing a course of philosophical study, I found the members of the Philosophy Department intolerably foolish, and so determined that I would take no more philosophy beyond the required logic course, and instead spend my remaining two undergraduate years qualifying for a second major in another subject. I picked chemistry because it was a natural science, and because, by taking a number of courses by examination, I could complete the requirements in my remaining four semesters, something I could not do in physics. Biology did not interest me at the time, and in Montana I had found the two courses I had taken in psychology to oscillate between banality and unintelligibility.

I took the introductory courses in chemistry, and organic chemistry as well, by examination, which was allowed at the University, and so saved considerable time. That would not do, however, for physical chemistry and quantum mechanics, both of which were required. There I was handicapped because I knew no more mathematics than high school geometry and algebra, absolutely nothing of calculus and differential equations. I managed nonetheless to obtain a better than average grade in both courses by a kind of ruse: in doing assignments, I teamed with a graduate student who could integrate and differentiate and understood the strange idea of logarithms, but who seemed baffled by problems stated in words. I learned more mathematics from doing problems with him than from the calculus courses in which I was enrolled at the same time.

I graduated in chemistry and philosophy, although the University thought the combination so improbable that my diploma read "English and Philosophy," and I enrolled as a graduate student in chemistry, all philosophy departments to which I had applied being unwilling to grant me that status. The summer between I spent climbing in the Tetons with my friend Don McCaig, in later years the owner of a farm in Virginia where I wrote my first book. I took along a single philosophical book, Stephen Toulmin's *Philosophy of Science*, which, having carried it to the exclusion of other reading in a full pack up a high mountain, I found so vapid that in disgust I threw it into a deep cavern. So there is another source: I came to formal philosophy in disappointment at the alternative. More accurately, by now I was disappointed in philosophy from all sides.

I had by this time, 1964, learned some calculus, some differential equations (a course I had to take twice, engaged the first time round principally in courting a young woman), and I had learned to program in Fortran— then practiced by producing quantities of punch cards, an exercise I very much disliked. I concentrated in inorganic chemistry, aiming to synthesize a molybdenum sandwich compound—a precursor of Buckeyballs. This required endless nights in the laboratory while chemicals gurgled away in racks of glass tubes, a setting made romantic by association with film images of the laboratories of mad chemists, which mine much resembled, but unproductive of molybdenum sandwiches. I was a

lousy lab chemist. In those laboratory nights I turned to reading mathematics, mostly topology and differential geometry, and
again to reading philosophy, this time Reichenbach's *The Direction of Time*, which I found fascinating.

It was not long before I was once more about to be dismissed
from the University, this time for instructing undergraduates in
the theories of Paracelsus. I was put in charge of an undergraduate chemistry laboratory supervising 20 or so undergraduates in
a course of experiments none of which required more than half an
hour to complete, but for each of which 3 hours had been allot-
ted. The harridan who had dominion over laboratory instruction
refused to allow me to release the students when they had completed their experiments, and so I had to keep them entertained
for more than 2 hours each week, first by playing poker, and then,
feeling that poker was inappropriate, giving the students lectures
on the history of chemistry. In an excess of seriousness, I decided
that if students received two hours of instruction each week on the
history of chemistry, they should be tested on the content. That
was my downfall. The chairman of the chemistry department came
across a copy of one of my little examinations, as it happened on
Paracelsus, and thinking I was teaching the students that modern
chemistry turns on the sulfureous principle, and the like, decided
to fire me. I calmed him a bit, but it became clear that I had no
future there. I applied to Indiana in History and Philosophy of
Science, and my beloved teacher at Montana, Cynthia Schuster,
prevailed on her old friend, Wesley Salmon, to admit me.

At Indiana I learned modern algebra and some serious logic
from a mathematician, Andrew Adler, and did chemical physics
as a minor subject, where I learned three things perhaps more
important than chemistry. I struggled through the graduate statistical mechanics course, full of long calculations that invariably
tripped me up, only to receive the highest mark in the course because of the final exam—an essay test. I learned this: mistakes
of calculation are easier to remedy than mistakes of conception.
In my graduate quantum theory course, the professor labored to
produce a clumsy theorem (I don't remember what) of the form
"if p then q." The contrapositive was more intuitive and I said so,
only to hear the professor adamantly deny the truth of the contrapositive formulation, and when presented with the general logical
principle, deny that too. I learned, as had better minds before me,
Boole's and Frege's included, that logic is not about people. The
man gave a final examination with no time limit, full of problems

each of which could be solved by a calculation requiring hours or in a moment by one or another trick. Some poor students labored over it for two days without sleep. I learned that cleverness is no excuse for cruelty.

My doctoral thesis was on logical empiricist accounts of scientific theories, and except for one little piece, it was not mathematics. It did leave me with a problem I have never solved: Consider the theory of infinity in the identity relation alone, in a first-order language with identity having another binary predicate. With Adler's help, I proved there is no logically weakest, consistent, finitely axiomatizable extension of the theory. Which raises the general question: when, if ever, does a recursively but not finitely axiomatizable theory have a logically weakest finitely axiomatizable conservative extension in extra predicates?

From Indiana I went to Princeton, where Richard Grandy and Dana Scott helped me to prove some things about equivalent theories, and I obtained an amusing result on indistinguishable spacetime models of general relativity, which helped me to win tenure. I spent several years trying to work out a formal theory of confirmation, vaguely inspired by Carnap and by my then colleague, Carl Hempel, and wrote a book about it, only to realize in the end that I could not make the formalism work because the project itself was ill-conceived: I had not answered, and worse had not asked, what confirmation has to do with finding the truth. That reflection, and conversations with Scott Weinstein, led me to an interest in formal learning theory, which Hilary Putnam had introduced fifteen years before and the philosophical community had largely ignored, and, regrettably, still does. I had at that point, thirty eight years of age, discovered nothing I thought of any real value, and in the bleakness of my self-imposed exile in Oklahoma thought my ambition to make a real intellectual contribution was lost. I wanted to contribute more in a life than the high brow book reports and whiggish histories of science that I found increasingly passed for philosophy of science, and that still do. Yet in the course of writing the book that disappointed me, I came across a statistical and social science literature on causal inference, where hypotheses were justified by statistical constraints on observed variables, and by 1980 or so I asked myself a question: what are the class of causal hypotheses, under what assumptions relating causation and probability, that can account for any specified set of probability constraints on observed variables? I never answered that question just as posed, but the fruits of the effort it prompted in collaboration with my then students, Peter Spirtes, Richard Scheines, and Kevin Kelly, did finally make me a kind of formal philosopher.

What example(s) from your work illustrates the role formal methods can play in philosophy?

The little puzzle I presented in *Theory and Evidence*, now often called the "problem of old evidence," illustrates a sensitivity to incoherence that is, I think, almost uniquely philosophical. The puzzle is simple: (1) Established phenomena can be evidence for new theories (the advance of the perihelion of Mercury was evidence for the general theory of relativity); (2) (according to Bayesians) E is evidence for H if and only if the probability of H conditional on E and other knowledge K is greater than the unconditional probability of H conditional on K; (3) Established phenomena have probability 1; (4) the probability of H conditional on K conjoined with a proposition of probability 1 is equal to the probability of H conditional on K. Hence Bayesians are inconsistent.

A lot has been written about this puzzle and variations on it. My view is that it is merely a dramatic way of making the point that there is no unique, normative way of redistributing probabilities when the algebra of events (or hypotheses) is altered—as by the introduction of a novel theory. What I think is interesting is that even very sophisticated statisticians don't get such arguments. Some weeks ago I had dinner with two distinguished statisticians, one a member of the National Academy of Science, and the other who ought to be. Both had just given lectures proclaiming themselves thoroughgoing subjective Bayesians. So what is this problem of old evidence they asked me, and I explained it: your degree of belief in the evidence is 1; so your degree of belief in the evidence conditional on a hypothesis is 1, so the conditional probability of the hypothesis given the old evidence equals its probability without the old evidence. "No, no" they protested: the evidence has a likelihood on the hypothesis that is different from one or zero. Though they claimed to be complete subjectivists, about likelihoods—i.e., probabilities conditional on hypotheses—they are radical objectivists.

More substantially, I think my work with Spirtes and Scheines, Richardson and Meek on causal Bayes nets illustrates the fruitfulness both for philosophy and for science, of axiomatization, mathematical proof, computational implementation, and simulation testing. The methods have found application in a wide range of applied sciences, some of which (in genetics and mineralogy, for example) I have been directly involved with. We have implemented some the basic algorithms for a scheduled 2009 NASA mission to Mars. One of the applications that most pleases me was quite unintended. For years I had talked with Alison Gopnik, a developmental psychologist at Berkeley, about Bayes nets and causality, and she talked to me about what babies can learn, taunting me that the algorithms of which I was so proud should be put to use doing something serious, like figuring out how babies learn what they do. Together we worked out some experiments, which Gopnik and her students conducted, to see whether young children make judgements in accord with causal Bayes net principles in simple problems. They do, and as the problems and principles got more difficult, the kids continued to perform as if they had Bayes nets in their heads. Whether they do or not, this work has opened up psychological thinking about causation and learning, and is even now being extended by a number of psychologists interested in child and adult cognition.

What is the proper role of philosophy in relation to other disciplines?

There are two roles of value: provocateur and innovator. As provocateur, the business of philosophy is to identify contradictions, purge nonsense, prompt clarification. For the sciences, the role of philosophy in innovation was announced more or less as I envision it, by Michael Friedman:

> Science, if it is to continue to progress through revolutions ... needs a source of new ideas, alternative programs, and expanded possibilities that is not itself scientific in some sense—that does not, as do the sciences themselves, operate within a generally agreed upon framework of taken for granted rules. For what is needed ... is precisely the creation and stimulation of new frameworks or paradigms, together with what we might call meta-frameworks or meta-paradigms—new conceptions of what a coherent rational understanding of nature might amount to—capable of motivating and sustaining the revolutionary transition to a new first-level or scientific paradigm. Philosophy, throughout its close association with the sciences, has functioned in precisely this way ... .
> —Michael Friedman, *The Dynamics of Reason*

Politics, religion and morality are practices, not disciplines, but I think philosophy has analogous roles with respect to them.

While I share Friedman's vision, his book describes no example of a 20th century philosophical contribution of this kind, nor did he provide one when I asked in recent conversation. There aren't many. Logic, and the idea of logical form, and its development by philosophers in the late 19th and in the 20th centuries, had considerable influence in mathematics, linguistics, and elsewhere. Philosophical logics of various kinds, although they became rather ritualized and sometimes overly technical for their own sake, had a considerable impact on computer science, especially artificial intelligence. Ramsey's work on decision theory and the foundations of probability helped to remake, or to create, many applied and theoretical subjects. Hilary Putnam's creation of computational learning theory, and developments from it by a few philosophers, makes another example. I suppose I should suppress modesty here and add my own work with Spirtes and Scheines, which created the interpretive and much of the mathematical fundamentals of graphical causal models, now finding many scientific applications.

What do you consider the most neglected topics and/or contributions in late 20th century philosophy?

Once when young I had the misfortune to be trapped at a Philosophy Meeting on the interior of a bench next to Roy Wood Sellars, who occupied the only exit from same. Roy Wood, father of Wilfred Sellars and briefly in the 1920s prominent in the American Critical Realist movement in philosophy, whatever that may have been, was then in his eighties and full up with a life time of opinions, most of them disapproving. Finding he had a literally captive audience, even if only of one, he provided me with the three hour version of the information that philosophy had gone wrong when it followed that fool, that whipper-snapper, that casuist, John Dewey. You, dear reader, if you exist, are at least not trapped, and can avoid my version of Roy Wood's diatribe. I too have a son in philosophy. Will parallels never end?

In Friedman's vision, which I share, philosophy of science should be judged in the first instance by its contributions to the advancement of the sciences; in parallel, ethics and political philosophy should perhaps be judged by their contributions to public morality and policy. By that standard, the assessment cannot be good.

Late 20th century philosophy drew up the bridges, locked on a chastity belt, and became so introspective that it has come close to swallowing itself. Real mathematical work with philosophical motives – Teddy Seidenfeld's collaborative work on the foundations of Bayesian statistics is a good example – is ignored or dismissed, and certainly undervalued, by philosophical audiences. Calculations are allowed as philosophy chiefly if they are exercises in finite probability, or bits of mathematical physics, or bits of logic. Computation theory, mathematical psychology, statistics, epidemiology, genetics, are alien territory, except as subjects for occasional book reports (e.g., the recent "philosophical" project to make an accounting of all of the ways biologists use the word "gene"). Except for misconceived and apparently indefatigable efforts to justify every methodological slogan from supposed subjective probability measures, late 20th century philosophy has handed over methodology to statistics and machine learning, to which only rare philosophers have anything to contribute. The little fresh air provided by developments in formal learning theory, those for example by Kevin Kelly and Oliver Schulte, is breathed chiefly by set theorists, not philosophers. There is excellent work here and there, but the preponderance is pretty dreary. The sorry state of philosophy of science is apparent among graduate students, who systematically avoid philosophically motivated problems that are sufficiently well-posed so that there is really something to discover.

I do not think things are much better with ethics and political philosophy, although I read less of it. The most original 20th century theory of a just state, John Rawls theory of course, prompted extensive commentary mostly internal to philosophy; the only public comment I have noticed is contemptuous dismissal by Anton Scalia. Rawls' theory did prompt some bad mathematics, Stephen Strasnick's thrice published but ever fallacious derivation of the difference principle from Arrow's theorem. There have been several philosophical defenses of libertarianism, most famously Robert Nozick's, but none that satisfactorily reconcile the doctrine of individual rights and the moral priority of property with simple facts about possession, the efficiencies of production, and the inefficiencies of distribution: for example, that pretty much everything owned by anyone was acquired through a history of transactions descending from some unjust taking, or that every manufactured good anyone in the world could reasonably consume could be made by one hundredth of the population of China alone.

Meanwhile, the issues of policy that affect the lives of millions are discussed in America without any useful philosophical contribution. The proper limits of state violence is surely among the most pressing philosophical issues, but philosophers can only offer a re-hash of just war theory. The responsibility of persons for the misdeeds of past governments that ruled them or their ancestors is at issue in everything from international debt payments to reparations for slavery, but there is no philosophical influence on public discussion. The ugly role of superstition – "faith" is the euphemism – in public morality and public policy has been challenged only faintly, by Dan Dennett, and more vigorously by Sam Harris. In America anyway, philosophy in the commons is represented, sad to say, by a failed philosophy graduate student, George Will, and a failed philosophy professor, William Bennett. For the most part, professional philosophical ethics and political philosophy is as far from contributing to political discussion as professional philosophy of science is from contributing to scientific discussion. Very far indeed. Were it not for Sam Harris and Peter Singer, there would be no connection at all.

What are the most important open problems in philosophy and what are the prospects for progress?

Oh, they are everywhere. All that is required is a well prepared mind, a willingness to collaborate, and freedom from the fear of actually discovering something or actually changing something.

8

Adolf Grünbaum

Andrew Mellon Professor of
Philosophy of Science
Research Professor of Psychiatry
Chairman, Center for Philosophy of Science
University of Pittsburgh, PA, USA

Why were you initially drawn to formal methods?

My interest in the foundations of geometry led me to appreciate Hilbert's demonstration that a number of alleged "theorems" in the 13 books of Euclid's *Elements* were actually non-sequiturs, begotten by the tacit assumption of additional postulates via reliance on diagrams. This major insight was afforded by *axiomatic rigor.*

What example(s) from your work illustrates the role formal methods can play in philosophy?

In my concern with the foundations of Einstein's special theory of relativity, I found great epistemological value in the 1924 German original of Hans Reichenbach's *Axiomatization of the Theory of Relativity* (1969): He endeavored to axiomatize that theory in such a way that its logically independent physical axioms were so chosen as to be each more or less separately accessible to test by known or envisioned experimental results.

What is the proper role of philosophy in relation to other disciplines?

In a nutshell, philosophy should serve as their intellectual conscience.

9

Susan Haack

Cooper Senior Scholar in Arts and Sciences

Professor of Philosophy, Professor of Law

University of Miami, Coral Gables, FL, USA

Formal Philosophy? A Plea for Pluralism

As I mulled over the questions put to me, what came first to mind was Frege's illuminating metaphor for the differences between formal and natural languages:

> We build for ourselves artificial hands, tools for particular purposes, which work with more accuracy than the hand can provide. And how is this accuracy possible? Through the very stiffness and inflexibility of parts the lack of which makes the hand so dextrous.[1]

Hot on its heels came this shrewd observation of Nietzsche's:

> In his heart every man knows very well that being unique, he will be in the world only once, and that no imaginable chance will for a second time gather together in a unity so strangely variegated an assortment as he is.[2]

Let me explain.

I was educated, in the late 1960s and early 1970s, first at Oxford and then in Cambridge—largely in the then-dominant linguistic-conceptual-analytical style. Quite early on, someone or something

---

[1] Gottlob Frege, "On the Scientific Justification of a Conceptual Notation" (1882), trans. Terrell Ward Bynum, in Bynum, ed. *Conceptual Notation and Related Articles* (Oxford: Clarendon Press, 1972), 83–9, p.86.

[2] Friedrich Nietzsche, "Schopenhauer as Educator" (1874), in *Untimely Meditations*, trans. R. J. Hollingdale (Cambridge: Cambridge University Press, 1983), 125–94, p.127.

led me to Quine, who led me to Carnap and Peirce,[3] who led me to the other classical Pragmatists. Over time, it has been Peirce's work that has come to influence me the most: his formal fluency and logical innovations, of course, but also his distrust of easy dichotomies, his idea of the growth of meaning, his attractively naturalistic theory of inquiry, his constructive reconception of metaphysics and its role—not to mention his penchant for neologisms. James hasn't been as strong an influence, but his observation that Pragmatism "'unstiffens' our theories" resonates with me;[4] for Pragmatism opened my eyes to a conception of philosophy broader and more flexible than, as Tony Quinton puts it, the "lexicographical needlework"[5] of pure linguistic analysis.

Over several decades, I have worked in logic and philosophy of logic; in metaphysics, epistemology, and philosophy of science; on questions of culture and society; and most recently on issues at the interface of epistemology and the law of evidence—and, of late, on the epistemological novel. So you shouldn't be surprised to hear that I think of philosophy, not as a sharply delineated and tightly specialized discipline, but as a loose federation of inquiries into a characteristic, though constantly evolving, class of questions—some of which are also of interest to inquirers in other fields. I see, for example, no bright line separating metaphysical questions about the nature, origin, and evolution of physical laws from questions in physical cosmology, or questions in philosophy of logic from questions in semiotics or theoretical linguistics, or questions in epistemology or ethics from questions in the jurisprudence of evidence or of culpability—and so on.[6]

---

[3] To Carnap by way of "Epistemology Naturalized," in *Ontological Relativity and Other Essays* (New York: Columbia University Press, 1969), 69–90; to Peirce by way of chapter 1 of *Word and Object* (Cambridge: MIT Press, 1960).

[4] William James, *Pragmatism* (1907), Frederick H. Burkhardt and Fredson Bowers, eds. (Cambridge: Harvard University Press, 1975), p.43; James notes that he borrowed "unstiffens" from the young Italian pragmatist Giovanni Papini.

[5] Anthony Quinton, "Character and Will in Modern Ethics" (1983), in Quinton, *From Wodehouse to Wittgenstein* (Manchester, UK: Carcanet Press, 1998), 39–55, p.39.

[6] On my conception of philosophy generally, see Susan Haack, "Not Cynicism but Synechism: Lessons from Classical Pragmatism," *Transactions of the C. S. Peirce Society*, XLI.2, summer 2005: 239–53; also forthcoming in John Shook and Joseph Margolis, eds., *Companion to Pragmatism* (Oxford: Blackwell).

So naturally I think there are many different talents useful to a philosopher, among them "logical acumen, textual sensitivity, creative imagination, analytic rigor, conceptual subtlety and penetration, etc.";[7] and many different legitimate ways of tackling the rich variety of questions within the purview of philosophy. The various members of the loose-knit family of approaches and techniques vaguely indicated by the phrase "formal methods"—which may refer, quite narrowly, to the syntactic methods of formal logic, but may also include Tarskian methods of extensional formal semantics, "Montague grammar," applications of the mathematical calculus of probability, etc., etc.; and which, at its broadest, encompasses any and every use of any and every kind of symbolic apparatus—are just a few among those "many legitimate ways."

Formal methods can be, and sometimes have been, very useful in philosophy; but I don't believe they are the only useful methods, or even that they enjoy any special privilege. Sometimes a formal approach is just what is needed; but sometimes it is inappropriate to the task at hand, sometimes it obliges us artificially to restrict the scope of our questions or the depth of our analysis—and sometimes it is little more than decoration, a superficially mathematical or scientific gloss on weak or woolly thinking (as the statistical apparatus deployed by social scientists sometimes is). Frege had it just about exactly right: for certain purposes the symbolism of modern logic is more powerful and more precise than natural language; but it is also less flexible and less versatile.

These days, however, with philosophy increasingly professionalized, increasingly self-conscious about its status as a discipline, and increasingly splintered into sub-specialisms, it seems that many philosophers seek to define themselves professionally by their allegiance to a specialized sub-field or to a specialized method of philosophizing. Of course, there is quite a long tradition of Continental philosophers scoffing at the persnickety logic-chopping of their analytic counterparts, and analytic philosophers scoffing, in return, at the pretentious vagueness of their Continental colleagues; and now even within neo-analytic philosophy there are internecine disputes about the relative importance of formal-logical tools, of close attention to ordinary language, to conceptual "intu-

---

[7] Here I am quoting myself, from an essay entitled "The best man for the job may be a woman ... and other alien thoughts on affirmative action in the academy," in Susan Haack, *Manifesto of a Passionate Moderate: Unfashionable Essays* (Chicago: University of Chicago Press, 1998), 167–87, p.175.

ition," or to the findings of this or that area of science. Worse yet, in the culture of boosterism and self-promotion that now pervades the universities, many are tempted to tout whatever philosophical questions most interest them as *the* most important or critical issues, and whatever way of going about philosophy best suits their temperament or talents as *the* most fruitful, *the* most rigorous, *the* most up-to-date, *the* most scientific, etc., method.[8]

If you are inclined, as I am, to a tolerantly expansive (but not boundless) view of the scope of philosophy and a flexibly pluralistic (but not promiscuous) attitude to its "method(s)," this situation seems—well, less than ideal. And since the questions before me seem in part to reflect the present unhappy situation, my responses will in part reflect my unease about it.

Why were you initially drawn to formal methods?

I have never thought of myself, as this question seems to presuppose, as a "formal philosopher"; but I can say something about how my interest in logic arose.

In my student days it was commonly taken for granted that logic was a *male* thing; women were supposedly more suited to ethics and such. (It is distressing, to say the least, that this idea has since been revived—in the name of feminism, yet!)[9] I suspect that my initial interest in logic may have arisen at least in part from my instinctive resistance to this ubiquitous presumption; at any rate, I still recall my disappointment on discovering that Dana Scott and Hilary Putnam were not, as I had innocently imagined, women. Whatever the initial motivation, though, what came to appeal to me was the rigor and clarity logic made possible, its clean elegance; but also—as, reading Frege and Peirce, I learned more about its history—the sense of modern logic as a remarkable, and still-evolving, intellectual achievement.

Reading in the history of logic taught me to distinguish an older, broader, Aristotelian conception of the subject, and a newer, narrower, Fregean conception. Logic in the broader sense, the theory of whatever is good in the way of reasoning, would include not only systematic, formal representations of deductively valid arguments, and meta-theoretical results about such systems, but also theories

---

[8]See my "Preposterism and Its Consequences" (1996), reprinted in Susan Haack, *Manifesto of a Passionate Moderate* [note 7], 188–208.

[9]See e.g. Andrea Nye, *Words of Power* (London: Routledge, 1990).

of non-deductive reasoning, and theories of the term, of propositions, truth, etc.. These days, however—rather as, thanks to the
success of particular brands, "Xerox" has become a generic word
for photocopying, and "Kleenex" for tissues—"logic" seems usually to refer, quite narrowly, to syntactically characterizable systems of valid reasoning, of which the Frege-Peirce-Russell propositional and predicate calculi would be the paradigm. Dewey's *Logic:
The Theory of Inquiry*, for example, though it surely is logic in
the older, broader sense, bears little resemblance to logic in the
newer, narrower understanding.[10]

I have long—at least since the time of my B.Phil. dissertation on
ambiguity and fallacies of equivocation—been interested as much
in the messy philosophical issues encompassed in the broader conception of logic as in the elegant formalisms of logic in the narrower
sense. Perhaps it is unnecessary for me to say that the fact that
my conception of logic is broader than Frege's doesn't mean that
I have any sympathy with the virtually-vacuous use of "logic" in
which philosophers of religion once routinely wrote of "the logic
of 'God'" and moral philosophers of "the logic of 'good'," and in
which cultural critics and literary theorists now routinely write
of the "logic of capitalism," the "logic of gender," and such.[11]
But probably it *is* necessary to say that it doesn't mean, either,
that I endorse the idea of "philosophical logic" as conceived by
those who take epistemic, deontic, or other intensional logics to
be somehow peculiarly philosophical. I don't see epistemic logic
as any substitute for substantial epistemology, nor deontic logic
for ethics; and I see philosophically interesting questions arising
with respect to just about every logical system.

What example(s) from your work illustrates the role formal methods can play in philosophy?

Once again, the question makes me uneasy. The best methodological motto for a philosopher, to my mind, is Nike's: "just do it."

---

[10] John Dewey, *Logic: The Theory of Inquiry* (New York: Henry Holt and
Co., 1938).

[11] See for example Fredric Jameson, *Postmodernism, or, the Cultural Logic
of Late Capitalism* (Durham, NC: Duke University Press, 1991); Marjorie
Garber, "The Logic of the Transvestite: *The Roaring Girl* (1608)," in *Staging
the Renaissance: Reinterpretations of Elizabethan and Jacobean Drama*, ed.
David Scott Kastan and Peter Stallybrass (New York: Routledge, 1991), 221–
34.

At any rate, I have always tried to use whatever tools—formal, conceptual, linguistic, phenomenological, etc.—are appropriate to the task at hand. And most to the present point perhaps, though there are numerous illustrations of the role of formal methods to be found in my work, there is also a long-standing preoccupation with questions about the scope and limits of formalism.

In my first book, *Deviant Logic*,[12] I explored various efforts to revise the "classical," Russellian, two-valued propositional and predicate calculi. I proposed a way of distinguishing extensions of classical logic from deviant systems; replied to a range of arguments purporting to show that classical logic was not revisable; assessed proposed interpretations of deviant logics in terms of reference failure, vagueness, future contingents, etc.; and studied many-valued, Intuitionist, free, and quantum logics. In my next book, *Philosophy of Logics*,[13] I explored philosophical issues in the interpretation of formal-logical calculi, including propositions, validity, truth, the semantic paradoxes, modality, etc., and metaphysical and epistemological questions about the logical enterprise, especially those posed by the existence of a plurality of logical systems.

In this second book—the first chapter of which opens with Kripke's observation that "there is no mathematical substitute for philosophy"—the question of the scope of formal methods arose first in the context of Tarski's pessimism about the applicability of his methods outside well-behaved formal languages, at that time an issue made urgent by the burgeoning "Davidson program," proposing those methods as the basis for a theory of meaning for natural languages. In 1978 I concluded, cautiously, that it could not be said with any confidence that Davidson had succeeded in answering Tarski's reservations. Now, I would say that—impressive as Tarski's achievement undeniably is from a technical point of view—the difficulties in Davidson's (now-abandoned) program suggest that Tarski was right all along about the restricted applicability of his extensional methods.

Writing *Philosophy of Logics* also gave me an opportunity to look at relevance and fuzzy logics, two families of non-classical systems that came to my attention only after *Deviant Logic* was

---

[12] Susan Haack, *Deviant Logic* (Cambridge: Cambridge University Press, 1974).

[13] Susan Haack, *Philosophy of Logics* (Cambridge: Cambridge University Press, 1978).

published. Both raised questions about the limits of logic. According to Lotfi Zadeh, the resolution of problems in electrical engineering requiring gradational variables reveals that we stand in need of a radically new, "fuzzy" logic: a logic in which the truth-values are themselves fuzzy, local and subjective; in which the set of such values is not closed under the usual logical operations, so that "linguistic approximations" like "very true" and "fairly true" are needed to guarantee closure; inference is approximate rather than exact, and semantic rather than syntactic; and considerations such as consistency and completeness are "peripheral."[14] In short, according to Zadeh "fuzzy logic" refers, not simply to a logic of vagueness, but to a logic which is itself vague. I didn't go quite so far as Scott—who, in a talk entitled "Deviant Logic: Fact or Fiction?", commented that fuzzy logic wasn't just fiction, it was pornography! But I did argue that fuzzy logic "lack[s] every feature that the pioneers of formal logic wanted logic *for*."[15]

Critics, pointing to the success of fuzzy thermostats, fuzzy dish-washers, the fuzzy braking system in the Tokyo subway, etc., replied that fuzzy logic must be right—after all, it *works*.[16] I suspected, but couldn't at that time be sure, that fuzzy technology (though perhaps it used fuzzy set-theory) *didn't*, indeed *couldn't*, really depend on the strange, vague pseudo-formal logic Zadeh had described. Eventually, I managed to figured out how fuzzy controllers for air-conditioners, cement kilns, etc., work: in effect, by mimicking human operatives' gradual adjustments of temperature; and then it was clear that the success of such devices does not require the adoption of a radically non-classical theory of truth-preserving inferences.[17]

The fact that some relevance logics *both* extend *and* deviate

---

[14]Lotfi Zadeh, "Fuzzy Logic and Approximate Reasoning," *Synthese*, 30, 1975: 407–25.

[15]Susan Haack, *Philosophy of Logics* [note 13], 162–9; "Do We Need 'Fuzzy Logic'?", *International Journal of Man-Machine Studies*, 11, 1979: 437–45; reprinted in Susan Haack, *Deviant Logic, Fuzzy Logic: Beyond the Formalism* (Chicago: University of Chicago Press, 1996), 232–42 (the quotation in the text is from p.237 of *Deviant Logic, Fuzzy Logic*). See also Susan Haack, "Is Truth Flat or Bumpy?", in *Prospects for Pragmatism: Essays in Memory of F. P. Ramsey*, ed. D. H. Mellor (Cambridge: Cambridge University Press, 1980), 1–20; reprinted in *Deviant Logic, Fuzzy Logic*, 243–58.

[16]See for example, J. Fox, "Towards a Reconciliation of Fuzzy Logic and Standard Logic," *International Journal of Man-Machine Studies* 15, 1981: 213–20.

[17]Haack, *Deviant Logic, Fuzzy Logic* [note 15], 230–31.

from classical logic revealed hitherto-unsuspected complexities in the apparently simple distinction I had made earlier; and the proliferation of rival formal systems all claiming to correct the classical neglect of relevance suggested that this concept might be far from simple. Anderson and Belnap had referred approvingly to F.C.S. Schiller's complaint that "the central doctrine of the most prevalent logic still consists in a flat denial of Relevance."[18] Noting that Schiller had intended this observation not as a call for formalizing relevance but as a critique of the ambitions of formal logic, I began to suspect that relevance might depend on content rather than form, and thus in principle resist syntactic characterization. Once again, in 1978 I was cautious in my conclusion. And once again, now—with yet more rival systems of "relevance" and "relevant" logic on offer—I would be less tentative: many years of work in epistemology have convinced me that the concept of relevance is not explicable in purely formal terms, but contains ineliminably material elements.

While *Philosophy of Logics* was in press, in the course of the work that was eventually presented in "Fallibilism and Necessity"[19] (hoping to shed light on our susceptibility to error not only in our empirical, but also in our logical and mathematical beliefs), I had initially adopted what seemed to be the obvious strategy of characterizing fallibilism formally in the language of epistemic logic. But everything I tried turned out, directly or indirectly, to collapse fallibilism into the thesis that some propositions are contingent. Eventually it dawned on me that I would have to go about things differently; and that a real epistemological understanding would require attention not only to the propositions known or believed, but also to knowing subjects and their interactions with the world and each other.[20]

One manifestation of this conception of the way to go about tackling epistemological issues was my decision in *Evidence and Inquiry* (1993) to take as *explicandum* "A is more/less justified, at t, in believing that *p*."[21] I called the resulting epistemological

---

[18] Alan Ross Anderson and Nuel D. Belnap, *Entailment* (Princeton: Princeton University Press, 1975), p.30, citing F. C. S. Schiller, *Logic for Use* (New York: Harcourt, Brace, 1930), p.75.

[19] Susan Haack, "Fallibilism and Necessity," *Synthese* 41, 1979: 37–63.

[20] An idea expressed, in what now seems to me a somewhat fumbling and preliminary form, in Susan Haack, "Epistemology *With* a Knowing Subject," *Review of Metaphysics*, XXXIII.2.130, 1979: 309–35.

[21] Susan Haack, *Evidence and Inquiry: Towards Reconstruction in Epis-

theory "foundherentism": like coherentism, it allowed the legitimacy of mutual support among a person's beliefs; like foundationalism, it acknowledged the relevance of experience to justification.
An analogy with crossword puzzles helped me explore the role
of experiential evidence (the analogue of clues), and reasons (the
analogue of already-completed entries), and to articulate the difference between legitimate mutual support and a vicious circle.

In this context I argued that the structure of evidence isn't linear, like a mathematical or logical proof; rather, reasons ramify,
as crossword entries do. And the determinants of evidential quality are multi-dimensional: supportiveness (analogue: how well a
crossword entry fits with its clue and completed intersecting entries); independent security (analogue: how reasonable those other
completed entries are, independent of the support of this one);
and comprehensiveness (analogue: how much of the crossword has
been completed). Moreover, I argued, supportiveness of evidence
is not a narrowly logical matter. For one thing, that evidence E
deductively implies p doesn't make E conclusive with respect to p;
for inconsistent evidence deductively implies any p you like, but
it certainly isn't conclusive evidence for anything—let alone for
everything! More radically, I suggested that lesser degrees of supportiveness of evidence, though often conceived as the realm of
"inductive logic," are not syntactically characterizable; and that
it may not be feasible to assign numerical degrees of justification,
or even a linear ordering.

At the time, however, though I had come to doubt that the
concept of supportiveness can be spelled out in purely formal
terms, I still approached it propositionally: so, in the last stage
of my account of evidential quality, experiential evidence had to
be represented by "A's experiential C-evidence,"[22] a phrase referring to a set of propositions to the effect that A is in such-
and-such a perceptual, etc., state. These propositional proxies for

---

temology (Oxford: Blackwell, 1993); see especially chapter 4. See also Su-
san Haack, "A Foundherentist Theory of Empirical Justification," in Louis
Pojman, ed., *The Theory of Knowledge: Classic and Contemporary Read-
ings* (Belmont, CA: Wadsworth, 2nd. ed., 1998), 283–93; reprinted in Ernest
Sosa and Jaegwon Kim, eds., *Epistemology: An Anthology* (Oxford: Black-
well, 2000), 226–36, in Michael Huemer, ed., *Epistemology: Contemporary
Readings* (New York: Routledge, 2002), 417–34, and in Steven Luper, ed.,
Essential Knowledge (New York: Longman's, 2004), 157–67.

[22] Throughout *Evidence and Inquiry* I relied on a distinction between belief-
states ("S-beliefs") and belief-contents ("C-beliefs") and, correspondingly, between S- and C-evidence.

experiential evidence were clumsy; and they apparently encouraged misunderstandings. Some readers thought I was suggesting that experiential events are themselves propositional; and one, Ryszard Wójcicki—despite my explicit and repeated statements to the contrary—misconstrued me as postulating a class of infallible "experiential beliefs."[23] In an equal and opposite confusion, Paul Thagard hoped to "subsume" foundherentism in his coherentist theory, apparently not noticing that his "Principle of Data Priority" ran together experiential *events*, someone's seeing or hearing this or that, with experiential *beliefs*, i.e., the person's beliefs about those experiential events—which I had been at great pains to keep distinct.[24]

A key theme of my next book, *Defending Science—Within Reason* (2003),[25] was that scientific inquiry is continuous with everyday empirical inquiry. All serious empirical inquirers, I argued—historians, detectives, investigative journalists, legal and literary scholars, etc., etc., as well as scientists—use something like the "hypothetico-deductive method"; what is distinctive about inquiry in the sciences is, rather, the vast array of local and evolving "helps" to inquiry that scientists have developed over centuries of work: models and metaphors to aid the imagination, instruments of observation to aid the senses, intellectual tools like numerals, the calculus, statistics, computer programs, etc., to extend reasoning powers, ... and so on. Moreover, the evidence with respect to scientific claims is continuous with the evidence with respect to ordinary empirical claims—only more so: the experiential evidence is more dependent on instruments, the internal connections of reasons are even denser and more complex; and, almost always,

---

[23] See Ryszard Wojcicki, "Foundationalism, Coherentism and Foundherentism: The Controversies from an Alternative Point of View," in Cornelis de Waal, ed., *Susan Haack: A Lady of Distinctions* (Amherst, NY: Prometheus Books, forthcoming) and my "Of Chopin and Sycamores: Response to Ryszard Wojcicki," in the same volume.

[24] Paul Thagard, *Coherence in Thought and Action* (Cambridge, MA: Bradford Books, MIT Press, 2000), pp.41 ff, and "Critique of Emotional Reason," in *Susan Haack: A Lady of Distinctions* [note 23]. Thagard also claims to have a formal algorithm for calculating evidential quality; but this seems to depend on intuitive assignments of weights to such vague constraints as "justification" [sic], "connectedness," "semantic relatedness," and "explanation." See my reply to Thagard, "Once More, With Feeling: Response to Paul Thagard," in the de Waal volume.

[25] Susan Haack, *Defending Science—Within Reason: Between Scientism and Cynicism* (Amherst, NY: Prometheus Books, 2003).

the evidence is a shared resource, pooled within and across generations.

Like ordinary empirical claims, scientific claims need to be anchored in experience. Fortunately, by the time of *Defending Science* I had figured out how to handle experiential evidence without the awkward apparatus of propositional proxies, and could write that "[e]xperiential evidence consists, not of propositions, but of perceptual interactions; and it contributes to warrant, not in virtue of logical relations among propositions, but in virtue of connections between words and world set up in language-learning" (p.63). However, I argued, the old distinction between ostensive and verbal definitions, consonant with a foundationalist approach, won't do; a better account, in harmony with a foundherentist conception of the structure of evidence, recognizes that the meanings of different words are acquired, in different proportions, partly by ostension and partly verbally. This explains how someone's seeing, hearing, etc., this or that can contribute to the warrant of a claim when key terms are learned by association with these observable circumstances; *and* why sensory evidence contributes more [less] to warrant the more [the less] the meaning of those key terms is exhausted by that association.

This represents a significant simplification and refinement of my earlier account of experiential evidence. But it is much more than that. It is also an expression of a newly-articulated, more comprehensive conception of the proper role of logic in epistemology generally, and in philosophy of science in particular—a conception that breaks quite radically with assumptions inherited from the Logical Positivists.

In contradistinction to older-fashioned forms of plain Positivism, "Logical" Positivism was so-called because of its reliance on the remarkable innovations made by Boole, Frege, Peirce, Russell, etc., in formal logic—which seemed the very model of rigor. Repudiating metaphysics, ethics, aesthetics, etc., as meaningless verbiage or at best bad poetry, the Logical Positivists found themselves obliged to reinvent philosophy; and so they did, as "the logic of science." Carnap announced the reinvented philosophical project in these words: "[t]o pursue philosophy can only be to clarify the concepts and sentences of science by logical analysis. The instrument for this is the new logic."[26]

---

[26] Rudolf Carnap, "The Old and the New Logic" (1931); English translation by Isaac Levi, in A. J. Ayer, ed., *Logical Positivism* (Glencoe, IL: Free Press,

This idea was at the root of the Old Deferentialism in philosophy of science, an approach focused on structure, on method, on logic. Well, actually the Old Deferentialism might be better described as an unruly, squabbling family of approaches; for there were several competing styles of "inductive logic" on offer, while Popper and his followers insisted that the logic of science is exclusively deductive. In due course, the Old Deferentialism was challenged by proponents of a radically different kind of approach, which originated among sociologists of knowledge but by now has more than a foothold in philosophy of science: the New Cynicism, skeptical of the supposed rationality of science, and focused on power, politics, and rhetoric. From the true premise that the scientific enterprise cannot be fully understood in purely formal terms, the New Cynics drew the false conclusion that science isn't a rational enterprise after all. But, just as the Old Deferentialists had, they still took for granted that, if science *were* a rational enterprise, its rationality would be a matter of logic.

The way forward, I realized, was to recognize that this shared assumption is flawed: the rationality of the scientific enterprise cannot be understood in narrowly logical terms. This prompted me to wonder what might be missing *both* from the narrowly logical approach of the Old Deferentialists *and* from the historico-sociologico-rhetorical approach of the New Cynics.[27] Once the question was clear, the answer was obvious: the world, and our interactions with the world. This is why the philosophy of science presented in *Defending Science* is not "word-y," but "worldly."[28] This worldliness is manifested not only in the simplified and refined account of experiential evidence I have described, but also in an amplified account of the role of content in evidential support, an amplified account that suggests a new perspective on the role of conceptual innovation in science.

So far from being, as the New Cynics imagined, an obstacle to the rationality of science, the introduction of new vocabulary and shifts of meaning in an existing vocabulary can advance the scientific enterprise by gradually developing a terminology which, corresponding more closely to real kinds, enables explanation.

1959), 133–46, p.145.

[27] And to recall a particularly shrewd observation of J.L. Austin's, that in every important thinker "there's the part where he says it, and the part where he takes it back."

[28] "Worldly" was my word (*Defending Science* [note 25], p.52); the contrast with "word-y" I owe to A. Philip Dawid.

And now the reservations I had expressed in *Evidence and Inquiry* about the prospects for "inductive logic" could be grounded. Carnap and Hempel were right, I argued, in assuming that there is such a thing as supportive-but-less-than-conclusive evidence; but Popper, though wrong in denying this, was right that there is no inductive logic. For, as Hempel seemed to be on the brink of acknowledging in his 1964 "Postscript on Confirmation,"[29] the moral of the "grue" paradox is that supportiveness of evidence does not depend on form alone; for "All emeralds are green" and "All emeralds are grue" have the *same* form, but different content. My account of supportiveness in terms of increment of explanatory integration of evidence with the claim in question led to the same conclusion, that the concept is not susceptible of purely formal treatment; for explanatoriness requires the identification of real kinds of thing or event, and hence is vocabulary-sensitive.

Of course, even while I was working all this out, I was uncomfortably aware that many philosophers of science (and some, though fewer, epistemologists) were cheerfully confident that probability theory could carry the burden of an account of quality of evidence. I had never shared this optimism; but it took a while to articulate why. Obviously, if the concept of warrant is anything like as subtle and complex as my account suggests, the probability calculus (devised originally to represent the mathematics of games of chance) couldn't constitute a complete theory of warrant. And neither, given the comprehensiveness condition, could the calculus of probabilities even be an adequate calculus of degrees of warrant—for the probability of p and the probability of not-p must add up to 1, but if there is insufficient evidence either way, neither a claim nor its negation may be warranted to any degree.[30]

So it was a relief to discover (unfortunately, however, only after the publication of *Defending Science*) that John Maynard Keynes had held that epistemic probabilities may not be susceptible of numerical values: "[s]o far from our being able to measure [the probabilities of arguments], it is not even clear that we are always able to place them in an order of magnitude"; and that Ludwig Von Mises, whose maxim was "FIRST THE COLLECTIVE—THEN THE PROBABILITY," had insisted that the calculus of prob-

---

[29] Carl G. Hempel, "Postscript (1964) on Confirmation," in Hempel, *Aspects of Scientific Explanation* (New York: Free Press, 1965), 47–51.

[30] *Defending Science* [note 25], p.78–9.

abilities applies only where we are dealing with a large class of uniform events, and *not* to epistemic probabilities: "[o]ur probability theory has nothing to do with such questions as: Is there a probability of Germany being at some time in the future involved in a war with Liberia?"[31]

The epistemological picture developed in *Defending Science* goes beyond the narrowly logical in other ways as well, not least in acknowledging the deeply social character of the scientific enterprise. *Evidence and Inquiry* had focused on the individual inquirer; *Defending Science* also aspires to represent the epistemological role of interactions among inquirers. This, however, posed a difficulty: the evidence with respect to scientific claims and theories is almost always a shared resource, pooled within or across generations of scientists; but the evidence with respect to any warranted empirical claim must include experiential evidence—which can be had only by individuals. Noting how different my approach is from Popper's "epistemology without a knowing subject," I handled this tension by taking as my starting point an account of the warrant of a claim for a person at a time, on which I built an account of warrant for a group of persons, and then an account of the warrant of a scientific claim at a time, period. This represented a further move away from the "logic of science" approach, and towards a kind of *rapprochement* of epistemology with sociology of science—and hints at one of the many cross-disciplinary connections that have drawn my interest.

What is the proper role of philosophy in relation to other disciplines?

Now, however, I am uneasy about the implied conception of philosophy as a clearly distinguishable "discipline" with a unique "proper role" in relation to other disciplines—a conception that seems to me faithful neither to the often vague and permeable boundaries of partially overlapping areas of inquiry, nor to the richness and complexity of the multifarious inter-relations of philosophy with other fields. Sometimes, for example, philosophy

---

[31] I learned this early in 2004, when I read Donald Gillies' *Philosophical Theories of Probability* (London: Routledge, 2000), which quotes Keynes, *A Treatise on Probability* (London: MacMillan, 1921), pp.27–8, on p.34, and Von Mises, *Probability, Statistics, and Truth* (London: Allen and Unwin, 2nd revised English edition, 1928), pp. 18 and 9, on p.97.

properly forges ahead into waters as yet uncharted by the sciences; sometimes it properly engages in underlaborer duties after scientific advances. Since it is quite impossible to do justice to the rich, complex, and multifarious inter-relations of philosophy with other areas of human endeavor in a few paragraphs, the best I can do is sketch a few examples from my own work first of how other disciplines bear on philosophy; next, of how philosophy bears on other disciplines; and finally of how philosophy contributes to our understanding of the relations among other disciplines or other human enterprises. In *Evidence and Inquiry* I urged the merits of a modest naturalism according to which the sciences of cognition—though they cannot replace epistemology—have contributory relevance to epistemological questions. This modest naturalism contrasted both with old, purely a priori conceptions of epistemology, and with new, scientistic forms of naturalism—such as Alvin Goldman's, according to which epistemological questions can be answered by cognitive psychology, or the Churchlands', according to which epistemological questions are illegitimate, and should be abandoned in favor of neurophysiological ones.[32]

My approach in *Defending Science* remained modestly naturalistic; but in this context I needed to explain how my style of naturalism differed, on the one hand, from Philip Kitcher's suggestion that a simple acknowledgment of the role of the inquiring subject itself constitutes naturalism and, on the other, from Larry Laudan's idea that empirical studies of science suffice to track the evolution of "the scientific method."[33] Writing that "it is not within the competence of the sciences to articulate core epistemological concepts and values," but that "nevertheless, they do have an epistemological contribution to make," I argued that the psychology of cognition has contributory relevance to an understanding of human cognitive capacities and weaknesses: how large

---

[32] *Evidence and Inquiry* [note 21]: chapter 6 disambiguates Quine's "Epistemology Naturalized," and offers a preliminary statement of my modest aposteriorist naturalism; chapter 7 explores the flaws in Goldman's reformist scientistic naturalism, and chapter 8 the flaws in the Churchlands' revolutionary scientistic naturalism.

[33] *Defending Science* [note 25], 306–10. The weaker idea is suggested by Philip Kitcher in *The Advancement of Science: Science Without Legend, Objectivity Without Illusions* (New York: Oxford University Press, 1993), p. 9; the stronger is suggested by Larry Laudan in "Progress or Rationality? The Prospects for Normative Naturalism," *American Philosophical Quarterly*, 24, 1987: 19–33, reprinted in Laudan, *Beyond Positivism and Relativism: Theory, Method, and Evidence* (Boulder, Colo: Westview Press, 1996), 125–41.

is the risk of experimenter bias, for example, and when can giving people additional information actually impair their judgment of evidence? And writing that "rather than a distinctive 'scientific method,' there is only ... the core epistemological values common to all inquiry, and ... the myriad local and evolving techniques and helps that make scientific inquiry 'more so'" (p.309), I argued that the history of science has contributory relevance to an understanding of the interplay between the underlying processes and procedures common to all serious inquiry, and the evolution of those special scientific helps.

In *Defending Science* I also took the opportunity to explore the potential for cooperation between epistemology and sociology of science—potential which, I argued, had been obscured by a false contrast between the rational and the social taken for granted by Old Deferentialists and New Cynics alike. No epistemological conclusions can be established by sociological investigation alone; but in conjunction with a sound understanding of the role of evidence-sharing in the warrant of theories, and a sound understanding of the determinants of better and worse conducted inquiry, sociological investigation of the peer-review system, of the incidence of scientific fraud and plagiarism, etc., of the politics of science funding, of science education, or of litigation-driven science, could illuminate what social factors help, and what hinder, good, honest, thorough, creative scientific work.[34]

Next, some examples of the bearing of philosophy on other disciplines: In the past several years I have devoted a good deal of time to applied epistemology—including exploring what an account of the determinants of evidential strength and of well-conducted inquiry could contribute to such diverse questions as the feasibility of economics-as-science,[35] the legitimacy of "weight of evidence" methodology in epidemiology,[36] or the benefits and drawbacks of "evidence-based medicine." But I have focused most intensively on the interface between epistemology and the law of evidence. Initially, my interest was piqued by the discovery that the "New Evidence Scholarship" in legal theory (so-called because of its new

---

[34] *Defending Science* [note 25], pp.194 ff.. See also Susan Haack, "On Scientific Secrecy and 'Spin': The Sad, Sleazy Saga of the Trials of Remune," forthcoming in *Law and Contemporary Problems*.

[35] Susan Haack, "Science, Economics, 'Vision'," *Social Research*, 71.2, Summer 2004: 223–34.

[36] Susan Haack, "An Epistemologist Among the Epidemiologists," *Epidemiology*, 15(5), September 2004: 521–2.

focus on the structure and content of evidence, rather than exclusively on legal rules of admissibility and burdens and standards of proof) was embroiled in a debate between "fact-based" and "story-based" approaches—i.e., to all intents and purposes, a debate between foundationalism and coherentism. In due course I found myself diagnosing the epistemological confusions at work in the U.S. Supreme Court's rulings on the admissibility of scientific testimony;[37] exploring the tensions between fallibilism and finality and between inquiry and advocacy that underlie the difficulties the U.S.legal system has encountered in handling scientific evidence;[38] and submitting arguments for and against adversarialism and exclusionary rules of evidence to epistemological scrutiny.[39]

Chapter 5 of *Defending Science* illustrates another, rather different way in which philosophy bears on other disciplines. The central question here is: what are the metaphysical presuppositions of the scientific enterprise—how must the world be for scientific inquiry to be possible? My argument is, in brief, that science would be impossible—as would everyday empirical inquiry of the most ordinary kind—unless there were particular things and events to which inquirers have some kind of sensory access, and unless those particular things and events were of kinds, and subject to laws. Whether or not my Innocent Realist answer is correct,[40] the question to which it responds identifies the kind of contribution that metaphysics might make to the sciences: not by underpinning this or that specific physical, cosmological, etc., theory, but by articulating the preconditions of scientific investigation.

It also falls to philosophy—this is my third theme—to inquire

[37] Susan Haack, "An Epistemologist in the Bramble-Bush: At the Supreme Court with Mr. Joiner," *Journal of Health Politics, Policy, and Law*, 26.2, April 2001: 217–48; "Disentangling *Daubert*," *American Philosophical Association, Newsletter on Philosophy and Law*, 03.1 (fall 2003): 118–22 (re"printed" electronically in *The Journal of Philosophy, Science and Law*, 5 (summer 2005), and in *Expert Witnessing in Forensic Accounting*, eds. Walter J. Pagano and Thomas A. Buckhoff (Philadelphia: R. T. Edwards, 2005), 176–80); "Trial and Error: The Supreme Court's Philosophy of Science," *The American Journal of Public Health*, 95, 2005: S66–73.

[38] Susan Haack, "Inquiry and Advocacy, Fallibilism and Finality, Science and Law," *Ratio Juris*, 17.1, March 2004: 15–26.

[39] Susan Haack, "Epistemology Legalized: Or, Truth, Justice, and the American Way," *The American Journal of Jurisprudence*, 49, 2004: 43–61.

[40] On Innocent Realism, see also Susan Haack, "Reflections on Relativism: From Momentous Tautology to Seductive Contradiction" (1996), reprinted in *Manifesto of a Passionate Moderate* [note 7], 149–66; and "Realisms and Their Rivals: Recovering Our Innocence," *Facta Philosophica*, 4, 2002: 67–88.

into the relations among other disciplines, or other fields of human endeavor. In chapter 6 of *Defending Science*, for example, the focus is on the ways in which the social sciences are like the natural sciences, and the ways in which they are different; in chapter 8, on the similarities and the differences between science and literature; and in chapter 10, on the relations between science and religion—between the content of well-warranted scientific theories and of religious creeds, between sensory evidence and "religious experience," between natural and supernatural explanations, between fallibilism and faith. (The concluding chapter, by the way, in line with my early preoccupation with ambiguity, focuses on distinguishing the many different philosophical, socio-historical, scientific, etc., ideas offered under the equivocal rubric, "the end of science": the threatened epistemological demotion of science; its inherent limits; and the prospect of its annihilation, of its culmination, or of its eventual completion.)

What do you consider the most neglected topics and/or contributions in late 20th century philosophy?

These would be perfectly appropriate questions to put to a natural scientist. Between 1952 and 1963, for example, most molecular biologists would probably have said with some confidence that at least *a* very significant outstanding issue was the "coding problem" for DNA (and by the time of the Cold Spring Harbor symposium for 1966, most of them would have said with some confidence that this problem was almost completely solved).[41] Asked about philosophy, however, these questions suggest an unrealistically "progressivist" picture—as if, like molecular biology, philosophy were on a clear (albeit steep and rocky) path of advance. Not a few problems once regarded as the province of philosophy have evolved into more readily soluble scientific questions; moreover, I believe, there *can* be, and sometimes is, progress in philosophy. Nevertheless, philosophy really *isn't* much like normal science; and neither, I'm afraid, does it presently seem to be on any clear forward path.

Instead, many seem to cling to the flattering and reassuring illusion that the ideas of our time are bound to be an advance over anything that went before, and so miss opportunities to build on

---

[41] See Horace Freeland Judson, *The Eighth Day of Creation: Makers of the Revolution in Biology* (New York: Simon and Schuster, 1979), p.488.

earlier insights. Proponents of "radical" theses are rewarded with attention and renown—even, perhaps especially, when those radical theses are radically implausible. Young people who aspire to join the profession are likely to be trained in aggressive but formulaic criticism or in over-ambitious speculation; urged to browse the *Philosopher's Index* to find a recent article to which they can reply; and pressured, ready or not, to publish *now*. But they are rarely encouraged to develop the patience they would need to work constructively and in detail. No wonder, these days, it often seems that philosophy is going backwards, sideways, or nowhere—any which way but forwards!

As a result of the "chauvinism of the present" characteristic of much recent neo-analytic philosophy, earlier contributions—when they are not neglected outright—are apt to be "co-opted": X, who is no longer alive, or just isn't one of the boys, is given a passing mention as having "anticipated" some contemporary or better-known Y; or an older approach is transmuted and its name adopted for a neo-analytic *ersatz*. The label "Pragmatism," for example, first kidnapped by Rorty and his admirers, now seems to be being adopted by neo-analytic philosophers proffering ideas at best vaguely reminiscent of something in the classical Pragmatist tradition.

Yet Peirce's constructive reconception of metaphysics as, not wholly *a priori*, but in part dependent on experience—on close, "phaneroscopic" attention to aspects of everyday experience ordinarily too commonplace to notice, not on the recherché kinds of observation that can only be made by means of scientific instruments— has been thoroughly neglected in almost a century of neo-Leibnizian, neo-Kantian, or outright scientistic, metaphysics;[42] and his distinction of existent particulars and real "generals," and its deployment in the resolution of the problem of induction and of cosmological issues about the evolution of laws, has been conspicuous by its absence from (almost all)[43] the recent literature in philosophy of science. Again, George Herbert Mead's remarkably suggestive theorizing about the ways in which the human mind is like animal mentality and the ways in which it is different, and about how our peculiar mental capacities might have arisen,[44] gets

---

[42] See Susan Haack, "The Legitimacy of Metaphysics: Kant's Legacy to Peirce, and Peirce's to Philosophy Today," forthcoming in *Kant Today*, ed. Hans Lenk.

[43] But not from chapter 5 of my *Defending Science* [note 25].

[44] George Herbert Mead, *Mind, Self and Society* (Chicago: University of

barely a mention despite the oceans of ink expended on philosophy of mind in the late twentieth century. And so on.

Another example: in all the excitement over "minimalism," "deflationism," "disquotationalism," etc., in the theory of truth, neither Tarski nor Ramsey is always given his due. Granted, Tarski's semantic theory, Ramsey's laconicist theory,[45] and contemporary minimalism, deflationism, etc., are all in intent or in effect attempts to articulate Aristotle's dictum that "to say of what is that it is, or of what is not that it is not, is true" in a completely generalized way; but they differ very significantly among themselves. Yet Quine suggests that Tarski may be classified as a disquotationalist[46]—even though Tarski himself had insisted that the enclosed expression in a quotation-mark name is not semantically a part of the name; which was precisely why he believed it was impossible to generalize his T-schema along the lines of "(p) ('p' is true iff p)." The editors of Ramsey's papers on truth observe that it is "remarkable how close [he] came to anticipating Tarski"[47]—even though Tarski himself says emphatically that his T-schema is not, and cannot be turned into, a definition of truth, while Ramsey had written that "*[my] definition of truth* is that a belief is true if it is 'a belief that p' and p, but false if it is 'a belief that p' and $\neg p$" (my italics). Scott Soames writes that Tarski's semantic conception is "the most famous and influential version of deflationism"—leaving it a mystery why Tarski himself took a hundred or so pages *beyond* the T-schema to articulate his (demonstrably materially adequate) definition of truth.[48] And so on.

Chicago Press, 1934).

[45] I owe the word "laconicism"—a much better label for Ramsey's approach than "redundancy theory"—to a former student, Dr. Kiriake Xerohemona.

[46] W. V. Quine, *Quiddities* (Cambridge: Harvard University Press, 1987), p.213. It is worthy of note that in his *Mathematical Logic* (1940: New York, Harper Torchbooks, 1962), p.26, Quine himself had endorsed the view that the expression enclosed in quotation marks is not a semantical part of the whole quotation-mark name.

[47] Nicholas Rescher and Ulrich Majer, eds., *On Truth: Original Manuscript Materials (1927–29) from the Ramsey Collection* (Dordrecht, the Netherlands, 1992), xiv.

[48] Scott Soames, *Understanding Truth* (New York: Oxford University Press, 1999), p. 238.

What are the most important open problems in philosophy and what are the prospects for progress?

For reasons that are by now too obvious to bear repeating, I am unwilling to be drawn into trying to identify "*the* most neglected topics" or "*the* most important open problems" in philosophy today. I am drawn instead to a passage in which, commenting on the "puny, rickety, and scrofulous" state of metaphysics in his time, Peirce proceeds "to set down almost at random a small specimen of the questions of metaphysics which press ... for industrious and solid investigation":

> Whether or not there be any real indefiniteness, or real possibility and impossibility? Whether there be any strictly individual existence? Whether there is any distinction ... between fact and fancy? Or between the external and the internal worlds? What general ... account can be given of the different qualities of feeling ...? Do all possible qualities of sensation ... form one continuous system ...? ... Is Time a real thing ...? How about Space ...? Is hylozoism an option, actual or conceivable, rather than a senseless vocable ...? ... What is consciousness or mind like ...?[49]

So here, set down almost at random (and following Peirce's agreeably antique style of punctuation), is *my* "small specimen of philosophical questions which press for industrious and solid investigation."

> Whether the grounds of validity of the laws of logic are to be found in language, in conceptual structures, in the nature of representation, in the world, or where? Whether Peirce's idea of necessary reasoning as essentially diagrammatic is defensible, or Russell's distinction of logical and grammatical form? How Aristotle's dictum could best be generalized to arrive at a satisfactory definition of truth? How, if this will

---

[49] C. S. Peirce, *Collected Papers*, eds Charles Hartshorne, Paul Weiss, and Arthur Burks (Cambridge: Harvard University Press, 1931-58) 6.6, c.1903. (References to the *Collected Papers* are by volume and paragraph number.) "Hylozoism" refers to a doctrine from early Greek philosophy to the effect that all matter has life (a doctrine with which Peirce's "objective idealism" has some, albeit distant, affinity). See also Haack, "Not Cynicism but Synechism" [note 6], and "The Legitimacy of Metaphysics" [note 42].

require propositional quantifiers, these can be interpreted without using "true"? Whether a unified interpretation of quantifiers is possible, and if so in what terms? Whether the semantic paradoxes are a sign of deep incoherence in the ordinary truth-concept, or a trivial verbal trick? Whether these paradoxes must be avoided by recourse to an artificial language in which they cannot be expressed, or resolved by probing the ordinary, informal concept of truth? Whether Tarski's definition really advances our understanding of truth beyond Ramsey's simple formula, and if so, how? ... How we are to understand the relation between the neurophysiological realization of a belief and its content? How belief-contents are best represented? How they should be individuated? How degrees of belief affect degrees of justification? How to articulate the desirable kind of interlocking or consilience that gives some congeries of evidence greater strength than any of their components? How to asses the weight of shared evidence when there is disagreement within a group, or when members give shared reasons different degrees of credence? What the proper relation is between belief and the will? What the mechanisms are of self-deception and of wishful and fearful thinking? ... How to understand "real," as applied to particulars? to kinds? to laws? to the world? Whether "real" has the same meaning as applied to social as to natural kinds and laws? How to distinguish the cosmological role of historical singularities and of laws? How to understand the evolution of laws? ... How works of imaginative literature can convey truths they do not state? Whether vagueness is always undesirable, or sometimes benign or even useful? How the precision sought by a logician differs from that sought by a novelist or poet? ...

Though I don't doubt that formal methods will play a part, I anticipate that the means of resolving such questions will prove as various as the questions themselves.[50]

---

[50] My thanks to Mark Migotti for helpful comments on a draft.

10

Sven Ove Hansson

Professor and Head of Department

Department of Philosophy and the History of Technology

Royal Institute of Technology, Stockholm, Sweden

Why were you initially drawn to formal methods?

I was attracted to formal models because of the chance that they give us to make philosophical discussions more precise. Later I have also discovered that formal philosophy is indispensable in studies of the foundational issues of other formalized disciplines, such as economics.

Of course, there are disciplines in which formal methods have a much larger role than in philosophy. We should confess that formal philosophy is on less safe ground than most other formalized disciplines. Think of physics. The formalized theories in that discipline give rise to predictions that can be empirically verified or falsified. This is of course a major reason why formal models have been so successful in physics. Nothing like that is possible in philosophy. Of course our formal models of preferences, beliefs, and inferences can be tested against actual human behaviour, but then they are tested from a psychological, not a philosophical point of view.

An interesting parallel can be drawn between today's formalized philosophy and pre-Galilean physics. Medieval physicists (the so-called calculatores) developed mathematical models of physical phenomena. However, these models were only tested against intuition, not against experiments or exact observations. This is how it still works in philosophy.

Nevertheless, formalization has many advantages in philosophy, and I would like to mention a few of them.[1] When we formalize an informal discourse, we have to make up our minds on issues

---

[1] SO Hansson, "Formalization in philosophy", *Bulletin of Symbolic Logic*, 6:162–175, 2000.

that are otherwise often neglected, such as the choice of basic concepts, the interdefinability of these concepts, and what principles of inference apply to them. Formalization also stimulates us to provide a reasonably complete account of the entities that we deal with. In particular, the rigorousness of a formal language makes it meaningful to search for a complete list of valid principles of inference. In my own work, I have put much emphasis on axiomatic characterizations of formal systems. One reason for this is that a representation theorem provides an overview of the properties of the construction. I have often discovered new axioms and other properties when searching for axiomatic characterizations, so at least for me this is also a good research strategy.

One of the major advantages of formal theories is that they can support delicate structures that we do not manage to deal with in an informal language. Perhaps the best example is the relation between truth and language. The philosophical impact of Tarski's semantical analysis of the notion of truth can hardly be overestimated. Of course its major ideas can be expressed informally, but I very much doubt that it could have been developed by a philosopher not using formal methods.

However, in spite of all its advantages, formalization also has its problems. Perhaps the most obvious pitfall is oversimplification. One example is the tendency in deontic logic to use one and the same notation for all if-sentences with deontic consequents. This is misleading since there are sentences with this grammatical form that differ fundamentally in their meaning and function. Why should counterfactual sentences with normative consequents have the same logical properties as normative rules?[2]

We can divide the philosophical and interpretational discussions on formal models into three types. Type one consists of new aspects on issues already discussed in informal philosophy. Type two consists of new philosophical issues that are discovered in the formalism, but have philosophical relevance apart from the formal models. Type three consists of issues that are peculiar to the chosen formalism and have no bearing on philosophical issues that can be expressed without the formalism.

Let me use the treatment of moral dilemmas in deontic logic as an example. If there is some p such that both Op (p is obligatory) and $O\neg p$ (not-p is obligatory) hold, then the dictates of the O

---

[2] SO Hansson, *The Structure of Values and Norms*, Cambridge University Press, 2001, chapters 11–13.

operator cannot be completely complied with; in other words we have a moral dilemma. This gives rise to issues of all three types.

The type one problem is that in the presence of conflicting obligations, no acceptable course of action seems to be available. This may be called the "compliance" problem. It is essentially the problem of moral dilemmas that is discussed in informal moral philosophy. Deontic logic provides more precision for instance in discussing the definition of moral dilemmas. Do we have a moral dilemma also when three obligations are involved, such as Op, Oq, and $O\neg(p\&q)$? Do we have a moral dilemma when Op, Oq, and $p\&q$ is impossible to achieve, rather than forbidden? If so, do we have a moral dilemma when Op and p is impossible to achieve?

In some moral dilemmas, practical action-guidance can be obtained by recognizing that although both alternatives are wrong, one of them is less wrong than the other. In deontic logic, this can be expressed by distinguishing between obligations of different strengths.[3] This gives rise to a long list of new questions about the properties of such a notion of strength. These are interesting philosophical issues that do not seem to have arisen without the formalism. They are issues of type two.

In standard deontic logic (SDL), it is possible to conclude from Op and $O\neg p$ that Oq for any argument q of the O operator. Hence, in the presence of a moral dilemma, everything is obligatory. Since the formal inference from Op and $O\neg p$ to Oq runs counter to the way inferences are made in non-formalized normative discourse, this is clearly a logical artefact that has little or nothing to do with moral philosophy. Hence, this is a problem of type three.

Formal philosophy can only be successful if we have a strong emphasis on issues of types one and two. When type three issues dominate, it is time to develop new and better formal models.

What example(s) from your work illustrates the role formal methods can play in philosophy?

I would like to give three examples that can hopefully illustrate more general points about formal models in philosophy.

The first example is the interdefinability of some of the central terms of moral discourse. There are two major proposals in the literature on how to define "good" in terms of "better". One is

---

[3] SO Hansson, "But What Should I Do?", *Philosophia* 27: 433–440, 1999.

Brogan's proposal to equate "good" with "better than its negation". The other proposal was put forward by Chisholm and Sosa.
They define "good" as "better than X", where X is some indif-
ferent state of affairs. Since both these definitions are intuitively
reasonable, an obvious question is under what conditions they are
equivalent. This is a question that can be asked informally, but
only answered with formal methods. It turned out that they are
only equivalent under what I would consider to be rather special
conditions.[4]

A similar and even more interesting issue concerns the interre-
lations between values and norms. Too little attention has been
paid to the distinction between these two categories. A value
statement does not have the inherent action-guiding or action-
motivating force that a normative statement has. So the two categories are distinct. Nevertheless, they are not unconnected. It
would be strange to say to someone what is the worst thing that
she can do in a certain situation, and then go on to tell her that
she ought to do it.

To make a long story short, I am convinced that George Moore
was right when he said that norms and values can be extensionally
but not intensionally equivalent. I believe that the essential (extensional) connection can be best expressed in the form of a very
simple principle on the negative side of the value-scale: "What is
worse than something forbidden is itself forbidden."[5] Note that
this is *not* equivalent to the idea that what is better than something obligatory is itself obligatory. It is morally obligatory for me
to offer a starving fellow-being a nourishing meal. Arguably, it is
also morally better for me to offer a meal that is both nourishing
and delicious. It does not seem to follow that it is obligatory for
me to offer the latter type of meal.

The very simple principle I referred to, "What is worse than
something forbidden is itself forbidden," is sufficient for building
a deontic logic in which we get rid of all the standard paradoxes
of deontic logic.[6] These paradoxes are, by the way, clear examples
of issues of the third type that I just referred to.[7]

---

[4] SO Hansson, "Defining 'good' and 'bad' in terms of 'better'", *Notre Dame
Journal of Formal Logic* 31: 136–149, 1990.

[5] SO Hansson, "Norms and values", *Critica* 23 (67): 3–13, 1991.

[6] SO Hansson, *The Structure of Values and Norms*, Cambridge University
Press, 2001. SO Hansson, "A new representation theorem for contranegative
deontic logic", *Studia Logica*, 77: 1–7, 2004.

[7] SO Hansson "Ideal Worlds – Wishful Thinking in Deontic Logic", *Studia*

The second example is the specification of different alternative sets. Again, a very simple insight can be used to clarify important philosophical issues. Again this insight has its full force only in a formalized treatment. The insight I refer to is that preferences are not sufficiently precise unless the set of alternatives is specified. Consider for instance the money-pumps that are so popular in decision theory. A money-pump is a hypothetical construction, obtained by appending monetary rewards to the alternatives in a decision that did not originally contain these rewards. Much confusion can be avoided by just explicitly constructing the new alternative set instead of performing the analysis in the original alternative set that contains no monetary rewards.[8] However, instead of going into details about that I would like to mention how the same basic insight can be applied in the analysis of social decisions.

Richard Wollheim's democratic paradox is illustrative. Wollheim asks us to consider an individual who endorses the democratic procedure, or "democratic machine". This person prefers a certain social state p to its negation $\neg p$, but as a democrat she also wants the democratic decision on p to be respected. It turns out that a democratic decision is made in favour of $\neg p$. Now, how should our democrat react? Since she wants the majority's will to be respected, she prefers $\neg p$ to p. But she regrets the majority's position for the simple reason that she in fact prefers p to $\neg p$. How can she both prefer p to $\neg p$ and $\neg p$ to p?

This problem can be solved if we use an adequate description of the states of affairs that her preferences refer to. These states include not only p and its negation, but also information about what the "democratic machine" has decided. We can use the predicate D to denote democratic decisions. Thus Dp means: "A valid democratic decision in favour of p has been made." Comparisons should then not be made between p and $\neg p$ but between the four states of affairs Dp & p, Dp & $\neg p$, $D\neg p$ & p, and $D\neg p$ & $\neg p$. A democrat who voted for p may nevertheless prefer $D\neg p$ & $\neg p$ to $D\neg p$ & p. That she prefers p to $\neg p$, in the sense mentioned by Wollheim, can be expressed as a preference that refers only to alternatives in which the democratic decision is respected, i.e. she prefers Dp &p to $D\neg p$ &$\neg p$. That she prefers $\neg p$ to p can be

---

Logica, in press.

    [8]SO Hansson, "Money-Pumps, Self-Torturers and the Demons of Real Life", *Australasian Journal of Philosophy* 71: 476–485, 1993.

expressed as a preference restricted to cases in which $D\neg p$ holds, i.e. she prefers $D\neg p$ & $\neg p$ to $D\neg p$ & p.[9]

More importantly, this insight about alternative sets can be applied in the formal study of social choices and decisions, in the tradition that was developed by Kenneth Arrow. In the standard social choice formalism, the individuals who take part in a voting procedure are assumed to have preferences that refer to the alternatives on which they vote. This is quite a natural starting-point. If we are going to vote on the alternatives x, y, and z, it is reasonable to assume that we all come to the meeting with preferences over the set consisting of these three alternatives, and vote accordingly.

However, as participants in collective decision procedures we often have preferences that do not refer exclusively to these options (decision-alternatives). Besides wanting the outcome to be as good as possible (according to your own standard), you may for instance prefer the decision to be taken by as large a majority as possible. Such preferences often lead a committee member to vote for her second or third best alternative in order to contribute to unanimity. Or you may prefer to be yourself part of the winning coalition, etc. I started to work in this area with the conviction that we need a representation of individual preferences that is capable of representing these types of procedural preferences. It turned out that this can be done surprisingly well with a very simple construction: The set of preference-alternatives (comparison classes) is equal to the set of possible voting patterns, i.e. the set of complete descriptions of how all participants vote.[10]

Consider three persons who vote, according to the simple majority rule, between the alternatives x, y, and z. Voting patterns can be represented by vectors, such that for instance $< y, x, x >$ represents the voting pattern in which the first participant votes for y and the two others for x. In Arrow's framework, each of the three participants has a preference ordering over the set consisting of x, y, and z. In the modified framework, each of them has a preference ordering over the set of voting patterns. This makes it possible to express procedural preferences like the ones I just mentioned. Suppose for instance that, informally speaking, one

[9]SO Hansson, "A Resolution of Wollheim's Paradox", *Dialogue* 32: 681–687, 1993.

[10]SO Hansson, "A Procedural Model of Voting", *Theory and Decision* 32: 269–301, 1992.

of the voters is in favour of x but is also in favour of unanimity, and that she gives higher priority to unanimity than to the difference between her preferred x and her second-best z. Such a person may prefer $< x, x, x >$ to $< z, z, z >$ and $< z, z, z >$ to $< x, z, z >$. Needless to say, a multitude of issues concerning strategic voting, coalition formation etc. can be expressed and analyzed game-theoretically in this framework.[11]

My third example concerns the definition of epistemic coherentism. According to the standard view, "all beliefs" in a coherentist system are capable of contributing to the justification of other beliefs. In studies of belief revision I was led to pay attention to beliefs that we have as "mere logical consequences" of other beliefs. For a simple example, since I believe that Paris is the site of the French foreign ministry (p) I also believe that either Paris or Quito is the site of the French foreign ministry ($p \lor q$). However, this latter belief does not have an independent standing; it stands or falls with the former. What role can such merely derived beliefs have in relation to coherentism? I hope to have shown that a coherence theory that includes all such beliefs has quite implausible consequences and that therefore, we have to revise coherentism.[12] If I am right, then coherentists will have to recognize that certain beliefs (the merely derived beliefs) are mere epiphenomena in the sense that they do not contribute to the justification of other beliefs. However, the rest of the beliefs, those that are not merely derived in this sense, do not correspond to the basic beliefs referred to in foundationalist epistemology. The relationship between coherentism and foundationalism seems to be different from what we have previously believed. Issues like this can only be investigated if we take the decisive step from the semi-formal style that has dominated in epistemology to a fully formalized framework.

What is the proper role of philosophy in relation to other disciplines?

No other academic discipline has such deep connections with so many other academic disciplines as has philosophy. When you

---

[11] SO Hansson, "Social Choice With Procedural Preferences", *Social Choice and Welfare* 13: 215–230, 1996.

[12] SO Hansson, "Coherence in Epistemology and Belief Revision", *Philosophical Studies*, in press. See also SO Hansson and E Olsson, "Providing Foundations for Coherentism", *Erkenntnis* 51: 243–265, 1999.

probe into almost any field of learning, interesting problems of a philosophical nature will emerge. Philosophy can therefore contribute to other subjects, and at the same time derive important insights from them. One would therefore expect philosophers to be at the forefront in all kinds of interdisciplinary research, working and writing together with scholars and scientists in other fields. But this happens surprisingly seldom, given the potentials of our discipline. I believe that this depends in part on an inconstructively isolationist view of the role of philosophy.

Instead of isolating philosophy from other disciplines we should, in my view, emphasize its role as one of many contributors to the unified corpus of systematic human knowledge. By this I mean the combined knowledge of the interdependent community of the disciplines that seek systematized knowledge about the world that we live in and about ourselves. This community includes both the sciences and the humanities. When I speak about unity I do not refer to any kind of reductionism but instead to the mutual respect that these discipline owe to each other's results and methodologies. An historian will have to accept the chemist's analysis of an archeological artefact. In the same way, a zoologist will have to accept the historian's judgment on the reliability of an ancient text describing extinct animals.

Historically, philosophy has always been part of this community of interdepending disciplines. But in recent years, some philosophers have tended to treat philosophy as another type of subject, not part of this community, not required to respect scientific knowledge in the way that scientists respect each other's disciplines. In my view, this would be a dangerous trend, leading almost unfailingly to the marginalization of our discipline.

Being a member of this community of disciplines is a matter of both giving and taking. As philosophers we have to respect the knowledge obtained in other disciplines, but we can also expect knowledge workers in other disciplines to respect achievements made by philosophers. It has to be said very clearly: We cannot with any credibility philosophize on natural or social phenomena without making use of the systematic knowledge about these phenomena obtained in other disciplines. A philosophy of time that is incompatible with the best available physical knowledge, or a philosophy of mind that fails to keep pace with neurobiology, is just as defective, just as incompetent, as a study of environmental pollution that gets the chemistry wrong.

We need more cooperation between philosophy and other disciplines. And I mean cooperation, which is very different from using scientists as objects of study. To take just one example, one of the most exciting recent developments in economics is the construction and use of new and more sophisticated representations of human beliefs, preferences, norms, and interactions. New foundations are being laid for important parts of economic theory. These developments are closely related to advances in philosophical areas such as value theory, moral theory, and epistemology. Philosophers who are active in this fertile interdisciplinary area are participants in the development of economic theory, not mere observers of it. The full combined force of the two disciplines can only be set free when we cooperate as equals to solve problems of joint interest.

In cooperations with other disciplines, our capacity to deal with formalizations is often essential. In the previous century, more and more disciplines became mathematized. Economics is perhaps the best-known example, but similar developments have also taken place for instance in branches of biology and psychology. It is ironic that interest in formal philosophy is declining in many quarters at the same time as more and more of our potential interdisciplinary cooperations require formalized work.

I have emphasized philosophy's continuity with other academic disciplines. But philosophy has at least one more important continuity issue, namely with everyday reflections on human life and its conditions. The ultimate concerns of philosophy are nothing less than the age-old questions of existence, knowledge, virtue, duty and beauty. These are the subject of reflection and speculation by men and women in all walks of life. Philosophy cannot claim monopoly on these issues but we have developed skills to attack them in a more systematic fashion.

Philosophy's two continuities need not be in mutual opposition. Science itself connects with our everyday reflections on the natural world. Philosophy can, without contradiction, be continuous both with science and with unsystematized everyday experience and reflection. It can perhaps even serve to connect them better with each other.

What do you consider the most neglected topics and/or contributions in late 20th century philosophy?

As I have already indicated, philosophy has many uninvestigated interdisciplinary connections that we should have looked into more carefully. Only relatively recently have philosophers begun to study the philosophy of chemistry. It turns out to be equally rewarding as the philosophy of physics and biology. Other disciplines are equally promising partners. I know from my own experience that there are a large number of fascinating philosophical issues in toxicology and ecotoxicology.[13] The same seems to apply to geology and the earth sciences, that have as yet attracted very little philosophical reflection. Being myself at a technological university, I know from numerous discussions with colleagues that there is a great potential to develop cooperations with the various technological disciplines such as structural mechanics, engineering design, etc.

For formal philosophy, it is particularly rewarding to look for cooperation with research areas that are either in a process of formalization or in a process of reconsidering dominating formal models. At present such areas can be found for instance in biology and economics.

A major "silent revolution" is underway in science, through the massive introduction of computer simulations, both to supplement experiments and—perhaps surprisingly often—to replace them. This new development has not been much discussed in the philosophy of science, but it seems unavoidable that it will in the future be a major topic. It is also far more suitable to formal treatment than many other topics in the philosophy of science.

What are the most important open problems in philosophy and what are the prospects for progress?

First of all: This changes. Philosophy does not deal only with eternal, unchanging issues. We also deal with issues that evolve with society and with the development of knowledge in other fields. To the extent that philosophy is concerned with reflection on the human condition—and I think it ultimately is—its very subject-matter changes as the human condition is changing. New philosophical problems and problem-areas are created. Old ones are

---

[13] SO Hansson, "Can we reverse the burden of proof?", *Toxicology Letters* 90: 223–228, 1997.

elucidated in new ways whereas others become obsolete. It is easy to give examples of developments in the previous century that had a deep influence on philosophy: the emergency of modern democracy, the holocaust, the threat of a nuclear war, computers, destruction of the environment, neurobiology, biotechnology, etc. Discussions about progress in philosophy have to take this into account. Since we have a moving target, progress in philosophy is less well-defined than progress in astronomy or ancient history.

It is not difficult to point at emerging new issues that will require philosophical reflection. New advanced medical technology gives rise to new ethical and even existential issues.[14] New developments in society give rise to complex issues related to new technologies, such as how to interpret the precautionary principle[15] and how to assess uncertain social effects of nanotechnology[16]. All this requires inputs from philosophy but of course also from other disciplines. We can expect formalized philosophy to have a role in many of these new endeavours.

There are also many well-established areas in philosophy in which substantial progress should be possible with formal methods. I will mention just three such areas. We still lack a reasonable representation of human beliefs that covers both probabilistic and non-probabilistic aspects. We still lack a reasonable account inductive reasoning. And we still lack a formalized account of most of the issues in informal logic, such as the common argumentative fallacies. It is almost an embarrassment to formal logic that we are yet not able to give good formal accounts of many common types of logical fallacies.

Formalized philosophy has an important mission. In spite of this, it is at present an endangered speciality. Much of the more technically involved work has been taken over by mathematical logicians, and recently much of the initiative for developing new formal systems has come from computer science. At the same time, formalization encounters an internal resistance in philosophy that is not present in these other disciplines. There is an urgent need to revitalize formal philosophy. This requires increased interaction with non-formal philosophy. Formal philosophers need to engage

---

[14]SO Hansson, "Implant Ethics", *Journal of Medical Ethics*, in press. SO Hansson, "The Ethics of Enabling Technology", *Cambridge Quarterly of Healthcare Ethics*, in press.

[15]SO Hansson, "Adjusting Scientific Practices to the Precautionary Principle" *Human and Ecological Risk Assessment*, 5: 909–921, 1999.

[16]SO Hansson, "Great Uncertainty about Small Things", *Techne* 8(2), 2004.

more in informal philosophy, and to put more effort into showing the general philosophical relevance of what they are doing. Philosophers not accustomed to formal language will have to give up their resistance. They have a fascinating new world of philosophical insights to discover.

11

Jaakko Hintikka

Professor of Philosophy

Boston University, MA, USA

The subject of formal methods in philosophy is intriguing but also—for me at least—puzzling, in more than one way. One puzzle is not unlike the predicament of the character in Molière who is surprised to hear that he had been speaking French prose all his life long. What else could he have done? What other methods should—or could—I have possibly used in the philosophical work I have done? The first two major philosophers to influence me were Eino Kaila and G.H. von Wright. Neither spoke self-consciously of formal methods, but neither one hesitated to use in areas like epistemology and philosophy of science concepts and arguments using logic, probability theory or other kinds of mathematics. I took such a methodology for granted.

The successes of such tactics encouraged and inspired me further. An early case in point in my education was the analysis of the phenomenon of bluffing in the game theory of von Neumann and Morgenstern. (I was introduced to this "formal method", not by my philosophy teachers but by one of my mathematics professors, Gustaf Elfing who taught the first lecture course in Finland on this subject.) On the face of things, bluffing is a purely psychological ad hominem ploy calculated to mislead an opponent. Yet a formal game-theoretical analysis shows precisely what is involved. In the rational eyes of a game theorist, bluffing is nothing more and nothing less than the use of a mixed strategy.

I was fascinated by this "hidden hand" analysis, and I believe that there are many more opportunities for such analyses than philosophers have exploited. For instance, I suspect that there is a much more striking rationale of appeals to coherence in epistemology than has been generally recognized. Another important example is the presence of two different kinds of identification principles in the conceptual and linguistic practice of all of us which nevertheless remains largely unacknowledged even by philosophers who pretend that they are practicing explication of concepts in our everyday logically unexamined life. It takes a cognitively disturbed patient like Oliver Sacks's "man who mistook his wife for a hat" to make us aware of the difference.

Although formal methods are thus for me the natural medium of philosophizing, my "philosophical mother tongue", I have come to realize that the very idea of formal *methods* is full of ambiguities and problems. Formal methods are important only when they actually do some work instead of merely being another notation. Keynes emphasized the mathematical skills of his great predecessor Alfred Marshall at the same time as he noted that Marshall used advanced mathematics only sparingly. Marshall knew when mathematics really does some work. In the same spirit, Pat Suppes used to respond to the news that some scientist or philosopher had formalized and axiomatized some theory by asking: "But how many theorems has he proved?"

Now that job that formal methods are drafted to do is in the last analysis indistinguishable from the substantial task they are tools of dealing with. Whether or not Marshall McLuhan is right or not, in philosophical analysis method is part of the message. For instance, in adopting the usual epistemic logic one is in effect adopting one particular interpretation of the notion of knowledge. If you do not see this at once, you may consider the parallel case of the logic of visual cognition. If one analyzes visual cognition in terms of the possible situations one's visual impressions rule out or admit, one is treating visual perception as pickup of information. In other words, one is in effect agreeing with a version of J.J. Gibson's ecological theory of perception according to which "there can be sensationless perception, but never informationless perception."

Likewise, the development of independence-friendly logic does not amount merely to a more flexible notation for the logical behavior of quantifiers. It means a deeper analysis of the very meaning of quantifiers, including a recognition of their role in expressing the relations of dependence and independence between quantifiers.

This point is not restricted to the use of formal methods e.g. mathematics, in philosophy. One of the most interesting conceptual issues in the foundations of quantum theory is the role of mathematics in it. Several positivistically oriented physicists, for instance Heisenberg, treat mathematics in the spirit of Quine only as a method of organizing and systematizing the information yielded by experiments. As against them, I have come to believe that the notorious conceptual conundrums of quantum theory, such as the measurement problem and the problem of nonlocality, are not only reflected in the mathematical formalism of quantum theory but perhaps could even be solved by developing a more appropriate logical and mathematical formalism. In thinking so, I have apparently have been unwittingly following the footsteps of no lesser a mathematician from John von Neumann. Even though he developed what now is the most widely used formalism for quantum mechanics, the Hilbert space formalism, he did not believe that it was the best one. He tried to find a better one, among other things creating a theory of operator algebras for the purpose, but died before he reached a definitive conclusion.

From this inseparability of form and substance it follows that in developing and using formal methods we must be aware of their substantive purpose. A tool is useless for you if you do not know what its function is. Acknowledging this insight amounts to recognizing an immense but largely unacknowledged philosophical problem. The problem faces us already in the case of ordinary first-order logic. Precisely how is it related to the uses of logic in our actual thinking and acting?

The philosopher who was most keenly bothered by this problem was Wittgenstein. He understood very well the idea of a purely formal system of logic and at the same time appreciated the role logical concepts and logical words play in our lives, our language games.

> "Cut down all the trees."— But don't you understand what "all" means?
>
> He left one standing.
>
> (*Remarks on the Foundations of Mathematics*, sec. 10.)

What Wittgenstein could not understand was what the formal manipulations with logical symbols contribute to our practices with logical words. He confessed that, although he understood what geometrical necessity means, he could not understand what logical necessity is.

For ordinary first-order logic, this problem is in the main solved by the interpretation of suitable normalized first-order proofs as frustrated counter-model constructions. This interpretation was put forward in different variants by Hintikka and by Beth in 1955. The philosophical and other theoretical opportunities of this line of interpretation have not yet been exhausted. This interpretation shows how logical consequence relations show up in our actual interaction with the world, and therefore it is the kind of interpretation that could have allayed Wittgenstein's apprehensions. In other directions, game-theoretical semantics offers different ways of bringing out the concrete meaning of formal logical operations.

In our day and age, which according to one book title is "the age of alternative logics", an analogous problem looms large prompted by the proliferation of so-called alternative logics. Such soi-disant logics may be the most conspicuous new "formal methods" that philosophers are likely to think of. But the very term "alternative logic" betrays the problem. This term is virtually a near no-brainer. Alternative to what? Presumably to classical logic. But what is classical logic? No clear criterion of classicism is found in the literature. For instance, it used to be thought that contradictory negation was the "classical" one. But it has been shown that in a suitable framework "classical" semantical laws lead to a stronger dual negation. Which is the "classical" one?

Even more importantly, speaking of alternativeness presupposes a common function. A saw is not an alternative hammer. But what is the function of logical rules? To guide us to truth, presumably. But how? The usual rules of inference do so cumulatively by leading us from truths to truths. But non-monotonic logics do not operate cumulatively; they can lead us from truths to falsehoods. Such rules can still eventually lead us to truths, but whether they do so depends on the strategies used. It is not guaranteed by the step-by-step rules themselves. But no non-monotonic logician has to the best of our knowledge tried to develop a theory of strategies of logical reasoning.

In some cases, alternative logics come with a built-in pragmatics, for instance in the case of some logics capturing the structure of certain particular kinds of games. But there are no grounds of thinking of such specialized exercises as serious alternatives to our ordinary logic.

In other cases, for instance in inferences by circumscription, it is made commendably clear what is going on. What is going on in such logics are inferences some of whose premises are left tacit. In traditional terms, such inferences are enthymemes. For instance, inferences by circumscription rely on the assumption that the other, explicitly stated original premises contain all the information that is relevant to the matter at hand. This assumption is a contingent one, and is in reality frequently false.

There is nothing wrong about a study of such enthymemes. But by itself, such a study cannot claim to be a logic alternative to the classical one. For the question whether genuinely new (or different) logical principles are needed in circumscriptive reasoning can only be answered by formulating explicitly its tacit premises. The perfectly genuine interest of circumscriptive reasoning does not lie in the logic that is being used, but in those tacit premises and in the reasons for the difficulty of spelling them out. What they instantiate are alternative premises, not alternative inferences.

This can be generalized. However useful formal methods are in philosophy and in science, we are sooner of later faced with the question of their true substantial meaning, whether that meaning is thought of as semantical or pragmatic. In the last analysis, an unexamined formalism is not worth formulating.

H. Jerome Keisler

Vilas Professor of Mathematics, Emeritus

University of Wisconsin, Madison, USA

Why were you initially drawn to formal methods?

I was initially drawn to mathematical logic when I discovered the book of Hilbert and Ackermann in the summer of 1956, after my first undergraduate year at Caltech. I was attracted by the fundamental nature of the subject, and by the prospect of reaching the frontier of research quickly. At the time, logic had an air of mystery for me because the field was small and there were no specialists on the faculty at Caltech.

In the fall of 1956 C.C.Chang (then at USC and later at UCLA) attended the algebra seminar at Caltech as a visitor. He became my primary mentor in my undergraduate years, when I got my start in research in model theory and produced two papers, and was later to be my co-author for two books and several articles. With ample warning, C.C. prepared me for the crucible of graduate study at Berkeley (1959–1961), which was aptly described in the wonderful book *Alfred Tarski. Life and Logic* by Anita and Solomon Feferman.

What example(s) from your work illustrates the role formal methods can play in philosophy?

The paper "From accessible to inaccessible cardinals" [1964] with A. Tarski is the starting point for the systematic study of large cardinals and strong axioms of infinity, which has since become a central theme in set theory and the foundations of mathematics. The paper gave evidence that the notions of weakly compact cardinals, measurable cardinals, and compact cardinals are natural analogues of the notion of an infinite cardinal which arise from a wide variety of mathematical problems. More recently, stronger axioms of infinity, such as the existence of many Woodin cardinals, have gained prominence.

The book *Model Theory* [1973] with C.C.Chang organized and became the primary reference for the subject that provides the fundamental justification of formal methods by providing the link between the syntax of a formal language and its meaning. Since the book was written, model theory has split into many branches, each with its own methods, such as the model theory of tame structures, finite model theory, models of set theory and arithmetic, nonstandard analysis, and model theories for a variety of non-first order logics and modal logics. Our book is now the trunk of the tree which supports all these branches. The book also has the following real-life illustration of the Russell paradox: "we dedicate our book to all model theorists who have never dedicated a book to themselves."

The model theory paradigm which was originally developed for first order logic in the first half of the 20th century is of central importance in many other settings. When investigating an area by formal methods, one often starts by developing a formal language suited for the area of interest, and then developing a model theory for the formal language. This general approach is illustrated in my monographs *Continuous Model Theory* [1966] with C. C. Chang, *Model Theory for Infinitary Logic* [1971], and *Model Theory of Stochastic Processes* with S. Fajardo [2002].

In my research I have been attracted to A. Robinson's nonstandard analysis, a formal approach that has been underused and captures some powerful intuitive ideas, such as hyperfinite sets and infinitesimals, which can help in the discovery of new concepts and results. (The importance of mathematical intuition in general will be discussed later in my answer to the next question.) As the history of calculus suggests, the intuitive idea of an infinitesimal can be grasped at an elementary level, and makes it easier for beginning calculus students to absorb and use the basic concepts of limit, derivative, and integral. To make the infinitesimal approach available to beginners, I wrote the book *Elementary Calculus, an Approach Using Infinitesimals*, (1976, 1986, open source online edition [2000]). I think of this as planting a seed, with the hope that early exposure to the intuitive idea of an infinitesimal will have long term benefits.

In the paper "The hyperreal line" [1994], I discussed some of the issues in the philosophy of mathematics that are raised by the concept of an infinitesimal. The series of papers [1984], [1986], [2006a],

[2006b] on the proof-theoretic strength of nonstandard analysis is motivated by the philosophical question of how and where one can expect nonstandard methods to lead to new mathematical results.

In the paper "An impossibility theorem on belief in games" [2005] with A. Brandenburger, we use formal methods to analyze the following new paradox on iterated beliefs: "Ann believes that Bob assumes that Ann believes that Bob's assumption is wrong".

What is the proper role of philosophy in relation to other disciplines?

As a mathematician, I will instead write about the proper role of mathematics, and in particular of formal methods in mathematics, in relation to other disciplines. In order to answer this question, it seems necessary to take a stance on the question of mathematical existence. According to the classification in P. Maddy's recent paper "Mathematical Existence" [M], my position is somewhere between arealism and thin realism. Briefly, mathematical intuition about infinite objects exists, but I reserve judgment on whether or not the infinite objects themselves exist.

Gödel [G] wrote in 1964 that "the question of the objective existence of the objects of mathematical intuition ... is an exact replica of the question of the objective existence of the outer world." "The mere psychological fact of the existence of an intuition which is sufficiently clear to produce the axioms of set theory and an open series of extensions of them suffices to give meaning to the question of the truth or falsity of propositions like Cantor's continuum hypothesis."

I agree with Gödel that a mathematical intuition exists which is sufficiently clear to produce the axioms of set theory and an open series of extensions of them. I also agree that mathematical intuitions exist independently of the observer. However, I reserve judgment on whether the intuition is or can be clear enough to give meaning to the question of the truth or falsity of propositions like Cantor's continuum hypothesis.

I view mathematical research as exploring mathematical intuitions. This is ordinarily done by a community of mathematicians collectively building a formal system and proving a large number of theorems. Formal systems are used to clarify, sharpen, and communicate intuitive observations. We use mathematical intuition to find new axioms, make conjectures, and find proofs of theorems which follow from the axioms. This provides evidence of the existence of mathematical intuition. As Gödel pointed out, the consequences of the axioms, in turn, can be checked against intuition, and provide evidence for or against the axioms, in a manner analogous to the scientific method of using observations to test a theory. Computers give mathematicians another tool for testing axioms, as well as for experimentation which can stimulate mathematical intuition.

Mathematical intuition occurs in a variety of settings, for example: the cumulative hierarchy in set theory; constructive mathematics; computational complexity; modal logic; nonstandard universes; category theory; probability theory; string theory; biological and social sciences. One should expect that completely different intuitive viewpoints are possible, and that some of them will be discovered in the future.

A successful example which is often cited is the use of the intuitive concept of the cumulative hierarchy of sets to find the basic axioms of set theory, add axioms of infinity, and draw conclusions about sets at the lower levels. One can formally represent most of mathematics within set theory. However, some caution is needed because it is often hard to transfer mathematical intuition from one setting to another, or even from one subarea of mathematics to another. For instance, when one is immersed in the usual set-theoretic hierarchy, it is hard to think intuitively in terms of functors in category theory, or hyperfinite sets in a nonstandard universe, or constructive existence. For this reason, I am in favor of a pluralistic approach which encourages the unrestricted exploration of mathematical intuition in different settings. Fruitful ideas can be discovered in one setting but obscured in others.

Robinson's nonstandard analysis is one of many examples where different mathematical intuitions have led to new concepts and results. Constructive mathematics is another example of this kind. It is a good idea to find out what can be done by constructive methods, but a bad idea to limit mathematics to such methods.

I see two roles for mathematics in relation to other disciplines. One role is to provide algorithms to solve practical problems. A second, more interesting role, where mathematical intuition comes into play, is to create models or theories which shed light on some phenomenon that one wishes to understand. From this standpoint, pure mathematics can be viewed as the study of a mathematical intuition for its own sake, rather than for some outside phenomenon.

One can get some insight into the role of mathematics in relation to other disciplines by looking at a particular area. For example, in the area of mathematical economics there is a very substantial literature on exchange economies. A real-life exchange economy has a large but finite set of small agents who interact in some way, and one would like to understand phenomena such as coalitions, equilibria, the movement of prices, and behavior under uncertainty. In the literature, three different ways of representing exchange economies have been developed and used extensively. These are: an increasing sequence of finite economies where one studies the asymptotic behavior, an economy with a continuum of agents, and an economy with a hyperfinite set of infinitesimal agents. Even though one knows that there are only finitely many agents in a real-life economy, many phenomena are best understood intuitively by using infinite structures. Moreover, the three different approaches involve different mathematical intuitions which are helpful in understanding different phenomena.

What is going on here is that well-behaved infinite objects are intuitively simpler than large complicated finite objects. In all real situations (even in physics) one wishes to explain a large but finite set of observations about the world. The role of mathematics is to use mathematical intuition, often about infinite objects, to help understand the observations. One does not try to give an exact description, but instead searches for an idea which is simple enough to be grasped intuitively and which somehow captures the essential features of the phenomenon. For this reason, mathematics can serve its role best if one has the flexibility to exploit different mathematical intuitions.

What do you consider the most neglected topics and/or contributions in late 20th century philosophy?

What are the most important open problems in philosophy and what are the prospects for progress?

As a mathematician rather than a philosopher, I will replace this pair of questions by the following single question.

Identify some problems in the philosophy of mathematics that you consider to be interesting and important, and discuss their prospects for solution.

I begin with a disclaimer. The problems which I mention are not new, have not been neglected at all, and have been discussed at length in the literature with a great deal of speculation.

The problem which underlies the whole discussion above is:

A. What is mathematical intuition?

I believe that this problem is closely related to the following two problems:

B. Do infinite mathematical objects exist?

C. How does the brain work?

I suspect that further progress on question A will depend on progress on question C. One would expect a great deal of progress in the future on how the brain works, more likely by biologists rather than mathematicians or philosophers. In order to make progress on question A, a person would need both experience with mathematical intuition, and knowledge yet to be discovered about how the brain works.

As for question B, we have only finitely many observations of the real world at our disposal, and these give us no way to tell whether or not infinite objects actually exist. There is also the possibility that infinite objects exist but do not fit any intuitive viewpoint. I have distinguished between mathematical intuition about infinite objects and the objects themselves. Perhaps a better understanding of mathematical intuition about infinite objects will tell us whether this distinction is tenable.

I will close by mentioning two other questions which I consider to be interesting and important, but see little hope for progress in the near future.

D. What would happen if a contradiction were found in a very weak system on which we rely, such as primitive recursive arithmetic?

E. Can there be an experiment which establishes the physical existence of an infinite object? If not, can one prove that there cannot be such an experiment?

References

[1964] H. J. Keisler and A. Tarski. "From accessible to inaccessible cardinals." *Fund. Math.* **53** (1964), pp. 225–308.

[1966] C. C. Chang and H. J. Keisler. *Continuous Model Theory.* *Annals of Math. Studies* **58** (1966), xii+165 pages.

[1971] H. J. Keisler. *Model Theory for Infinitary Logic* (1971), North-Holland 1971, x+208 pages.

[1973] C. C. Chang and H. J. Keisler. *Model Theory* (Second edition 1977, Third edition 1990), North-Holland (1973), 554 pages.

[1984] C. W. Henson, M. Kaufmann, and H. J. Keisler. "The strength of nonstandard methods in arithmetic," *J. Symb. Logic,* **49** (1984), pp. 1039–1058.

[1986] C. W. Henson and H. J. Keisler. "On the strength of nonstandard analysis," *J. Symb.Logic,* **51** (1986), pp. 377–386.

[1994] H. J. Keisler. "The hyppereal line." *In Real Numbers, Generalizations of the Reals, and Theories of Continua,"* ed. by P. Erlich, Kluwer Academic Publishers, pp. 207–237, 1994.

[2000] H. J. Keisler. *Elementary Calculus, An Approach Using Infinitesimals,* xviii+940 pages. (First edition, Prindle, Weber and Schmidt 1976, Second Edition 1986, Online Edition with Creative Commons License 2000).

[2002] S. Fajardo and H. J. Keisler. *Model Theory of Stochastic Processes.* Lecture Notes in Logic, Association for Symbolic Logic (2002), xii+136 pages.

[2005] A. Brandenburger and H. J. Keisler. "An impossibility theorem for beliefs in games," accepted, *Studia Logica.*

[2006a] H. J. Keisler. "The strength of nonstandard analysis." To appear.

[2006b] H. J. Keisler. "Nonstandard arithmetic and reverse mathematics." To appear.

[G] K. Gödel. "What is Cantor's continuum problem?" *In Philosophy of Mathematics,* Selected Readings, edited by P. Benacerraf and H. Putnam, Prentice-Hall 1964.

[M] P. Maddy. "Mathematical existence." *Bulletin of Symbolic Logic* **11** (2005), pp. 351–376.

13

Isaac Levi

John Dewey Professor Emeritus

Columbia University, NY, USA

I do not think I was ever attracted to "formal methods in philosophy" nor do I think I am drawn to them now. For a long time I have been interested in the topic of justifying changes in points of view. I use the term "point of view" to encompass an agent's convictions, judgments of uncertainty, and values. I claim that such justification is itself "practical" in the sense that it requires adopting the best means available to the agent relevant to realizing the agent's current goals.

All of the notions I have just mentioned are, as they stand, highly obscure. It has seemed to me that structures studied by logicians, statisticians, economists and decision theorists could be helpful aids to alleviating this obscurity. I have felt compelled to learn something about the technical ideas in these disciplines in order to improve my understanding of some of the concepts with which I must deal. And these technical ideas and structures have, of course, an irremediably formal character. To the extent that I use formal methods in philosophy, I do so because I have to.

I was early on in my career concerned with the extent to which ampliative scientific inference (statistical inference, inductive inference and theory choice) could be rationalized within the framework of a general approach to rational decision making. I always thought that the expected utility principle was an excellent starting point for giving an account of ampliative scientific inference except for the fact that the principle required the specification of numerically determinate probabilities and utilities for its application. In the 1960's, I bracketed my concern and built a model of "cognitive decision-making" founded on the injunction to maximize expected utility.

This model was published in a book *Gambling with Truth* (1967) and shortly after modified in "Information and Inference" (1967).

Subsequently, I sought to address my worry concerning where the numbers come from according to Bayesian decision theory. For many authors, this question boils down to asking how elicitation from choice behavior may be employed, at least in principle, to obtain judgments of credal probability, judgments of utility for consequences and judgments of expected utility for options from judgments as to how the agent would choose among the available options in appropriately specified decision problems.

The classical approach to such hypothetical elicitation did not seem to me to answer the question in which I was interested. That approach presupposed that the ideally rational agent had numerically determinate probabilities, judgments of utility and of expected utility and that such an agent maximized expected utility. By "numerically determinate", I mean that the agent's state of belief or credal or subjective probability is representable by a unique probability function over the relevant algebra of states, the agent's evaluation of consequences (his extended value structure as I came to call it) is representable by a utility function unique up to a positive affine transformation and the agent's expected utility function (the agent's "value structure") is representable by a set of expected utility functions obtained by taking any utility function from the given set and the unique credal probability and determining the expected utility. [This too is unique up to a positive affine transformation.]

It seemed to me extremely doubtful that a rational agent should always be committed to such numerically determinate judgments. My worry was not that in practice it would not be feasible to measure or identify the agent's probabilities, utilities or expected utilities precisely. The classical Bayesian tradition already conceded that, as in physics, so too in psychometrics, perfect precision in measurement is not to be achieved with or without the Heisenberg principle. The classical Bayesian tradition could concede that no one can meet the demands of rationality (including numerical precision in probability and utility judgment) in practice while insisting that ideally rational agents were, nonetheless, committed to numerically determinate probabilities, utilities and expected utilities and that researchers studying such agents could treat such commitments as theoretical magnitudes.

My dissent from the classical Bayesian tradition related to the standards of ideal rationality that classical Bayesians endorsed. I insist that ideally rational agents ought not to be committed to numerical determinacy in probability, utility and expected utility.

Rational agents ought in some contexts to be prepared to remain in suspense or doubt concerning probability, utility and expected utility just as they ought to be prepared to remain in doubt or suspense in the sense of withholding full belief that proposition h is true or, equivalently, refusing to rule out as a serious impossibility that h is false and that $\sim h$ is false. Allowing ideally rational agents not to be opinionated concerning truth-value bearing propositions is recognized as part of an adequate account of rationality. Indeed, in many contexts, ideal rationality requires refusal to be opinionated.

I contend that an account of ideal rationality ought to allow refusal to be opinionated in probability, utility and expected utility judgment to be rationally coherent and in many contexts to be mandatory.

I take insistence on this as part and parcel of a way to integrate the approach to ampliative reasoning I adopted in *Gambling with Truth* into a more comprehensive study of justifying changes in attitudes not only of full belief, but of credal probability judgment, utility or value judgment, and expected utility judgment and how changes in such attitudes relate to practical deliberation. I understand this project to be one way to develop the belief-doubt model of inquiry pioneered by Peirce and extended by Dewey.

This project in the hands of Dewey (though perhaps not Peirce) did not appear to be part and parcel of "formal philosophy". And Dewey himself seems to have had (wrongly I believe) a tendency to avoid formal investigations. I agree with many of those hostile to formality that the core of the project focuses on preaching a sermon. The sermon addresses the question: What is required of an ideally rational agent engaged in problem solving inquiry according to the belief-doubt model? I am convinced that the text of the sermon requires appeal to formal structures.

To my way of thinking, all of the concepts involved in the belief-doubt model and most especially the concepts of belief and doubt call for elaboration in ways that unavoidably require technical developments. The gist of these elaborations may, perhaps, be indicated without appeal to technical elaborations. But any one who thinks that one can obtain a genuinely philosophical understanding of this approach to inquiry without a modicum of understanding of some formal structures is not, to my way of thinking, philosophically serious.

Having said this, I remain reluctant to take myself to be a formal epistemologist or a formal philosopher. Whatever modest use I have made of formal structures in my own work has been for the sake of the concept or problem I seek to clarify. Those who are engaged with formal structures more than I am may wish to consider the formal structures in their own right. I have no objection to purely formal investigations. But I am suspicious of formal investigations that as such pose as philosophy.

To illustrate the relevance of formal considerations to philosophical issues and also why they are not totally decisive, let me briefly summarize an episode in my own intellectual history. In *Hard Choices*, I argued that the value structure for a set of available options is representable by a set of utility functions that is convex. The condition of convexity may seem of underwhelming philosophical significance. But I argued that when two (expected) utility functions represent permissible ways of evaluating options then so must all potential resolutions in the sense that they preserve the evaluations that are settled according to the two utility functions. I claimed further that every potential resolution should be a weighted average of the two initially conflicting utility functions. Hence, the convexity condition on value structures.

Seidenfeld, Kadane and Schervish demonstrated in 1989 that if the two utility functions are expected utility functions derived from probability-utility pairs (p, u) and (p', u') where $p \neq p'$ and $(u \neq u')$, the only potential resolutions could be the expected utilities derived from these two pairs. If the value structure for options is representable by permissible expected utilities derivable from permissible probability-utility pairs as seems mandatory according to the qualified Bayesian view I favor, it appears that imposing convexity on value structures cannot consistently be imposed as well. Something is, therefore, wrong with my potential resolution condition.

In response, I offered a modification of the potential resolution condition. A potential resolution needs to preserve the common assessments of the two probability utility functions and the two pairs (p, u') and (p', u). This is because the second two pairs are themselves appropriately considered potential resolutions of the conflict between the first two. It turns out then, that a cross product rule gives the set of permissible expected utility functions in the value structure. This value structure is not convex. But the set of permissible credal probability functions will be as will the set of utility functions representing the extended value structure (the evaluations of potential consequences of the acts). Seidenfeld, Kadane and Schervish did not convince me that the motivation for my initial convexity requirement was wrong. I was motivated by a certain conception of what it is to have an open mind. The results of Seidenfeld, Kadane and Schervish required me to modify my view of doubt, the open mind, being in a state of suspense concerning how to evaluate options. And it emphasized for me the importance of the separability of probability and utility judgment. They take a different lesson from their results. Whatever the merits of our differing views, the formal results do not settle the philosophical issues by themselves but they force clarification of the potential resolution condition in an unexpected and important manner.

Very recent results obtained by the Carnegie Mellon trio show that it is possible to show that when there is a single utility function in the extended value structure (unique up to a positive affine transformation) and a set of two or more permissible probabilities in the state of credal probability judgment so that the issues over which I and they disagree do not surface, it is possible to identify hypothetical decision problems that uniquely identify the credal state according to the criterion of E-admissibility I favor. Seidenfeld, Kadane and Schervish seem to think that the representation theorem they can obtain in this fashion argues strongly against a convexity condition on credal probabilities.

In this case, the technical result does not require me to correct anything I have claimed previously. I endorse E-admissibility as a choice criterion. I agree that it can be applied without assuming convexity of credal states. But I contend that we should respect the demand that the potential resolution condition amended to address the 1989 result of Seidenfeld, Kadane and Schervish should also be satisfied. And this will insure convexity of the set of permissible expected utilities in the value structure.

This second Seidenfeld, Kadane and Schervish result is important because it shows how to test in terms of hypothetical choices whether an agent satisfies the convexity condition on credal states – at least in principle and not because it undermines the convexity condition as a demand of rationality.

I do not pretend to have great powers as a logician, mathematician, statistician and probabilist or decision theorist. But I think it important for a philosopher to be as open to the contributions of those who are proficient in these areas when their ideas are relevant to philosophical issues. It would have been better for me if I could have been a master of all these formal studies. But barring that, I think that philosophers should listen to workers in these areas as best they can and benefit from their insights.

I agree with Richard Rorty on one point. Although scholars and teachers ought to be professional, I do not think of Philosophy as a profession, discipline or *Fach*. Nor do I care much for controversies concerning the drawing of boundaries between different disciplines. I am interested, as I have suggested, in conditions under which changes in points of view are warranted. I have learned as much from psychologists, economists, decision theorists, statisticians, and computer scientists about topics relevant to my concerns as I have from logicians, epistemologists and value theorists. And my worries about the unholy marriage of game theory and evolutionary biology match my reservations about Dewey's famous analogy between adaptation in an amoeba and the process of problem solving inquiry.

I am not sure that I can rate topics with respect to undeserved neglect. But I can at least mention an open problem in which I am interested and which is widely neglected and for which I do not at present see an adequate solution. That concerns provision of a more or less systematic account of how conflicts in value judgment are legitimately resolved.

I mentioned that one of Dewey's many great insights is to have recognized that moral problems are not merely challenges to live up to what we know we ought to do. The most important kinds of moral problems arise when the agents involved do not know what they ought to do. It is to Dewey's credit that he recognized the distinction. Few moral philosophers have taken up the challenge it poses. To be sure, many writers speak of moral dilemmas and some may even acknowledge them to be predicaments where agents do not know what they ought to do—although this is rare. Few reflect on the methodology of conflict or problem resolution as a matter for inquiry rather than for persuasion. It seems to me that exploring this topic and the parallel topic relevant to resolution of political conflict are the most important open problems we face.

For my part, I have failed to make much headway on these topics. And I doubt that much headway will be made until we can understand better the kinds of formal structures required to make sense of value conflict and its resolution.

14

Ruth Barcan Marcus

Reuben Post Halleck Professor of Philosophy

Yale University, New Haven, USA

Why were you initially drawn to formal methods?

I had an early interest in mathematics and the role of proof. When in my later focus on philosophy, common-sensical or relatively non-formal understanding of philosophical questions often required, the use of formal methods for further clarification. By formal methods I'm thinking of uses of formal logic, formal semantics, formal mathematical theories such as set theory and model theory, proof theory and the results of such theories. This does not exhaust the extent to which formal theories have either illuminated philosophical and logical questions or fuelled the adoption of novel approaches. In my view the tools of formal methods have lead to many dramatic advances in the twentieth century but they are sometimes misused. Sometimes the preoccupation with formalisms displaces what is of centrally philosophical interest.

What example(s) from your work illustrates the role formal methods can play in philosophy?

(A)

I had a pre-formal interest in the modal concepts of necessity and possibility which can be traced back to Aristotle. This led me to study, with the encouragement of my undergraduate tutor J.C. McKinsey, the work of C.I. Lewis who had developed modal systems of propositional logic. As a graduate student at Yale this interest was pursued with the support of F.B. Fitch. At that time, and through the early forties, a prevailing view about interest in modal logic was that of W.V. Quine who claimed that its source was in a misguided confusion between use and mention. It was also claimed that any attempt to develop a system of quantified modal logic would lead to deep problems of interpretation, including incoherence.

I set about extending some of the Lewis systems to first- and then second-order (*JSL*, 11, 1946 and *JSL*, 12, 1947) under Ruth C. Barcan. included is an attribute forming abstraction operator and the "Barcan formula" taken as an axiom:

$$\Diamond(\exists x)Fx \rightarrowtail (\exists x)\Diamond Fx$$

On the given formalizations the converse is provable. The "Barcan Formula" and its converse remains a subject for debate.

The system Quantified Modal Logic (QML) had some outcomes which answered to some non-formal speculation and debate about modalities such as:

a. A formal proof of the necessity of identity.

b. Despite Lewis' claim that strict implication was supposed to capture the relation of deducibility or logical consequence the strict analogue of the deduction theorem in unmodalized predicate logic was *not* provable. A weaker more plausible deduction theorem is provable in some of the Lewis systems. *JSL* 11, 1946. (See also *JSL* 18, 1953 for a more extended account.)

c. A substitution theorem which *proscribes* the substitution of non-necessary equivalences in the scope of the necessity operator.

(B) Interpretation of QML

a. I defend Smullyan's claim that Quine's examples of substitution failures in modal contexts are mistaken. Russell's formal theory of descriptions is adopted as well as a linguistic theory of direct reference for proper names, (Proper names are not taken to be disguised descriptions.) *JSL*, 13, 1948.

b. "Modalites and Intensional Languages," *Synthese*, 1961. Several issues are addressed using formal methods:

   i. A direct reference view for genuine proper names is defended. I called them *tags* since they are unmediated.

On such a direct reference view of proper names in conjunction with the theory of descriptions, the much advertised "failures" of substitution for identity in modal contexts are dispelled within interpreted QML.

ii. The necessity of identity is defended. (The "=" in identity formulae is flanked by individual variables or constants. Only proper names are individual constants.)

iii. A substitutional alternative to objectual quantification is proposed for consideration in some contexts. It is seen as of interest but not urged. See also "Quantification and Ontology", *Nous*, VI, no. 3, 1972 where Quine's claim that the substitutional account leads to a contradiction is formally shown to be fallacious.

iv. A non-formal account of essentialism challenges the claim that essentialism is "invidious". Formal accounts within QML are given in *Nous* 1, 1967, some versions of which have been adopted, often without attribution.

v. A sample model-theoretic semantics with fixed domain is given in which the Barcan formula is provable. Metaphysically understood, domains of interpretation contain only actual objects. Possibility concerns properties actual objects might have. My arguments against *possibilia* are linguistic and empirical and discussed in *The Proceedings of The American Philosophical Association*, 1975. *Grazer Philosophicshe Studien*, vol. 25, 1985/86, *Revue Internationle de Philosophie*, 1997.

vi. The paper here considered was delivered in 1962 and was followed by comments from Quine and a discussion with Quine, Kripke, Føllesdal *et al.* which were published in *Synthese*, 1962. There Quine says that "the distinction between names and descriptions is a red herring." That distinction (the red herring) was later adopted by Kripke (1971) and others. The historical chain account of name transmission was first proposed by Peter Geach in "The Perils of Pauline", *Revue of Metaphysics*, 1969.

(C) Moral dilemmas and Consistency

An analogue of the formal model theoretic definition of consistency is used to dispel the received claim that when a moral code can mandate incompatible actions in a particular case, it must be inconsistent. But, what is formally required for consistency is that there is a *possible* world which is dilemma free, e.g. where keeping promises does not conflict with saving lives as in Plato' s example. There are ethical conclusions to be drawn; we ought to arrange our lives and institutions to minimize occasions of conflict. *Journal of Philosophy*, LXXVIT, no. 3, 1980 and in Homer Mason, editor, *Moral Dilemmas and Moral Theory*, OUP, 1996. This account runs counter to many formalizations of deontic logic where conflicts of obligations in a particular case entails inconsistency.

(D) Set Theory in a Modal Framework

The syntax and semantics of QML can be enriched to accommodate a theory of collections described by inventory and sets described as satisfying some attribute not given by inventory e.g.

$$\widehat{x}(x \text{ is a planet})$$

from

$$\widehat{x}\left(\begin{array}{c} x = N \vee x = V \vee x = M \vee x = P \vee \\ x = Ma \vee x = U \vee x = S \vee x = E \vee x = J \end{array}\right)$$

where the upper case letters are names of the actual planets.

Any two attributes given by inventory, if they describe the same collection then they are necessarily equivalent. No axiom of extensionality is required. This is just an extension of the necessity of identity for the singular case. That does not hold for attributes which may be satisfied by the same things where the equivalence is not necessary but analogous to a material equivalence.

This paper was written in two versions; there was a problem of making the *vocabulary* and symbolism perspicuous. *Acta Philosophica Fennica*, XVI, 1963. *American Philosophical Quarterly*, 1974.

(E) CODA

The list above is partial account of the way that formal methods have been essential to my philosophical work. In recent years I have been writing on epistemological issues such as belief and rationality. Here I have rejected most received accounts of propositional attitudes and attempts to systematize epistemic logic. The entire project is in a formative stage so it has been omitted from the discussion.

What is the proper role of philosophy in relation to other disciplines?

Philosophers should not in their own work, close out advances in other disciplines as being irrelevant. This attitude is widespread among even the most exacting analytical philosophers, who are often inclined to say that searching out advances in other disciplines in the pursuit of ones own philosophical research isn't "doing philosophy." I've heard this from some in philosophy of mind who ignore brain and neurological research, and from some in ethics and epistemology who ignore research in the behavioral and social sciences. But philosophers who are not ignorant of work in other disciplines not only stand to gain in their own projects they have also proved to be incisive critics. There has been and could be fruitful collaboration as in linguistics, law and cognitive science.

What do you consider the most neglected topics and/or contributions in late 20th century philosophy?

I am too much a part of the late twentieth century to feel confident about my judgement in answering this question. I am not schooled in recent continental philosophy and my research interests have been in analytic philosophy and its history. What I do notice is that there is a tendency to latch onto the work of a single figure to the neglect of the substantial and sometimes more original work of others. More broadly speaking, recent history has been given short shrift. Often where narratives of philosophical developments are presented as historical accounts they are not. There is a tendency to neglect original sources and to carry along the misrepresentations of others. This is not just a question of settling matters of priority or provenance. There is much to be learned in tracing the actual history of emergent views.

What are the most important open problems in philosophy and what are the prospects for progress?

I have given this question considerable thought but I am not in a position to judge with any confidence which are the *most* important open problems in philosophy. I am confident about frivolous or dead end pursuits but weighing importance eludes me.

Bibliography
(exclusive of abstracts and many reviews)

BOOKS

Alan Ross Anderson and R.M. Martin, eds., *The Logical Enterprise*, pp. 31–38. New Haven: Yale University Press, 1975.

Logic, Methodology and Philosophy of Science, VII, eds. R. Barcan Marcus *et al*, North Holland, 1986.

Modalities: Philosophical Essays, pp. 102–109. New York: Oxford University Press, 1993.

ARTICLES

Published under "Ruth C. Barcan"

"A Functional Calculus of First Order Based on Strict Implication." *Journal of Symbolic Logic* (1946), 11: 1–16.

"The Identity of Individuals in a Strict Functional Calculus of First Order." *Journal of Symbolic Logic* (1947), 12: 12–15.

"The Deduction Theorem in a Functional Calculus of First Order Based on Strict Implication." *Journal of Symbolic Logic* (1946), 11: 115–118.

Review of Arthur Smullyan's "Modality and Description." *Journal of Symbolic Logic* (1948), 13: 149–150. Reprinted as "Smullyan on Modality and Description" in *Modalities: Philosophical Essays*, pp. 36–38. New York: Oxford University Press, 1993.

Published under "Ruth Barcan Marcus" sometimes indexed under "Barcan-Marcus"

"The Elimination of Contextually Defined Predicates in a Modal System." *Journal of Symbolic Logic* (June 1950), 15: 92–93.

"Strict Implication, Deducibility, and the Deduction Theorem." *Journal of Symbolic Logic* (September 1953), 18: 234–236.

"Extensionality." *Mind* (January 1960), 69: 55–62. Reprinted in Leonard Linsky, ed., *Reference and Modality*, pp. 44–51. Oxford Readings in Philosophy. London: Oxford University Press, 1971.

"Modalities and Intensional Languages." *Synthese* (Dec. 1961), 13(4): 303–322. Reprinted in Marx Wartofsky, ed., *Boston Studies in the Philosophy of Science*, pp. 77–96. Dordrecht, Holland: Reidel, 1963. Reprinted with corrections in Irving M. Copi and

James A. Gould, eds., *Contemporary Readings in Logical Theory*, pp. 278–293. New York: Macmillan, 1967. Reprinted in Farhang Zabeeh, E.D. Klemke and Arthur Jacobson, eds., *Readings in Semantics*, pp. 837–853. Urbana: University of Illinois Press, 1974. Reprinted in Irving M. Copi and James A. Gould, eds., *Contemporary Philosophical Logic*. New York: St. Martin's Press, 1978. Translated into Hungarian in the Hungarian version of Irving M. Copi and James A. Gould, eds., *Contemporary Readings in Logical Theory*. Budapest: Gondolat, 1967. Reprinted in *Modalities: Philosophical Essays*, pp. 5–23. New York: Oxford University Press, 1993.

"Discussion of the paper of Ruth B. Marcus", W. V. Quince, S. Kripke, D. Follesdal, *et al, Synthese*, 1962. Reprinted in Marx Wartofsky, ed., *Boston Studies in the Philosophy of Science*, pp. 77–96. Dordrecht, Holland: Reidel, 1963.

"Interpreting Quantification." *Inquiry* (1962), 5:252–259.

"Classes and Attributes in Extended Modal Systems." *Acta Philosophica Fennica* (1963), 16: 123–135.

Part of Proceedings of a Colloquium in Modal and Many-Valued Logics, Helsinki, 1962.

"Reply to Dr. Lambert's 'Quantification and Existence'." *Inquiry* (1963), 6: 325–327.

"Iterated Deontic Modalities." *Mind* (October 1966), 75(300): 580–582.

Reprinted in *Modalities: Philosophical Essays*, pp. 40–43. New York: Oxford University Press, 1993.

"Essentialism in Modal Logic." *Nous* (March 1967), 1: 90–96. Reprinted with revisions in *Modalities: Philosophical Essays*, pp. 46–51. New York: Oxford University Press, 1993.

"Modal Logic." In Raymond Klibansky, ed., *Contemporary Philosophy: A Survey*, Volume 1: Logic and Foundations of Mathematics, pp. 87–101. Florence: La nuova Italia, 1968.

"Essential Attribution." *Journal of Philosophy* (April 8, 1971), 68(7):187–202. Translated into Italian in *Individui e mondi possibili: problemi di semantica modale*. Scritti di Ruth Barcan Marcus et al. Edited by Daniela Silvestrini. Milan: Feltrinelli, 1979. Reprinted with revisions in *Modalities: Philosophical Essays*, pp. 54–70. New York: Oxford University Press, 1993.

"Quantification and Ontology." *Nous* (September 1972), 6(3): 240–249. Reprinted with revisions in *Modalities: Philosophical Essays*, pp. 76–87. New York: Oxford University Press, 1993.

"Classes, Collections, and Individuals." *American Philosophical Quarterly* (1974), 11(3): 227–232. Reprinted in a revised form as "Classes, Collections, Assortments, and Individuals" in *Modalities: Philosophical Essays*, pp. 90–100. New York: Oxford University Press, 1993.

"Does the Principle of Substitutivity Rest on a Mistake?" In Ruth Barcan Marcus, Alan Ross Anderson and R.M. Martin, eds., *The Logical Enterprise*, pp. 31–38. New Haven: Yale University Press, 1975. Reprinted in *Modalities: Philosophical Essays*, pp. 102–109. New York: Oxford University Press, 1993.

"Comment on Wiggins." In Stephan Körner, ed., *Philosophy of Logic: Papers and Discussion*, pp. 132–146. 3rd Bristol Conference on Critical Philosophy, 1974. Oxford: Blackwell, 1976. On David Wiggins' "Identity, Necessity and Physicalism," pp. 96–132.

"Dispensing with Possibilia." *Proceedings and Addresses of the American Philosophical Association* (1975–76), 49: 39–51.

Review of Leonard Linsky's *Names and Descriptions*. *Philosophical Review* (1978), 87(3): 497–504.

"Nominalism and the Substitutional Quantifier." *Monist* (July 1978), 61(3): 351–362. Reprinted in *Modalities: Philosophical Essays*, pp. 112–124. New York: Oxford University Press, 1993. Reprinted in Dale Jacquette, ed., *Philosophy of Logic*, pp. 161–168. Mass.: Blackwell Publishers, 2002.

(with B. Kucklick and S. Bercovitch.) "Uninformed Consent." *Science* (1979), 205: 644–647. Reprinted in Samuel Gorovitz, et al., eds., *Moral Problems in Medicine*. 2d ed. Englewood Cliffs, NJ: Prentice–Hall, 1983.

"Moral Dilemmas and Consistency." *Journal of Philosophy* (March 1980), 72(3): 121–136. Reprinted in *The Philosopher's Annual* (1981), 4: 133–148. Reprinted in Christopher W. Gowans, ed., *Moral Dilemmas*. New York: Oxford University Press, 1987. Reprinted in James P. Sterba, ed., *Contemporary Ethics*. Englewood Cliffs, NJ: Prentice-Hall, 1989. Reprinted in *Modalities: Philosophical Essays*, pp.127–141. New York: Oxford University Press, 1993.

"Hilpinen's Interpretations of Modal Logic." In G.H. von Wright, ed., *Logic and Philosophy*, pp. 31–36. International Institute of

Philosophy, Symposium in Düsseldorf, August 27-September 1, 1978. The Hague: Nijhoff, 1980.

"Modal Logic, Modal Semantics and their Applications." In Guttorm Floistad, ed., *Contemporary Philosophy: A New Survey, Vol 1: Philosophy of Language—Philosophical Logic*, pp. 279–298. The Hague: Nijhoff, 1981. Reprinted in a Chinese translation, in a collection *Modalities*, Chenbol, Peking, ed.

"A Proposed Solution to a Puzzle about Belief." In Peter A. French, Theodore E. Uehling, Jr. and Howard K. Wettstein, eds., The *Foundations of Analytic Philosophy*, pp. 501–510. *Midwest Studies in Philosophy*, 6. 1981. Minneapolis: University of Minnesota Press, 1981.

"Rationality and Believing the Impossible." *Journal of Philosophy* (June 1983), 80(6): 321–338. Reprinted in *Modalities: Philosophical Essays*, pp. 144–161. New York: Oxford University Press, 1993.

"Bar-On on Spinoza's Ontological Proof." In Nathan Rotenstreich and Norma Schneider, eds., *Spinoza: His Thought and Work*, pp. 110-120. International Institute of Philosophy, Entretiens, 1977, Jerusalem. Jerusalem: Israel Academy of Sciences and Humanities, 1983.

"Spinoza and the Ontological Proof." In Alan Donagan, Anthony N. Perovich, Jr. and Michael V. Wedin, eds., *Human Nature and Natural Knowledge: Essays Presented to Marjorie Grene on the Occasion of her Seventy-Fifth Birthday*, pp. 153–166. *Boston Studies in the Philosophy of Science*, 89. Dordrecht, Holland: Reidel, 1986. Reprinted in her *Modalities: Philosophical Essays*, pp. 164–176. New York: Oxford University Press, 1993.

"Is There Irrationality in the Existence of a Plurality of Philosophical Theories?" *Dialectica* (1985), 39(4): 321–328.

"On Some Post-1920s Views of Russell on Particularity, Identity, and Individuation." In Jules Vuillemin, ed., *Mérites et limites des méthodes logiques en philosophie*. Paris: Vrin, 1986. Reprinted in *Modalities: Philosophical Essays*, pp. 178–188. New York: Oxford University Press, 1993.

"Possibilia and Possible Worlds." *Grazer Philosophische Studien* (1985–86), 25–26: 107–133. Reprinted with revisions in *Modalities: Philosophical Essays*, pp. 190–213. New York: Oxford University Press, 1993.

"A Backward Look at Quine's Animadversions on Modalities."
In Robert B. Barrett and Roger F. Gibson, eds., *Perspectives
on Quine*, pp. 230–243. Perspectives on Quine: An International
Conference, April 9–13, 1988 at Washington University in St.
Louis. Oxford and Cambridge, Mass.: Blackwell, 1990. Reprinted
in *Modalities: Philosophical Essays*, pp. 216–232. New York: Oxford University Press, 1993. Reprinted in Dale Jacquette, ed., *Philosophy of Logic*, pp. 308–317. Mass.: Blackwell Publishers, 2002.

"Some Revisionary Proposals about Belief and Believing." *Philosophy and Phenomenological Research* (Fall 1990), 50(Supplement): 133–153. Reprinted in Gordon G. Brittan, Jr., ed., *Causality, Method, and Modality: Essays in Honor of Jules Vuillemin*,
pp. 143–173. *The University of Western Ontario Series in Philosophy of Science*, 48. Dordrecht, Holland: Kluwer, 1991. Reprinted
with revisions in *Modalities: Philosophical Essays*, pp. 234–255.
New York: Oxford University Press, 1993.

"Ontological Implications of the Barcan Formula. " In Hans Burkhardt and Barry Smith, eds., *Handbook of Metaphysics and Ontology*. Munich: Philosophia Verlag, 1992.

Several entries in Ted Honerich, ed., *The Oxford Companion to
Philosophy*. New York: Oxford University Press, 1996.

"More on Moral Conflict." In Homer Mason, ed., New York: Oxford University Press, 1996.

"Are Possible Non-Actual Objects Real?" *Revue Internationale
de Philosophie* (1997).

IN PROGRESS

Book length manuscript on Epistemology, Belief, and Reference

Article on Russell's departure from the theory of descriptions

15

Rohit Parikh

Distinguished Professor

Brooklyn College and CUNY Graduate Center, NY, USA

Why were you initially drawn to formal methods?

When a graduate student at Harvard, I took a logic course with Quine. I was not turned on by that course, although I found Quine quite helpful in personal interactions. I then took a second course with Burton Dreben. Dreben was quite disorganized, and the course was rather chaotic, but Dreben brought to the course the enthusiasm of a young man, and that caught. Indeed, Dreben remained a 'young man' until his death in 1999 at the age of 71. Moreover, after an unsuccessful attempt to introduce us to Herbrand's thesis (it was discovered later that there were mistakes in that thesis) Dreben abruptly switched to Martin Davis's book *Computability and Unsolvability* (McGraw Hill, 1958). I had spent the previous summer as a programmer for Minneapolis Honeywell, and Davis' Turing machine based treatment went down as easy as pie. I decided to do my dissertation in Logic.

But Dreben suddenly took a leave of absence, and many of the students at Harvard decided to study with Hartley Rogers at MIT. Rogers was an absolutely first class teacher in Recursion theory, and after studying with him, problems in that area started to seem quite easy. I did my dissertation in *transfinite progressions*, influenced by and extending some work of Kreisel.

A different acquaintance with formal methods came about as a result of my work with Noam Chomsky as a research assistant. I introduced the notion of semi-linearity for studying context free languages, and proved that inherently ambiguous context free languages existed. (This last result has been attributed by Hopcroft and Ullman – *Introduction to Autmata Theory, Languages, and Computation*, to Gross, but since Gross himself attributes the result to me, Hopcroft and Ullman must be mistaken!) This work became much better known than my dissertation but had little influence in the purely logical work which was my main concern.

But there had also been an earlier 'logical' influence on me. As a first year graduate student I had come across a copy of Wittgenstein's *Remarks on the Foundations of Mathematics*. I did not really follow what he was saying, but I realized that he was a genius and that some day I must understand him. This event happened only many years later, with the help of my then colleague, Arthur Collins, and Mr. Saul Kripkenstein. Kripke did not correctly represent Wittgenstein, in my view, but he was extremely clear, and after reading Kripke on Wittgenstein, it became much easier to understand the master himself. Wittgenstein's treatment has always remained with me and kept me away from falling into a groove which, while well traveled, is an impediment to understanding.

What example(s) from your work illustrates the role formal methods can play in philosophy?

One example is my paper 'Existence and Feasibility in Arithmetic' which appeared in the *Journal of Symbolic Logic* in 1971 and which was influenced by the ideas of the Russian mathematician Yesenin Volpin, as well as by Wittgenstein and Dummett. Volpin had argued that the set of one's heartbeats in childhood is an inductive set, i.e., closed under a successor function. For if b is a beat *in childhood*, so is b', the next one. After all, no one ceases to be a child in the course of just one heartbeat. And yet, the set of such heartbeats is easily seen to have cardinality less than two billion, counting (at most) two heartbeats per second over at most 18 years. So a finite set could be inductive! Volpin proposed to use such "finite" inductive sets to prove the consistency of ZF set theory, a project which did not much interest me, even though I was interested in Volpin's ideas themselves, which I and everyone else had immense difficulty following.

So my failure to understand Wittgenstein was paralleled by my failure to understand Volpin's methods. But I did use conventional methods to prove the following result. Suppose some theory T extending Peano Arithmetic postulates that there is a set of *small* numbers which includes 0, and is inductive, but such that some explicitly described very large number is *not small*, then T of course will be *inconsistent*. For starting with 0, and repeatedly applying the inductive property we can prove of *any* particular number that it is small. But still, every formula ϕ proved in T which is strictly about the usual theory of numbers (i.e., does not contain the symbol for *small*) and whose proof is short (with an explicitly given upper bound) will be true. Indeed ϕ will already be provable in Peano Arithmetic. The method was not strictly speaking conventional in that few now use it—it was the ϵ-calculus. But it was conventional in the literal sense that Hilbert and Bernays, and W. Ackermann had already used it. What we can conclude from this result is that Volpin's idea had some merit. It is interesting that Ackermann used the ϵ-calculus to prove the consistency of Peano Arithmetic. Such a consistency proof does not make use of a model (the usual infinite set of natural numbers) for all the axioms at one fell swoop in order to establish consistency, but instead provides a finite model for each *proof*.

Another example is my work on vagueness. Quite early on I became convinced that the use of vague words was a *human* practice and could not be reduced to a semantics or even to a precisely defined logic. But I was able to show that the use of vague terms has utilitarian value. Thus suppose that Ann asks Bob to look for a blue book on her shelf and bring it to her at the university. Now it is well known, for instance from the work of Berlin and Kay (*Basic Color Terms; their universality and evolution*) and many others, that human beings do not assign the same extension to color words as other human beings. So the extensions of *blue* as used by Ann and by Bob are likely to be different. However, since Ann and Bob belong to the same linguistic community, these extensions will have a positive correlation. *Learning* the use of color words does not imply that we acquire the *same* extension for color words as others, but that the differences decrease and we can all agree on whether the light is green and we can go, or that the light is red, and we must stop.

This fact of positive correlation of extensions of color words can then be used to show that even with his different interpretation of *blue*, Bob will spend *less* time looking for the book than he would have if he had not been told anything by Ann. Indeed the saving for Bob will be greater if the correlation between the two extensions of *blue* is greater. Thus Ann's statement that the book is blue helps Bob, even though he 'misunderstands' it, not having the extension for 'blue' intended by Ann in mind. Thus, to put it in Wittgensteinian terms, a successful language game can be played using vague terms, even though such terms have no well defined semantics or even a logic. Lewis' signalling games rely on a similar idea. Whether signalling is successful or not is independent of whether we can give a clear semantics to the signals themselves.

What is the proper role of philosophy in relation to other disciplines?

To encourage other disciplines to examine their methods and to be more explicit about their own foundations.

What do you consider the most neglected topics and/or contributions in late 20th century philosophy?

I think the influence of materialism in philosophy and the desire to appear scientific has been very harmful. Perhaps materialism is true, and everything reduces to matter. But it is hardly explanatory. We just do not look inside John's brain to see what he wants for dinner; we ask him. It is by far the more efficient method. I think that the influence of materialism shows itself in the importance given to model theory, for a mathematical model is a sort of actual world. Thus a materialistic outlook in philosophy very naturally leads to a Platonic view in mathematics and logic, away from proof theory or more general techniques.

I think our failure to understand important questions in set theory is directly traceable to this 'realistic' view. More than a hundred years after Russell's paradox we still do not really understand it, and brilliant young set theorists are wasting their time inventing stronger and stronger 'large cardinal' axioms. The possibility that set theory is not 'about' something, but represents our thinking processes, an insight which Brouwer would have urged on us, is completely lost.

Luckily, Artificial Intelligence (AI) has stepped into territory which Philosophy left. For AI wants to understand how people think and communicate, and human communication goes well beyond "informing each other about the real world." Both Modal Logic and Non-monotonic reasoning (known to philosophers as defeasible reasoning, and deeply involved in the Gettier puzzles) are older than any convincing semantics for these two areas, and I think this is healthy. AI forces us to look back to human practices, and while these practices can sometimes be explained in terms of a semantics, quite often the practices have their own life.

A very nice example of this sort of situation comes up with the Morning Star, Evening Star puzzle which is more than a hundred years old. Recently it was discovered that the person who sent re-tired diplomat Joseph Wilson to Niger was his wife Valerie Plame who was also a CIA operative. Here we have three definite descrip-tions with a single denotation—exactly like the situation with the two descriptions of the planet Venus. However, this issue not only has political ramifications, it also encourages us to ask questions about how a logic of knowledge with notations for descriptions would handle such issues. A former student, Eric Pacuit, and I have written about these logical questions which belong to AI but can be traced back to purely philosophical roots.

Currently there is a sort of divide among two communities inter-ested in knowledge. One is the community of epistemologists for whom the 1963 paper by Gettier has created a fruitful discussion. The other community is the community of formal epistemologists who trace their roots back to modal logic and to Hintikka's work on knowledge and belief. There is relatively little overlap between the two communities, but properties of the formal notion of knowl-edge, e.g., positive and negative introspection, have caused much discussion. I would suggest that knowledge statements are not actually propositions. Thus unlike "There was a break-in at Wa-tergate," "Nixon *knew* that there was a break-in at Watergate," is not a *proposition* but sits inside some social software. It may thus be a mistake to look for a *fact of the matter*. The real issue is if we want to hold Nixon *responsible*. The American people did hold Nixon responsible, and I think that was a good choice, but I think it would be a mistake to conclude from that that there was a *fact of the matter* which would meet stringent conditions on assignment of knowledge.

What are the most important open problems in philosophy and what are the prospects for progress?

At least to me, two very important problems are consciousness, and understanding the workings of natural language. The prospects for understanding (large parts of) natural language are much bet-ter of course, because at least we are not looking in the wrong direction.

Another issue, of interest personally to me, is having some re-alistic progress in Ethics so that we are not torn between denying morality on the one hand, and relying on religious dogma on the other. This is an area in which philosophy could be doing much more in the *public* sphere, outside the ivory tower, than it is cur-rently doing.

16

Jeff Paris

Professor of Mathematics

University of Manchester, UK

Why were you initially drawn to formal methods?

I can't really say that I was 'drawn to formal methods' because I arrived there by accident, firstly through arithmetic and secondly through uncertain reasoning. It was only later that I realized why I felt at home there.

For most of my career I've seen myself very much as a mathematical rather than philosophical logician. It's only been over the last decade or so that I've started relating to philosophers and more philosophical questions, and I still only feel comfortable with the authority of proven theorems to back me up.

I suppose that sums up one of the two main reasons why I 'do' formal methods. A correctly proved theorem tells you that if you assume (a),(b),(c) (including some underlying logic) then (d) must hold. You may feel that in your context some of (a),(b),(c) do not hold, in that case the theorem has nothing to say to you. But if you think they do hold then you should also think that (d) holds. Or putting it another way, if you reject (d) then you had better also reject at least one of (a),(b),(c). Results like this are worth having, the more so if (a),(b),(c) appear widely valid. Time and philosophical considerations may make (a),(b),(c) seem less, or more, generally applicable, but that makes not a jot of difference to the fact that *if* they do all hold *then* so does (d). Within the corrosive atmosphere of philosophy there is little else with this sort of permanence.

The second main reason why I do formal methods is because I really believe that such theorems can tell us something, that the (a),(b),(c) can be such that it's harder to reject them than accept them whilst the conclusion (d) tells us something at best surprising, and at the very least comforting.

To give an example, it would seem clear to most of us that we have some 'knowledge' about the world and that we have a process of reasoning with it to produce 'new knowledge', conclusions we were not initially patently aware of. Furthermore one imagines (least ways *I* imagine) that any alien from this, or any other, universe, also has 'knowledge' and 'does reasoning'. What I intuitively feel here (for whatever that's worth), and what I would like to *prove* here are very general results of the form that within certain natural constraints the representation of the knowledge and the reasoning process are inevitable, determined, fixed. Much of my own work, largely with collaborators, has been aimed at proving limited (or toy) versions of this.

As I have said I believe such results can have a positive, illuminating, effect within Philosophy. Unfortunately they do not always seem to me to work this way, at least not in the short term, and that's because they are not appreciated for what they are, simply conclusions from assumptions. The first form of misinterpretation is when the assumptions are overlooked or simply ignored. As a result the conclusion is given an authority it doesn't deserve and cannot support. It's consequent fall from grace is then equated at large with the underlying theorem having been 'disproved'. For example I have heard it said that de Finetti's Dutch Book Theorem is *wrong* when further enquiry simply showed that the nevertheless influential speaker had dropped some of the assumptions on which it was grounded (though pointing this out was not enough to erase his belief that the theorem was wrong).

A second somewhat negative effect is rather the complement of this, wanting to have the assumptions of the theorem without the conclusion. Thus if the conclusion of the theorem is an unpleasant surprise then any number of devices will be employed to re-interpret the, at least initially acceptable, assumptions so that the intervening proof fails. This is certainly better than wanting the conclusion without the assumptions but can seem like an opportunity wasted, an undue desire to make the unpleasant go away. The Liar Paradox serves as a good example here.

What example(s) from your work illustrates the role formal methods can play in philosophy?

In the mid 1980's I got involved with a pathologist colleague in creating an 'Expert System' (or Knowledge-based System as they later became known) for diagnosing slides. Scanning through the literature I became dismayed at how *ad hoc* many of the deductive methods being employed in these systems seemed to be. So, based on the limiting assumption, which commonly prevailed at that time, that the expert's knowledge base consisted of a finite (satisfiable) set of linear constraints on a probability function (the expert's 'belief function') I sat down with my co-worker Alena Vencovská to try to formulate what it means to say that on the basis of such knowledge, and such knowledge alone, a certain conclusion is 'common-sense'.

To give an informal example of what I mean here suppose I am tossing a penny and know nothing more about that coin. Then it seems only 'common-sense' for me to assign belief (i.e. probability) 1/2 to it landing tails. As a second example, again with a coin, suppose that I did know something: that it was raining in Manchester and there was an errant lump of gum stuck to the head side of the coin. Then in this case it would again seem 'common-sense' that the information about Manchester's weather was irrelevant, and hence that I should assign the same belief (though now not necessarily 1/2) to tails as I would if it was sunny instead of raining.

From idealized everyday examples of this sort, some of which were already well known in the literature, we gathered a handful of such 'principles'. Our interest then was whether these were mutually consistent and if so to what extent these common-sense requirements limited the possible beliefs/probabilities one could assign on the basis of such knowledge sets. In other words, is common-sense at this level doomed from the start and if not how far can it take us? Is there a point at which we have to throw up our hands and admit that any way of proceeding further has to be *ad hoc*?

In fact it came as a great surprise to us (I can remember clearly the moment when the mathematics suddenly fell into place like a jigsaw puzzle) when we realized that we had the best of all possible worlds: not only were these common-sense principles mutually consistent but their observance led to a unique answer. In other words two individuals armed with the same such knowledge (i.e. a finite satisfiable set of linear constraints on a belief/probability function) and obeying common-sense as captured by these principles would always be led to assigning the same beliefs.

Over the next decade or so we proved a number of refinements of this result. It still holds if your initial knowledge was simply of the form of qualified beliefs in particular events (like for example *I believe a tossed drawing pin will land spike up with probability 2/3*), and indeed it even has a version which applies to completely general finite satisfiable sets of constraints provided they are closed in the topological sense. Of course one should not lose sight of the fact that despite these refinements the assumption that the knowledge base has such a primitive form is, at anything more than the broadest of brushes, almost always unrealistic for real world examples involving human reasoning—except in mind experiments. (Failure to fully appreciate this underlying assumption has caused some terrible non-sense to have appeared in the literature.)

What is however the case is that *if* an agent's knowledge is simply of this form, and in particular this certainly has applied to many expert systems, *then* the agent's failure to come up with this unique answer will mean that the agent is contravening, or at least neglecting, to act according to our understanding of common-sense as captured by these principles.

Much of my subsequence research, usually joint, has been aimed at formulating principles of common-sense, or rationality, within the framework of some very simplified representation of 'knowledge' and then delineating the consequences of applying these principles. As I have already said, in practice the knowledge that humans call on when reasoning currently appears so far from any such simple representation that results along these lines would rarely seem to be directly applicable to human (as opposed to artificial agent) reasoning. Nevertheless such results have value in that they cut down the search space, reduce the playing field: if one doesn't like the conclusion then one must move outside the area of the assumptions and say why certain other factors are crucial.

As an example of this process an early paper by Ian Maung and myself (and related results appear elsewhere in the literature) showed that if one assumes that reasoning involved attempting to assign belief/probability values consistent with a finite knowledge base of satisfiable linear constraints then this is computationally infeasible (according to the current viewpoint in that subject). Indeed even the process of checking the satisfiability of such a linear knowledge base is infeasible. Taking the position that this amounted to a serious drawback Alena Vencovská and I posited an entirely different model of knowledge representation and reasoning (essentially knowledge is just a store of past examples and the reasoning is by association) called the *Ent model* which avoided both these shortcoming. I still retain a soft spot for these Ents whose cause I vainly try to promote at every possible opportunity!

What is the proper role of philosophy in relation to other disciplines?

The main role that I see philosophy playing is to continue what I believe it does best, to step back from the the world and experiment with ideas and ways of seeing. Whilst this advisary 'think tank' role is hardly new, emphasizing it gives the subject a vitality and purpose that sometimes seem to those of us at the fringe less than self evident.

What do you consider the most neglected topics and/or contributions in late 20th century philosophy?

Considering the number of papers, theses, books, lectures in Philosophy over this period it would be hard to find any topic or contribution with more than provincial aspirations which had been truly neglected, even when that was what it thoroughly deserved.

Down at the level my own, local interests, however, an area which seems to me to have remained strangely quiescent for the past 40 years is Inductive Logic in the sense of Carnap. Following its birth with the papers of W.E. Johnson in the 1920's and 30's, its independent discovery by Carnap some 20 years later and the subsequent flurry of activity with important contributions from de Finetti, Jeffreys, Kemeny et al. further developments have indeed been few and far. Indeed that whole approach to understanding induction now seems to be out of fashion. This comparative lack of activity is especially surprising given that in Schilpp's well known 1963 volume of collected papers on *The Philosophy of Rudolf Carnap* Kemeny sets out a clear agenda for the future development of the topic. In part this might be explained by the increasing technical complexity of the mathematics involved though there were certainly philosophical logicians around for whom this would not have have been overly daunting.

Failing to respond to this challenge seems to me to have been an unfortunate missed opportunity. For one thing I believe that recent research shows that there are philosophically, and mathematically interesting new results in inductive logic so that without the intervening (mainly) dark age this could by now have been a flourishing and stimulating area. Apart from the obvious intellectual pleasure that has been lost, or at least postponed, the period has seen the rapid development of other disciplines, AI and Cognitive Science in particular, who are covering much the same ground (basically predicate probability logic). Though their emphasis and aims may be different to have had in place, a well thought through body of knowledge and theory(ies) with which to inform would certainly not have done our subject any harm.

A second philosophical problem, which is often remarked on by Mathematicians though I am not aware of any convincing explanation, concerns the way 'natural mathematical examples' tend to occupy 'distinguished positions' in classifications. To give a specific, and particularly vivid, example of this phenomenon, we can classify the complexity of sets of natural numbers by their Turing degrees (for this example it is not important to know what this actually means). In this classification the bottom position is taken up by the class O of recursive sets and above that we have it's so called jump, the class O' which contains, for example, the set of codes for Turing Machines which halt (eventually) when run on their own code. There are known to be many classes strictly between these two 'distinguished positions'. However it is striking that whenever one has a 'natural', as opposed to artificial, set of numbers which lies somewhere in this range then it either lies in O or in O', never in one of the many intermediate classes between them.

Such situations are common throughout Mathematics. Why?

What are the most important open problems in philosophy and what are the prospects for progress?

I'm not sure it is a very good idea to view Philosophy as being in the business of *answering* problems in the sense that Mathematics, or Engineering, or even Physics, answer problems. Philosophy is better at posing problems.

17

Gabriel Sandu

Directeur de recherche, Professor

IHPST, Paris, France
Department of Philosophy, University of Helsinki, Finland

Why were you initially drawn to formal methods?

I could say it was not a matter of choice but rather one of necessity. I arrived in Helsinki in the late 70s. The department of philosophy had people like von Wright, Stenius, Hintikka (visiting quite often), Pörn, Rantala, Kivinen, Hilpinen, Niiniluoto, Knuuttila, Saarinen, Tuomela and others. On top of all this, there was once a year a joint picnic with the members of the department of philosophy of Uppsala's university. Stig Kanger presented once a year a paper, often on the proof of the existence of God. The fact that in Helsinki you had to have a huge portion of formal logic was common knowledge. I did my Master Dissertation with I. Pörn who had just arrived at that time from Great Britain. I was driven by him towards deontic logic, a natural topic to investigate in von Wright's department. After that I had Jaakko Hintikka as the supervisor of my doctoral thesis. It went without saying that I was supposed to master formal methods, although Jaakko continuously warned me and everyone else about the danger (!) to be too much preoccupied with technicalities. There was no sign of Snow's two cultures in the intellectual climate of the department of philosophy of the University of Helsinki in the 70s. Hintikka lectured and supervised students from mathematics, philosophy and linguistics departments. It was another piece of common knowedge that at the doctoral level there are no disciplinary barriers: one just sees to it that he or she acquires the proper education in all the departments where the topic of the dissertation might lead her or him to. As a curiosity, it is in this very department that few years ago, shortly before his death, von Wright predicted that this century will not be that of logic, as the preceding one, but that of speculative philosophy ...

What example(s) from your work illustrates the role formal methods can play in philosophy?

I remember having read the proceedings of a workshop, which took place in Israel around the seventies and which was devoted to the role of formal logic in philosophy. The workshop was chaired by Bar-Hillel who, in his opening speech, launched a challenge to the participants (who included, among others, Hintikka, Stenius, Montague, Dummett, Soames, Katz and many others) to evaluate what according to him was one of the greatest scandals in the intellectual history of humankind: has anybody ever seen a piece of natural language reasoning validated by an argument in formal logic? And who was to be blamed for that? I think that the worries expressed by philosophers and logicians then are more or less the same that concern us today. Chomsky criticized Bar-Hillel in the 50s for trying to introduce formal logical relations in linguistics. He used more or less the same arguments that Quine used against Carnap earlier on: formal languages and formal relations do not stand by themselves, and thereby their role cannot but be very limited. Nevertheless, I think all the parties agreed then as they agree nowadays that relating an argument or an assertion to a formal schematism (one of the many formal methods used in philosophy) fills in the gaps left over by the ambiguities, vagueness and vagaries of informal reasoning in natural language. I shall give just two examples among many.

Take a classical philosophical problem like that of truth. Tarski's work on the concept of truth in formalized languages is a beautiful piece of philosophy. Many logicians before him, Frege, Wittgenstein and Ramsey, fought with the same problem, that is, with the problem of defining truth. Frege and Wittgenstein could only commit themselves to assert that the truth of a proposition amounts to nothing else than the assertion of the proposition itself. When they tried to say more (the status of concepts, objects, or the picture theory of language, etc), that was not meant to be taken as a full-fledged semantical theory, but only as some kind of elucidation, or nonsense. Ramsey almost gave an inductive definition of truth, but he finally gave up, seeing no hope to regiment natural languages in such a structural way that would make possible the application of an inductive (compositional) definition. Tarski agreed with him on this point, but found, nevertheless, a family of languages for which that kind of definition could work. Those are the formalized languages, that is, the interpreted languages abstracted from those used by mathematicians for a long time, like the language of arithmetic or the language of the calculus of classes, coming in pairs with an underlying theory with which they had grown together. Once he isolated them into the object of his considerations, thus literally transforming them into object languages, he could apply his inductive method and give a truth-definition for many of them in the metalanguage. Moreover, he could produce a beautiful result to the effect that the metalanguage had to be stronger than the object language, and thus show that the truth predicate cannot be defined in the object languages themselves. The benefit of Tarski's formal method are undeniable: its setting (formalized languages) could allow the application of a method (compositionality) that led both to a positive and negative result. No wonder that logicians after him tried to get English, look like a formal language! His negative result bothered, of course, many. Kripke showed how one can get the truth predicate definable in the object languages themselves, provided it is partially interpreted. In the late eighties Hintikka was convinced that this result could be improved. I was working with him on the so-called IF languages and in the same time I did some work with Joukko Vaananen on the model theory of branching quantifiers. The idea of putting all these things together into a truth-definability result for IF-languages came quite naturally.

Results like this one have ramifications of all sorts and connect to other kinds of formal methods. Since the time of Hilbert, conservativity arguments have been devised in order to avoid ontological commitments to abstract entities. Hilbert introduced a distinction between real statements (involving only finitistically meaningful entities) and ideal statements. He was concerned with the status of highly abstract mathematical entities like those figuring in Cantor's set theory. His goal was to show that if we add to a mathematical theory containing only real statements a theory containing ideal statements and if the latter were conservative over the former (it did not prove real statements that the former theory could not prove), then one would not need to bother about the ontological status of the abstract entities. Their role would be purely heuristic. The same idea has been applied over and over again in philosophy. For instance, conservativity arguments have been used to show that mathematics is conservative over physics and that a deflationist theory of truth (i.e. a theory which asserts that everything we need to know about truth is contained in the axioms of the form "It is true that A if and only if A") is conservative over almost any theory. Conservativity is thus supposed to be an indicator of how substantial the ontological commitment over a particular notion is. Roughly, if after adopting the notion in question, I cannot prove more statements than I could prove before endorsing it, then there is a clear sense in which the notion in question is ontologically thin. Using this measure, Tarski's theory of truth is ontologically more committing than disquotational theories and truth in IF languages is certainly more committing than Tarskian truth. True enough, Hilbert's program did not work in the end, neither did Field's fictionalist program. But it is important, I think, to be able to show in what conditions and in what sense something works or doesn't work.

What is the proper role of philosophy in relation to other disciplines?

To address foundational issues about the limits of the subject matter ... . Recall, for an example, the great debate between Chomsky and Quine on the nature of linguistics, one of the most fascinating in the histories of human thought. Quine launched a typical philosophical argument: there is no epistemology, which could show that grammatical distinctions can be objectively specified. For him, Chomsky's distinction between linguistic competence and performance is just another way to resuscitate the analytic-synthetic distinction. There is no such thing as a correct grammar, for any criterion to select one is bound to go beyond the permitted behavioral evidence. The debate brought to the surface many interesting things about the relation between natural language and formal logic, the limits of grammatical schematisms, the justification of scientific theories, and, most importantly, the nature of evidence in linguistic theory. In fact, I believe that often, interesting philosophical ideas are the ones which lead to interesting developments elsewhere. A good example is Hintikka's analysis of intentional notions in terms of possible worlds (scenarios, situations, etc). Think about the impetus it has given to the modelisation of cognitive notions in artificial intelligence ...

What do you consider the most neglected topics and/or contributions in late 20th century philosophy?

I think the problem of the logical fallacies is one of them. It is always fruitful to deal with the pathology of a subject. Too much

attention has been devoted to the semantic paradoxes, and too
little to the traditional fallacies themselves.

What are the most important open problems in philosophy and what are the prospects for progress?

I think the question of what is our home logic and logical language,
if any, is one of them. After an age of an undisputed "first-order
thesis", certain developments in artificial intelligence in natural
language compelled us to take seriously the question of computational complexity. It is now argued that decidable sub fragments of
first-order logics (e.g. modal logics, etc), which have lower computational complexity, are better suited for many purposes and that
expressive power should not be the first priority. This particular
issue, which bears on logic, is part of a broader problem. In the
last quarter of last century, many philosophers (Davidson, Kripke,
Putnam, Dummett) have been defending normativity and holism
as a particularity of language, logic and thought. Very often the
notions a philosopher has been traditionally concerned with, like
the nature of meaning, concepts, logic, knowledge, etc, have a normative flavor which is not exhausted by empirical investigations.
The space of reasons and arguments is not that of physical contingencies. Well, it is obvious that with developments of the kind
just mentioned, and parallel ones in cognitive sciences, this philosophical view has to be qualified. There is more talk nowadays
about a psychological turn in logic, as there is more talk about,
let's say, the computerization of science. I do not mean that traditional philosophical notions will lose their normative force. Logical reasoning will still be qualifiable as correct or incorrect, but
progress into the nature of the contingencies which make possible
logical reasoning is bound to have relevance for what is our logic
in concrete, information bound situations. I think that part of the
reason why, much of the research in say logic takes place elsewhere
than in philosophy departments, as do also research on concepts,
or ontology, is that philosophers have been slow to assimilate the
significance of results obtained elsewhere. Of course, this is not
the only justified philosophical attitude, but if we are ready to
talk about problems in philosophy, then progress in my opinion
can come mainly from that kind of interaction.

18

Krister Segerberg

Professor Emeritus

Uppsala University, Sweeden

Why I was initially drawn to formal methods

In primary school I dreamt of becoming an astronomer, in secondary school a physicist, at university a mathematician. But as an undergraduate math major at Columbia I had two encounters that were to change my plans once more: one with logic, the other with history of ideas.

One of my math courses was in logic, and I found that logic suited me. But I also liked the compulsory courses in Western Civ for which Columbia is famous. I was impressed by the great thinkers, however dead and white and male, who had thought so deeply about important issues and evidently had shaped so much of modern thought. After graduation I could only find one department in which it was possible to pursue both these new interests, and that is where I ended up: in the philosophy department. An academic philosopher can think about almost anything as part of the job. I liked that freedom.

From a logical point view Uppsala, where I began graduate study in philosophy, was a desert, and to transfer to Stanford was an epiphany (as they say in the U.S.). I had already become interested in modal logic and, as I was to find out, California in those days—the latter part of the 60s—was a hotbed of modal logic. I never looked back.

An example from my own work

My work falls almost entirely within modal logic, in a wide sense of the word. Thus when asked about formal methods my immediate thoughts go to methods of logic (even though I am not sure I could give a very satisfactory definition of either 'formal' or 'method').

There are of course other formal methods, but in my own research they have played a minor rôle.

For the last two decades my major concern has been to try to develop what I call DDL and DΔL: a dynamic doxastic logic in which to formalize some of the (nowadays extensive) work on belief change, and a dynamic deontic logic in which to formalize notions of actions of various kinds and norms. The example selected here is taken from the former project. Actually, what I will describe is matters belonging to the conceptual analysis that precedes formal logic.

Philosophical questions of the type "What is knowledge?" seem too big for an ordinary mortal to address. By contrast, the question "What is a belief state?" appears to be more manageable. Writers in other walks of philosophy have addressed this question at length, holding for example that belief states are (or are not) brain states. That kind of approach is of course alien to logicians: a logician could not *qua* logician answer the question "What is X?" if X is something empirical. But there is a related question the logician might be able to tackle, namely, "What would be a good way, or some good ways, of representing X?"

Before trying to give a formal representation of belief states we first have to agree on a context or background—to lay down the rules of the game, as it were. To this end, let us assume that there are two components, (A) an environment and (B) an agent able to hold beliefs about the environment.[1] To make this precise, let us assume that the agent's beliefs are restricted to aspects of the current state of the environment. A simple example would be a meteorologist equipped with a set of instruments: "northerly wind 5 m/s, 18°C and sunny" might be the contents of a possible belief.

The simplest would be to treat the entire set of the agent's beliefs—let us call it the agent's *belief set*—as a representation of the agent's belief state. To streamline our analysis we may assume that the belief set is (alternatively, gives rise to) a theory in Tarski's sense (that is, a set of propositions that contains all logical tautologies and is closed under logical consequence). Simple as it is, this definition permits at least a preliminary discussion of the ways of belief of the agent and its logic of beliefs. For example,

---

[1] A human agent is either *he* or *she*, a collective agent may be *they*, an inanimate agent such as a robot or a program or a system seen as an agent is *it*. Always writing *he* might seem sexist, always writing *she* obsequious (if the writer is male). And always writing *he or she* is tiresome. So in this paper, the agent will be *it*; please bear with me and this tribute to political correctness.

it becomes possible to say something about what distinguishes rational from nonrational belief. (In *Knowledge and Belief* Jaakko Hintikka took a further step: he allowed the agent to hold beliefs about its own beliefs, which is like treating the agent and its beliefs as part of the environment.)

Now let us add the assumption that the agent receives new information over time and as a consequence may modify its beliefs. In other words, the agent may replace its current belief state by another. This transition from belief state to belief state must then be examined. It now appears that it was premature to identify an agent's belief state with its belief set. For presumably two rational agents with the same set of beliefs about the current state of the environment can react differently to the same new piece of information.

Instead of casting the agent's belief state as a theory, let us now represent it by what I like to call a *hypertheory*, a set of theories the exact nature of which will not be explained here. It is interesting that this concept can be reached along two quite different routes: by formal considerations or by intuitive reasoning. In the actual development of AGM theory (the dominant paradigm named for Carlos Alchourrón, Peter Gärdenfors and David Makinson), the two routes were travelled independently: the introduction of hypertheories was made on formal grounds, the intuitive rationalization came later (although it was clearly foreshadowed in earlier work).

What actually happened was this. It occurred to Adam Grove that a representation theorem for the theory of AGM could be proved in terms of David Lewis's theory of sphere systems. Grove's theorem was a formal result, the details of interpretation were left vague. Now, in modellings of the kind Grove used it is natural to identify a sphere (a closed set) with a theory. Therefore a sphere system (a prime example of a hypertheory) may be seen as a set of theories in which the belief set is the strongest and the other spheres represent weaker theories serving as defaults—*fallbacks*, to use a term later suggested by Sten Lindström and Wlodek Rabinowicz. The idea is that if the agent's current belief set becomes untenable in the light of new information, then the current belief state (the sphere system, the hypertheory) will be helpful in determining a new belief set with the help of a suitable fallback. That default must be weaker, of course, the question is only how much weaker. This is the problem of belief change in a nutshell: to give up enough and yet keep enough.

This way of thinking was congenial to AGM, even though they had originally expressed themselves in different terms. Early on they had defined an operation they called *expansion*: in order to expand one's beliefs with a new belief, add the new belief to the current belief set and then close under logical consequence. If the added new belief is consistent with the old belief set, then this operation seems like a reasonable way of arriving at a new belief set that accommodates the new belief. Unfortunately, in the general case this will not do, for there is the danger that the agent's new belief set is inconsistent. In fact, this will always be the case in the only really interesting case, namely, when the new belief-to-be-added is inconsistent with the old beliefs. The solution recommended by AGM was to proceed in two steps. First (assuming that the new belief to be added is consistent by itself) adopt as an intermediate belief set what we may now describe as the strongest fallback that is consistent with the new belief (assuming that there is such a fallback). Then (but only then) expand by adding the new belief. The result is the desired new belief set, and thanks to the way in which it was constructed it is consistent.

Of course, to complete the theory we must specify, not just the new belief set, but the entire new hypertheory (that is, the new belief state). How that can be done is controversial and will not be discussed here.

This was a short sketch of the development of the AGM paradigm of belief change. There is also another paradigm for which KGM may be an appropriate moniker (in honour of Hirofumi Katsuno, Gösta Grahne and Alberto Mendelzon). It is generally accepted that the former paradigm makes sense in a setting where the information about the environment may vary but the environment itself does not change. By contrast, the latter is useful when the new beliefs concern changes in the environment. It turns out that we are actually dealing with two different kinds of belief change, *revision* and *update* as they have come to be called; and their logics differ in interesting ways. Thus AGM is a paradigm for belief revision, while KGM is a paradigm for belief update. Accordingly, when I have tried to combine both these paradigms in a single theory, I have had to distinguish two kinds of beliefs about the environment, one belief about what is the current state of the environment, the other belief about environmental change. In this combined theory, a hypertheory can still be seen as representing the belief state, but only against a set of fixed beliefs about how the environment can change—a background theory (which is neither revised nor updated).

In other extensions of the theory, further kinds of beliefs may be distinguished, for example, beliefs about one's beliefs (as in Hintikka's theory), beliefs about the self (what sort of agent the agent believes itself to be: reliability, memory capacity, relative state of information, decision principles), beliefs about others (what beliefs other agents have but also what sort of agents they are), and so forth. How these extensions affect the question as to how to represent the agent's belief state will then have to be considered.

How the example illustrates the role of formal methods

The case just described motivates the following observations, some of which are related. They are not terribly original, and most of them have been made many times by other authors (which does not mean that they are uncontroversial).

Deep philosophical questions are never fully answered. Even the question what a belief state is—a much simpler question, it would seem, than the question what knowledge is—cannot be completely answered by a merely formal theory. Perhaps it is a defining property of a (deep) philosophical question that one can always prolong any analysis by asking for a fuller or better answer. That this is a popular technique with our youngest philosophers, the two- and three-year olds, is hardly an accident. My youngest grandchild, two-and-a-half-year old Fia-Stina-Lotta, who like many of her agegroup devotes much time to philosophical discussion, ends every conversation in precisely that way: "What *is* that?" or "What *are* you *talking* about?" And, with devastating gravitas, "*Why?*"

Formal methods generate new questions. In order to tackle the chosen problem, an abstract set-up is defined. In terms of new, sometimes very technical concepts it becomes possible to formulate precise new questions. One point of the formal exercise is that, unlike the deep philosophical questions with which the investigation began, those questions can often be answered.

Formal methods are typically precise. This has an obvious advantage: rigour. But it is also indirectly one reason why those of our nonformal colleagues who don't like us don't like us. The price for increased precision is decreased scope. The advantage of the microscope over the naked eye: you see more sharply, but in some sense you see less. Let me add one remark and one question (not meant to be rhetorical). The remark: Formal methods do not have a monopoly on precision. The question: Are there significant domains in the analysis of human endeavour that are incompatible with precision?

There is a constant back-and-forth between formal modelling and intuitive understanding. One way to try to understand something—let us call it the object of study—might be to build a model. Studying the formal properties of the model may help to see the object of study in a new light and may suggest new questions about it; these in turn may lead to new formalisms. (For example, if belief change is seen as a binary relation in a collection of hypertheories, one can formally distinguish different kinds of change and compare them with informal notions.) There is also the important phenomenon that Hintikka has remarked upon: the re-education of intuition.

Formalisms once defined tend to take on a life of their own. There are both good and bad examples of this tendency. The bad examples arise when formal investigation begins too early, or if the formalism does not have emough structural richness to reward technical work. The good examples include modal logic, currently a very active field being extended in many different directions. Today it is studied most intensely by mathematicians and computer scientists, but it was initiated by philosphers who were driven by genuinely philosophical concerns. (Here I might mention my own experience. By the time I came to modal logic it was already a well established, if not very respected, discipline on the verge of reaching maturity. For years I was happily submerged in completely formal, purely mathematical problems.)

All thinking has to begin somewhere. Linguists will tell you that the Whorf hypothesis has been thoroughly discredited. But it is difficult not to think that there is something to it: that the way we speak and think is a selective result of the efforts of previous generations to survive in a challenging environment. Surely there were stone age philosophers. And surely they had they same influence on their contemporaries as, for better or worse, philosophers have always had. So there is reason to think that our everyday thinking has been imbued by the thought habits of many previous generations and therefore, perhaps, is unwittingly biassed or "infected". For example, the notion of states of various kinds is intelligible to normal folk; you don't have to be a philosopher to talk about someone's emotional state, state of anxiety, state of doubt, state of ignorance, or state of belief. Yet, if you think about it, these are highly sophisticated terms, perhaps dependent on presuppositions and ways of looking at things of which speakers—men and women in the street, who use these terms with perfect ease—are not aware. In fact, it may be very difficult to articulate what those "ways of looking at things" might be.

There is something "oxymoronic" about formal methods in philosophy. In order to treat a philosophical question formally, it must first be rephrased in formal terms ("formulated"), only then does real work become possible. If the work is not successful, the analysis will ossify and/or will eventually be abandoned. On the other hand, if it is successful it may take off on its own, a new discipline resulting. In fact, the latter has happened several times in the history of philosophy. It may be happening right now, when formal logic is becoming a *lingua franca* in computer science, at the same time as—this is just my impression, I can only hope that I am wrong—beginning graduate students in philosophy increasingly turn to nonformal areas of philosophy. A number of central philosophical questions are at the bottom of much foundational work in computer science and AI: about knowledge, the growth of knowledge, inference, change, perception, action, norms, to mention a few. If the computer scientists are successful, as they probably will be, they will change philosophy as we know it. (A point of historical interest: Of AGM, A was a professor of jurisprudence, G is Sweden's first professor of cognitive science, and M is a logician who went from UNESCO to a computer science department. All three of KGM are computer scientists.)

Succinctness is a virtue. With an efficient formal language or a well-wrought formal theory, complicated relations may be stated in a concise form that can easily be surveyed. Mathematics is of course the shining example (with today's notation, Cardano's sixteenth century treatise on how to solve equations of the third degree can be reproduced in a couple of pages). Could it be that the human mind, being what it is, requires methods that provide this kind of succinctness in order to advance certain areas of knowledge?

Truth may be unique, but modellings need not be. Some, even some philosophers, seem to expect one answer to each question, one solution to each problem. But in modelling, plurality is the rule rather than the exception. And plurality is welcome! Sometimes different modellings can be proved to be equivalent, alternatively proved not to be equivalent. Results of both kinds may be of interest: equivalence suggests that an important feature has been captured, nonequivalence may show the need for an important distinction.

The gap between representation and reality needs to be explained.
Modal logicians—but also other formal analysts—habitually fail
to discuss the detailed relationship between their abstract modellings and the reality to which those modellings are meant to
apply. How to apply the theory is taken for granted. Perhaps the
pragmatists have the beginning of an answer: perhaps there is
a practice that connects theory and application, even though it
would be difficult or even impossible to describe it. On the editor's
questions about what are the most important neglected topics or
the most important open problems in philosophy today, I respect-
fully pass. But among the problems facing me in my own work,
this one—the connection between the formal and the actual—
stands out. To paraphrase Fia-Stina-Lotta: "What *am* I *doing?*"
And the inevitable follow-up: "*Why?*"

What I think about the role of formal methods

I will end by considering four slogans, rejecting two and endorsing
two.

I am a supporter of formal methods in philosophy. This is not to
say that I believe that all philosophy must be made with their help.
My friend and older colleague, the late Stig Kanger, who liked to
provoke, used to say that *philosophy that cannot be mathematized
is not philosophy.* And there is Quine's famous line: *philosophy
of science is philosophy enough.* I don't subscribe to either slogan
(and I don't know whether Kanger or Quine really did either). My
own view is that formal methods are important for some parts of
philosophy and indispensable for a few.

The value of formal methods lies in what they let you do but also
to some extent in what they don't let you do. That they allow you
to do things you cannot do without them is obvious. Rich Thomason once said something like this (in conversation about philosophers who spurn formal methods): Aristotle was very smart; today's philosophers cannot realistically hope to improve on what he
said without resorting to methods that were not available to him.
This is a striking observation that would deserve to be hammered
into a slogan, for example, *Don't think you can outsmart Aristotle!*
or *To go beyond a great philosopher, go beyond his methods!*

But there are also things formal methods will not let you do.
Formal methods impose discipline. It is of course possible for a
formalist to devote himself to triviality. Even reputable technical

journals occasionally contain nugatory papers that probably owe their existence to their authors' need for tenure or promotion. But formal methods bring with them fairly definite standards of excellence, and so it is very difficult to get absolute rubbish published in a technical journal. For parts of the humanities, standards of excellence are, relatively speaking, less clear. For philosophy in particular, this lack is sometimes a problem. This is one reason why I deplore that the logic component in philosophy curricula in the countries with which I am familiar appears to be diminishing. It must be good, it seems to me, for all students of philosophy to be confronted with rigour at least once in their lifetime, a concept they are unlikely to meet outside mathematics or logic.

My exit line is due to Esaias Tegnér, Swedish poet and bishop of Lund in the early nineteenth century. I don't know what he would have thought of having his words cited as a slogan in support of the use of formal methods in philosophy, but I like to think that he would have condoned it:

The words and thoughts of men are born together:
to speak obscurely is to think obscurely.

19

Wolfgang Spohn

Professor for Philosophy and
Philosophy of Science

Department of Philosophy

University of Konstanz, Germany

Why were you initially drawn to formal methods?

My occupation with God and religion, quite intense for a child, I recall, was somehow exhausted at the age of 14, forever, I suppose. My interest then turned to philosophy, a most natural follow-up. It was vacillating at first and without much guidance. With 17 I read the *Hauptströmungen der Gegenwartsphilosophie* by Wolfgang Stegmüller (1952). He presented a number of philosophers, Husserl, Scheler, Heidegger and others, which I found quite obscure. Chapter IX, though, was devoted to Rudolf Carnap and the Vienna Circle. I think I was imprinted by this chapter like the little duck is by the call of its mother. I was firmly decided since to study philosophy at Stegmüller's institute. 38 years later and after rich reflection and experience I still cannot think of a sounder way of doing philosophy than I encountered there.

What example(s) from your work illustrates the role formal methods can play in philosophy?

I am firmly convinced of the crucial importance of formal methods for philosophy. I know many excellent philosophers who do not use formal methods and are not able to profitably do so, and I know a lot of formal papers that are terribly boring, since they neither make much philosophical sense nor are particularly deep from a formal point of view. Still, properly applied formal methods achieve an inestimable philosophical surplus out of reach of any other means. Of course, different philosophical fields are amenable to formal methods to largely varying degrees, and the most difficult and valuable work often consists in making a field so amenable in the first place. Generally, I believe that the fruitfulness of formal methods extends much further than is usually thought. Clearly, though, one needs a good sense of self-constraint.

As far as my own papers are concerned, I sense that I tend to overdo the formal methods (to the detriment of their accessibility). There are great masters of leaving formal methods implicit; compare, e.g., the formally explicit book of Lewis (1969) and his formally implicit twin paper (1975). However, there is a fine line between leaving formal methods implicit and not having them in the back at all, and I want to keep a clear distance from this line by all means. Whence my tendency.

Own examples? The example I have made the biggest fuss about is ranking theory. This is an elaborated account of Baconian probability (as opposed to the real Pascalian probability) or theory of the rational dynamics of (plain) belief. Since any theory of doxastic change is nothing but an account of the problem of induction, the importance of this example is obvious. However, let me refer to my most recent survey article Spohn (forthcoming b) concerning that example and turn to another less known one.

It is about decision theory. Since Nozick's (1969) famous presentation of Newcomb's problem philosophical decision theory is split between causal decision theory (the majority opinion) the adherents of which recommend two-boxing and evidential decision theory some adherents of which favor one-boxing. The issue is still contested, mainly, I think, because the majority is not stable, but rather plagued by the question "Why ain'cha rich?" which is not soothed by the answer: "Because irrationality is rewarded in this situation." In Spohn (2003) I have developed a sophisticated argument *justifying one-boxing within causal decision theory*. Here, I want to give a very rough sketch of the argument in order to afterwards explain the quite obvious role of formal methods in this example. The sketch proceeds in eight steps:

The *first* ingredient of the argument is the theory of *Bayesian nets*. A Bayesian net is a directed acyclic graph the nodes of which represent factors or (random) variables plus a probability measure over the algebra of propositions (or events) generated by these variables such that the measure agrees with the graph. The latter means that the set of parents of each node is the smallest set such that this node is probabilistically independent from all its non-

descendents given this set; cf. Pearl (1988, sect. 3.3). The fact
that this notion is well defined and that indeed for each measure
there is such a graph is due to the so-called graphoid axioms for
conditional probabilistic independence among sets of variables;
cf. Pearl (1988, sect. 3.1). These properties are crucial for the
whole mathematics of Bayesian nets and were already discovered
by Dawid (1979) and Spohn (1978, 1980).

The *second* step is that Bayesian nets have a *causal interpretation* provided that the nodes or variables are temporarily ordered
and the vertices agree with the temporal order, i.e., the endpoint
of a vertex is always later than its starting point. The causal interpretation then is simply that each vertex represents a direct
causal dependency; its endpoint directly causally depends on the
starting point. At this point, however, I have an argument with
most other causal theorists working in this paradigm. The common opinion is that a vertex in a Bayesian net is symptomatic of
a causal dependence (cf. Spirtes et al. 1993, ch. 3, and Pearl 2000,
ch. 1), whereas I say that it is definitive of a direct causal dependence. (I have more carefully analysed this difference in Spohn
2001)

My stronger claim makes sense only because, in the first analysis, I take causal dependence to be frame- or model-relative; insofar only the variables in the Bayesian net are considered and no
more, the causal dependencies run as represented in the net. Of
course, we think that causal dependence is an objective relation
in the world not relative to the frame we happen to consider. The
only way I can do justice to this thought is by referring to the
universal frame embracing all variables whatsoever. The universal
Bayesian net, as it were, displays the causal dependencies as they
objectively are.

One may wonder whether the universal frame is really well defined. Therefore, I am, in a *third* step, more interested in how
the causal dependencies relative to smaller and larger frames relate. This can only be judged from the point of view of the larger
frame. Hence, I am more specifically interested in the *reduction
of Baysian nets*. That is, if one node of a Bayesian net is deleted,
how do the vertices get rearranged? Basically, the answer is: the
vertices between the remaining variables stay the same, and if C
is the deleted node, then $A \rightarrow C \rightarrow B$ reduces to $A \rightarrow B$ and $A
\leftarrow C \rightarrow B$ reduces to $A \rightarrow B$ (provided A precedes B). Reversely,
this means that, whenever there is an apparent direct causal de-
pendence $A \rightarrow B$ relative to a small frame, this may turn into an

indirect causal dependence $A \to C \to B$ or into a common cause relation $A \leftarrow C \to B$ relative to an enlarged frame.

Well, this is roughly so. There is a third possibility that turns out to play no role for the rest of my argument. And there are conditions to my claims that should be carefully considered.

Now, what have Bayesian nets and their causal interpretation to do with decision theory? This is the *fourth* consideration. Let some Bayesian net be given and suppose that you can directly manipulate some variable. You can choose any value for it you like. We might then call that variable an action variable. What should you do? This depends, of course, on your utilities for all possible realizations of the variables in the net. And it depends on your beliefs. Should you just use the probabilities conditional on the envisaged value of the action variable in order to determine the conditional expected utility of that value? And maximize expected utility on this basis?

In opposition to evidential decision theorists, the causal decision theorist says no, you must not. By manipulating the action variable directly, you cut it off from its causal dependencies as represented in the Bayesian net, you treat it as uncaused by the other variables in the net or exogenous and at best caused only by you or your will. This means, however, that instead of the original Bayesian net you have to consider the so-called *truncated Bayesian net* which one obtains from the original one by deleting all vertices ending at the action variable and by substituting the original probability measure by its so-called truncated factorization that agrees with the truncated graph. The terminology is that of Pearl (2000, sect. 3.2) where the procedure is described in detail, but the substance may already be found in Spohn (1978, sect. 5.2). It should be clear that it is the reasonability of just this step that is at issue between causal and evidential decision theory. And I clearly take the causal side.

So far, we have only prepared the grounds for the argument to come. My point will be that the combination of reduction and truncation produces most interesting effects. So, let us, in a *fifth* step, start from the decision theoretic point of view, i.e., from a truncated Bayesian net with exogenous action variables. And let us think about how one might undo the truncation. This means thinking about on what the action variables causally depend. At first, this appears irrelevant from the decision theoretic point of view. When taking a decision, one does not think about the possible causes of one's actions, one rather evaluates the possible actions (according to their expected utility) and decides for one of the best. Still, the consideration will bear fruits:

In a way, it is obvious how our actions are caused. An action is caused precisely by the decision situation in which it is best, where a decision situation is a subjective state of the agent consisting of desires and beliefs and represented by a truncated Bayesian net with a distinguished action variable and a utility function. Hence, it is also clear how to complete the truncated Bayesian net. Each action node is to be preceded by a decision node, a variable taking as values all possible decision situations deciding about that action node. It is precisely this decision node on which the action node causally depends, indeed directly, as long as we do not attend to how mental states eventually issue in bodily movements.

I call the truncated Bayesian net (plus a utility function) a *simple decision model* and the completed Bayesian net (plus a utility function) a *reflexive decision model* because it contains nodes reflecting on the truncated simple decision models. Fully spelled out, such reflexive decision models are enormously complex, but most interesting structures which I strongly recommend for further inquiry.

Here, however, we need not consider the whole of that complex structure. Let us, in a *sixth* step, only focus for a while on the *causal place of these new decision nodes*. The following assumptions are natural and crucial.

1. Each action node has exactly one decision node as a parent. It cannot have two decision parents; you cannot decide twice about the same action, the first decision would then be causally idle and not a genuine decision. It must have at least one decision parent, because rational (or irrational) action is precisely characterized by being caused in this way. And it cannot have other than decision parents; decision situations are the complete direct cause of the ensuing action.

2. Each decision node has at least one action node as a child, since a decision must decide about some action. It may have several action children; one may decide about several actions or about a whole course of actions at once.

3. Each decision node may have many parents. Indeed, a decision situation is a very rich item causally depending on a host of other factors; simply consider in which complex ways your beliefs and desires are caused.

4. Each decision node may have other than action children. Your propositional attitudes are not exclusively expressed by your actions. You may look a certain way when you are determined. Some uncontrolled behavior, your mimics, etc., may be indicative of your desires. Other persons may observe all this and draw their conclusions. Or think of the lie detector assessing your beliefs not via your actions. And so on.

5. No decision node need temporally immediately precede its action children; I can now decide what to do tomorrow or in a month or in five years. One must not confuse here causal and temporal immediacy. Of course, when I now decide what to do in five years, decision and action must somehow be mediated, by memory, by staying determined, etc. However, this is only a difference of degree to allegedly immediate decisions, as everyone painfully knows who forgets from one second to the other what he wanted to do. This mediation is not modeled in reflexive decision models.

Each of these assumptions may be contested, and each makes a big difference for the resulting reflexive decision theory.

In a *seventh* step, we must now consider more closely the relation between the truncated simple and the completed reflexive decision model. The simple model is not simply the truncation of the reflexive model. Note that truncation does not diminish the nodes, it diminishes only the vertices and modifies the probability measure so that it agrees with the truncated graph. Yet, the reflexive model, by attending to the causes of actions, additionally contains decision nodes not at issue in the simple model. Hence, we must first reduce the reflexive model by the decision nodes and then truncate it with respect to the action nodes. The simple model is the *truncated reduction* of the reflexive model. The task then is to account for these truncated reductions in detail. I have given a rough idea of reductions and of truncations. However, in combination they generate the final crucial twist that supports my initial claim about Newcomb's problem.

I am not going to explain this final *eighth* step in abstract; my presentation has already become too imperspicuous. Let me rather exemplify it with two important philosophical puzzles, the Toxin case and Newcomb's problem; this at the same time illustrates our abstract considerations so far.

In the *toxin puzzle*, someone, the predictor, approaches you at noon and promises you a lot of money for managing to form the firm intention or to decide before midnight to drink a glass of toxin tomorrow noon, which makes you feel sick for some hours; in any case, the reward by far outweighs the sickness. And, the predictor adds, he has a cute cerebroscope that reliably tells whether you really have the intention. Note the reward is for the right intention, not for the drinking. The puzzle is that you do not seem to be able to get the reward even though you would like it.

Let us represent the situation by a decision model. There are five variables involved: your mental state M before midnight, the signal C of the cerebroscope at midnight, the reward R soon afterwards, your possible drinking T of the toxin tomorrow noon, and your possible sickness S for some time afterwards. My convention is to use squares for action nodes, triangles for decision nodes, and circles for the other nodes. So, prima facie the relevant Bayesian net looks like this:

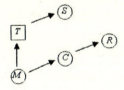

FIGURE 19.1.

However, where is the decision node for the action node T? There are two possibilities. Either, the mental state M is already the intention or decision D to drink, or not to drink, the toxin. Or, as most say, the decision D about T is definitively taken only briefly before tomorrow noon; in that case, though, the mental state M is not one of resolution and the cerebroscope will tell so.

Let me graphically represent the two alternatives together with their truncated reductions (this illustrates at the same time how they work). One model is this: (figure 19.2)

There, in the simple model on the right side it is clear what maximizes conditional expected utility: it is not drinking the toxin, but there is no way to get the reward (unless the cerebroscope makes an error). Hence, those attached to this model despair of getting the preferred reward.

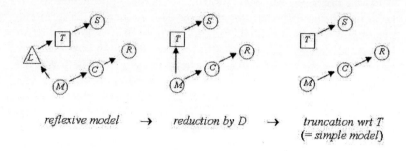

reflexive model   →   reduction by D   →   truncation wrt T
(= simple model)

FIGURE 19.2.

The other model is this: (figure 19.3)

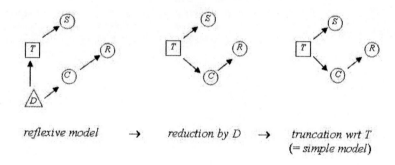

reflexive model   →   reduction by D   →   truncation wrt T
(= simple model)

FIGURE 19.3.

We observe here a crucial anomaly in the reduction, a causal arrow from T to C running backwards in time. Do I suddenly plead for backward causation? Of course not. The point is rather this: According to the reduction rules explained above we should have an arrow running from C to T, which, however, would have to be deleted in the truncation. This seems unjustified. Compare this case with another scenario in which the cerebroscope takes 24 hours to process its data and to give a verdict, so that T precedes C. Intuitively, this should make no difference whatsoever. However, the above reduction rules say that reduction results in an arrow from T to C in this scenario, which would not fall victim to the subsequent truncation. Hence, I propose to change the reduction rules *only for this special case* as indicated in the graph above. Recall that an arrow in the reduced graph represents a direct or an indirect causal dependence *or* a common cause relation.

And it represents the latter (and no backwards causation) in the reduced graph. Hence, I am far from assuming causal absurdity.

Once this step is accepted, it is clear that truncation runs empty in this case (since T is exogenous already in the untruncated graph). And it is clear that it is drinking the toxin that maximizes conditional expected utility in the resulting simple model. So, this is what you rationally decide before midnight. By "decide" I mean "decide" without any afterthought or reconsideration, and this includes actually drinking the glass of toxin (or at least seriously attempting to do so).

The crucial point here is the reduction anomaly, the necessity of which emerges only with the subsequent truncation. This is the important special effect announced earlier of combining reduction and truncation.

The story is much the same for *Newcomb's problem*. Its representation by a simple model involves three variables: there is first the prediction P of the predictor and the corresponding filling of the opaque box, a bit later you take the opaque box or both boxes (action node B) and finally you get the reward R depending on the prediction and your action. This yields the simple model:

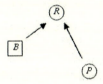

FIGURE 19.4.

in which it is clear that two-boxing maximizes conditional expected utility, as causal decision theorists have said all the time.

How may we extend this simple model to a reflexive one? There are again two ways. The reflexive model must somehow account for the surprising correlation between the predictor's prediction and your action. One possible explanation is to assume some common cause X of the prediction and your decision D. Then the reflexive model and its truncated reduction looks like this: (figure 19.5)

According to the simple model of figure 19.5, as in the model of figure 19.4, only two-boxing is rational. This is precisely the account of Eells (1982, ch. 8). He calls it a justification of two-boxing in terms of evidential decision theory. However, I would rather say that he has thereby laid grounds to reflexive decision

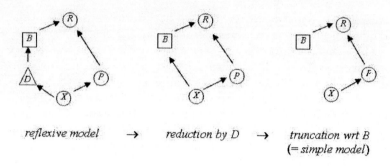

reflexive model   →   reduction by D   →   truncation wrt B
                                                (= simple model)

FIGURE 19.5.

theory.

There is another explanation for the correlation, namely that your decision D influences the prediction P. Then the reflexive model and the truncated reduction look like this: (figure 19.6)

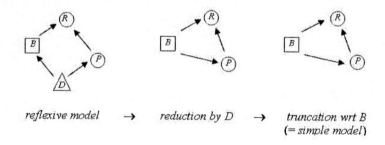

reflexive model   →   reduction by D   →   truncation wrt B
                                                (= simple model)

FIGURE 19.6.

Note again the reduction anomaly resulting in an arrow from B to P backwards in time, which, however, indicates merely that B and P have a common cause in some decision node. In the resulting simple model one-boxing is obviously the rational thing to do. This is what I take to be a rationalization of one-boxing within (a reflexive extension of) causal decision theory.

You might object that the decision D cannot influence the prediction P because you take it only when you are standing before the boxes. Recall, however, my remarks about the temporal relation between decision and action node. When standing before the boxes you might as well think that as a rational person you were committed all along to take only one box and that the predictor had sufficient time to observe your rationality and to infer your commitment. I indeed find that this explanation of the correlation between prediction and action is more plausible than Eells' common cause scenario.

The upshot of the whole argument is this: There are rationalizations both of two-boxing and one-boxing according to where you place the decision node. But there is no doubt what the more profitable rationalization is. Hence, since you have a choice where to place the decision node, you should place it so early that you resolve in one-boxing.

Note, by way of comparison, that you cannot thereby rationalize non-smoking in Ronald A. Fisher's smoking gene scenario. In that scenario the smoking gene is a common probabilistic cause of your desire to smoke and the lung cancer. This corresponds to the first reflexive model of Newcomb's problem, and then it is certainly rational to yield to your desire and smoke. If we would want to carry over the second reflexive model, we would have to assume that smoking still does not cause lung cancer, but that the desire to smoke somehow activates the dangerous gene. However, this was not Fisher's story.

So much for my argument. There is no point here in fighting it further (and I am sure it needs further fighting). Let me only add that these considerations have much wider application. For instance, McClennen (1990) has carefully explained two decision rules, sophisticated choice and resolute choice. The latter appeared unintelligible to many commentators. My considerations offer, I think, further rationalization of resolute choice and indeed integrate sophisticated and resolute choice into one model instead of treating them as competitors.

More generally, commitment was tacitly the key notion of my considerations. Commitment is a most central notion to practical philosophy, but it receives only informal treatment and somehow remains ill-understood. My above considerations have the potential, I believe, to improve this situation. Moreover, my real focus in Spohn (2003) was to rationalize cooperation in the single-shot prisoners' dilemma, at least a plausible attempt in view of the fact that the prisoners' dilemma may be conceived as a two-sided Newcomb's problem.

Let us finally return to the original purpose of this exposition. What does it show about the role of formal methods in philosophy? I think, three quite trivial things which I state nevertheless, because they are so clearly exemplified here:

First, it is serious and important philosophical problems that are successfully addressed by formal methods. This is clear from my last remarks; also, Newcomb's problem is not just an odd puzzle, it lies at the heart of our understanding of rational agency.

Secondly, what I have sketched is a relatively sophisticated formal reasoning. By turning it formal, one can and must make explicit all the assumptions and conditions needed. One could certainly give a purely informal version of the reasoning, and this would certainly result in a plausible story. However, an opponent could easily tell an equally plausible counter-story. And the ensuing argument would get hopelessly lost in confusion. I am not claiming that the formal reasoning proves my case. Hardly any philosophical thesis can be strictly proven. Still, the formal reasoning greatly helps in getting clear what the issues are.

The third point is stronger than the second. Even the heuristics of my reasoning requires formal methods. In this case I cannot imagine that I first have an informal sketch of the argument, then try to formalize it, and in the end come up with the formal version. In order to see the argument at all it was important to already have a trustworthy formal model of decision situations in terms of Bayesian nets with action nodes and to think about the formal properties of the model.

In this way, my example shows that formal methods are required and useful at every stage of inquiry.

What is the proper role of philosophy in relation to other disciplines?

Philosophy has many roles and many proper roles, in relation to human life in general, a relation not at issue here, and in relation to other disciplines. Here, I see at least five proper roles:

The *first* important role is that philosophy is a *speculative fore-runner* of scientific issues. Thinkers are often beset with pressing questions of a broadly empirical nature, not knowing how to turn them into sound scientific questions to be tackled in a sober empirical way. They engage then in speculation, develop models and perspectives, and thus open possibly quite influential ways of how to think at all about such issues. This is often called philosophy, with some justification, since it requires intellectual freedom (or lack of control) hardly to be found elsewhere.

There are many great historic examples for this role of philosophy, Democritus' atomic theory being perhaps the most famous one. In our times when the disciplines have become extremely specialized and ramified, this role is certainly diminished. Sketchy philosophical models for our highly advanced and sophisticated cosmology, e.g., would simply be ridiculous. Things differ, though, in relation to psychology. We still find a lot of speculative mental model building within philosophy which is not without influence on psychology.

Philosophy is not only a forerunner, however, it is *secondly* even the *mother* of many scientific disciplines (though I do not claim parthenogenesis, of course). This is a familiar phrase with which one mainly associates the times of Enlightenment, roughly from late 17th to early 19th century, which generated the basic differentiation of scientific disciplines. The philosophical origins of analysis (perhaps the most powerful tool of mathematics), Newtonian physics, psychology, sociology, economics, the political sciences, etc. are well known.

These may seem to be past merits. However, the process continues, perhaps in a less speculative manner, till today; and one should emphasize this point whenever the current social or political significance of philosophy is critically discussed. A prominent case is Artificial Intelligence, which has certainly more than one parent; but one should read how much Marvin Minsky and other fathers of AI say they have learned from philosophy. Another example is linguistic semantics and pragmatics that started establishing as a separate discipline only 30 years ago and are still dominated by ideas developed by philosophers.

Yet, I do not want to deny that times have changed. The current role of philosophy is, *thirdly*, rather that of a *sister* of sciences and humanities. What has been a mere boundary has often developed into a larger research field promoted by philosophy and other disciplines in a cooperative way. Again, there are many important examples. Perhaps the most comprehensive example is cognitive science, a collective enterprise of neuroscience, psychology, linguistics, AI, and philosophy. Science studies are due to the joint efforts of sociology (of science) and history and philosophy of science. Philosophy, economists, and politologists equally contribute to social choice theory. Applied ethics is philosophical ethics in collaboration with medical, biological, environmental, or economic studies, to mention only the more prominent connections. Moreover, there are various issues without a disciplinary name that have turned interdisciplinary. The theory of causation is belabored by philosophers, physicists, statisticians, economists, and even AI researchers. After philosophers have learned general relativity theory, space-time is again a joint topic. And so forth.

It seems obvious to me that philosophy essentially contributes to all these cooperative efforts; they would be poorer without philosophy. This is perhaps an even stronger argument in critical discussions of the current significance of philosophy. However, one must never forget that philosophy does not exhaust itself in mother- and sisterhood. It is able to cultivate these kinships only because of the productivity of its core disciplines: ontology and metaphysics, epistemology, philosophy of mind and language, and ethics. Philosophy stands and falls with its independent worth endowed by these core disciplines.

So far, I have described the kind of relation philosophy has to other disciplines. My examples displayed the legitimacy of these relations. Still, it must be in virtue of some contents that philosophy can engage in these relations, contents delivered by philosophy rather than any of the other disciplines participating. What are they? There are two fundamental kinds of contents, I believe, that characterize the two substantial roles philosophy will forever play for other disciplines.

The first kind of content is *normative content*. Normative discussions take much space in philosophy, and they do so explicitly. Theology and jurisprudence are also firmly aware that they are dealing with normative contents. In all other disciplines, in particular in the natural, but also in the social sciences, the normative dimension remains, as far as I can see, largely implicit; apparently, this dimension does not fit into the picture these disciplines have of themselves. This does not mean, however, that this dimension does not exist. On the contrary, and it is philosophy's task to bring to bear its normative wisdom to the other disciplines (and it is obviously philosophy rather than the other normative disciplines mentioned that is called for here). This, then, is the *fourth* proper role of philosophy: to provide the normative input for the cooperative cognitive enterprise.

In fact, the normative dimension of empirical science has at least three aspects, and at least two are genuinely philosophical:

One kind of normative issue is that of allocation: How much of our bounded means should we spend on the questions in which our unbounded curiosity might take interest? These issues are most involved, often left to the market, often hotly politically disputed. By and large, philosophy has no special competence here. However, such allocation issues often have a moral dimension, I suspect indeed much more often than is usually thought. To this extent philosophical advice may well be sought.

Another kind of normative issue is that of methodology. Once it is decided which question to investigate, the follow-up question is how to do it: how to set up the inquiry, what to conclude from its possible results, how to assess the various hypotheses at hand, and so on. These are methodological issues, and as such they are normative, though their normative character is usually veiled. For instance, statistics, better manned than philosophy, is fundamentally methodological and hence normative in character, but this fact almost disappears behind all the sophisticated mathematics.

Of course, methodology is no exception to ubiquitous ramification and specialization. However, general methodological issues are genuinely philosophical; they belong to normative epistemology and philosophy of science. And these issues are far from being exhausted. Philosophy has still a lot to teach to, and to learn from, other disciplines about them.

There are, finally, general normative issues: how to behave rationally, how to behave morally or, rather, simply how to behave not only in scientific contexts, but in life as such. Again, on a general level these are genuinely philosophical issues. They may not appear relevant to empirical research (except insofar as researchers are also agents). However, this is not so. As I have argued several times, most recently, albeit briefly in Spohn (forthcoming a), normative theorizing does not only tell how we should behave, but also how we ideally behave; and deviation from the ideal is to be described as such (unless we adhere to an, I think, highly implausible eliminativist program in psychology). In this way, normative theorizing becomes an essential part of empirical research on all human affairs; psychology is essentially normative. This is a third aspect of the normative dimension in which at least the human sciences are tied to philosophy, even though the awareness of this fact remains wanting.

The other kind of content for which philosophy has a special expertise is *modal content*. What do I mean? Well, all scientific disciplines seek the truth, claim to find it, and sometimes actually do; each scholar is a truth authority for his field. The philosopher's task then is to sort out the (alleged) truths found; and this is his authority. There are many kinds of truths, and the modalities are there to classify them. There are necessary and contingent truths, and there are half a dozen different senses of necessity (or more). There are analytic and synthetic truths, and the notion of analyticity is as difficult as the whole theory of linguistic meaning.

There a priori and a posteriori truths, and Kant's suggestion that apriority is wider than analyticity opened new, though debated philosophical spaces. Among the a posteriori truths, one may distinguish empirical and theoretical truths, due to the suggestion that the meaning of theoretical terms differs very much from that of empirical terms. Causation is presumably a modal notion, explanation definitely is. There are methodological, i.e., normative claims which many call true or false as well. And so on. All these distinctions are subsumed under the label 'modality'.

It is difficult to know one's way through the jungle of modalities. Even philosophers who think for decades about them get easily confused. Some claim to have gained clarity in the end; alas, the alleged clarities differ wildly, and so the collective state is again one of confusion. This, however, is due to the complexity of the subject matter, and even though it is contested among philosophers, they know so much more about it than scholars from other fields.

And it is important to accomplish the classificatory work of applying the modal categories. Each modal category has its characteristic grounds of truth, and all scientific discourse essentially depends on the character of these grounds. Arguments for an empirical truth, for instance, radically differ form those for an analytic truth, and both have nothing to do with justifying a normative truth. Hence, discourse is bound to end up in confusion if the modal classification of the focal claims is unclear. Here philosophy is called to bring in its expertise. This is the *fifth* and last proper role I see for philosophy in relation to other disciplines.

Sometimes I sense that scientists feel patronized by this role of philosophy; they suspect that philosophers want to be the better scientists. There are perhaps some such presumptuous philosophers. This would be a severe misunderstanding, though. Philosophy indeed has some competence concerning the claims made in other disciplines, namely in the way indicated. Scientists are well advised to acknowledge this competence, and philosophers are well advised not to confuse this with an authority on the scientific field.

What do you consider the most neglected topics and/or contributions in late 20th century philosophy?

One must be aware how radically the academic condition has changed since World War II. We have seen an unprecedented academic explosion due to increased needs and a fabulous wealth in the western world. I use to say that half of the professional philosophers ever existing are still alive; and though it is difficult to count (who in the ancient or medieval times is a professional philosopher?), my guess is probably not off the mark in magnitude.

Moreover, the communication conditions have changed even more radically. Philosophy has become so easily accessible. The living philosophers have read so much of the dead, I assume much more than the dead read of the dead (whereas the dead had little opportunity to read texts of the living). There are so much more publishers, journals, conferences, guest lectures, etc. Internet and e-mail has further accelerated communication in an unbelievable way.

Often it appears to me that these dramatically changed conditions and relations have received insufficient attention in the still wide spread history-biased understanding of philosophy.

Hence, I find the title question misplaced; it is a question for conditions of scarcity, not for conditions of abundance. And we are living in the latter. A sure sign of this, and one I perceive with great skepticism is the tremendous increase of encyclopedias, handbooks, companions, introductions, etc., in the last 10 or 15 years. If they are well made, one is grateful for them; but they show at the same time that there are many philosophers who have no good idea how to occupy themselves.

What I find much more fascinating is the issue of the power relations in the modern unprecedented philosophical market. From where to where do the influences run? Why do they run as they do? Do the power relations produce systematic distortions or even (unintentional) suppression? Such a market needs and has opinion leaders. How do they get their role? Certainly in virtue of their charisma, their quality und originality. I suspect, though, there are many more factors at work. How, then, do the opinion leaders structure the discussion? For good or for bad? The communication mechanics is presumably not so different in other disciplines. So, which observation can be generalized and which are special to philosophy? These would be the questions to investigate.

I have not seen any study directed to philosophy, though it would be worthwhile. I am certainly not the one to do it. However, I would like at least to mention that one factor appears to me still to be of utmost importance: language. Of course, international communication requires a common language, and as the world has developed (this is part of the power relations), this language is English. There are those who master English perfectly and those

who master it imperfectly; the large majority of foreigners belong
to the second group. This is an inevitable asymmetry which seems
particular relevant for philosophy, because philosophers pay much
more attention to phrase and style than many other disciplines
and because it is still less natural for philosophers to adapt to a
common language than for most other scholars.

The long and the short of all this is that I find it unlikely
under the present circumstances that there really are forgotten,
though important topics and contributions. Almost the only way
how there could be such things is that some philosophers entirely
withdraw from the academic fuss and develop their thought in
obscurity, which might nevertheless be ingenious. There are such
philosophers – should I say: fortunately? – but, of course, it is
difficult to know of them.

Actually, I know of at least one: Ulrich Blau from the University of Munich. For almost 30 years he is working on the logic of
paradoxes and indeterminacies, pursuing deep perspectives in the
theory of truth, semantics, philosophy of mathematics, and much
further. To some extent, his ideas are similar to known accounts
of semantic paradoxes (though I cannot decide issues of priority), but in many respects they go far beyond. He has published
only in German, and the last publications are about 20 years old.
Now, finally, his opus magnum, Blau (forthcoming), a book of
1000 pages, the fruit of 30 years of thinking, is intended to go in
print. I am unable to reliably assess this incredibly rich work, but
I am sure it contains an exceptional lot of ingenuity and definitely
deserves much wider attention. This is the first positive answer to
the fourth question that comes to my mind.

What are the most important open problems in philosophy and what are the prospects for progress?

I said already that hardly any of the philosophical problems are
forgotten or neglected, and I also mentioned that hardly any of the
philosophical problems are or will be solved; they will remain open.
They are usually not that kind of problem that can be solved;
rather, the spectrum of possible answers can be widened, ramified,
substantiated, clarified, and united, and this process is clearly a
progressive one, even if no one answer can be distinguished as the
true one.

Which among all those problems are the most important ones?
This is presumably a matter of taste. In any case, I am convinced

that philosophy as a whole will be of increasing importance. I see two historical long-term tendencies in both of which philosophy is centrally involved.

Despite contrary appearances of an increased religious influence on the historic course of events, I am first convinced that Enlightenment is not yet finished and that in the long run secularization will be the dominating tendency (I am a philosopher, after all). My minor reason for this conviction is that growing prosperity and education always has a moderating effect on religious affairs. My major ground, though, is that I think that epistemic rationality is a slow, but very strong force. The major religious doctrines are thoroughly interwoven with epistemic irrationality. This is why I think they are doomed in the long run; we cannot forever maintain beliefs against reason simply for their real or alleged good consequences.

I am not claiming that a secularized world is a better one. I hope that religious mania gets controlled, but I am also opposed to uncontrolled egocentrism on an individual, social, or political level, which often accompanies secularization. I fear, for example, the delusion of eternal life in both forms: as the ultimate ground of many religions conceptions and as an ultimate motive of modern biomedical research (which it surely is).

Here, mankind faces a huge ongoing task. If secularization is unavoidable, at least its bad consequences must be avoided. Philosophy has to certainly play an important role in this task. It is, for instance, often claimed that certain morally valuable attitudes are not to be had without their religious justificatory superstructure. If this were so, all the worse for the attitudes. However, I do not accept the premise; of course, the morally valuable attitudes are amenable to an enlightened justification. And philosophy is there to provide it.

The other great tendency I see at work is that of self-destruction, and I do not know at all which of the two processes, secularization or self-destruction, will be the faster one. It seems obvious to me that mankind has reached a critical stage. There is too much wealth and too much need at the same time, and both are ruining the world. I wonder for how long the earth will carry six billion men (as present) or even nine or ten billion (as predicted); not for many centuries, I fear. This is an even bigger challenge to mankind, to its science and technology, but even more to its social and political forms. Indeed, it will be the biggest challenge we will have ever faced. Mastering it, there is still hope, will require the best of our human capacities, and again philosophy will have to play here an important foundational role.

This sounds as if only practical philosophy would be called upon. However, in the end, theoretical and practical philosophy form an inseparable unity. So, both challenges concern philosophy as a whole. Still, since I am rather a theoretical philosopher and since I guess the title question rather asked for my taste, let me give a second, quite different answer.

Ontology is the one core discipline of theoretical philosophy, epistemology is the other. For me, the deepest problem of theoretical philosophy is the relation of its two core disciplines. The long-known, ongoing wavering between ever more sophisticated forms of realism and idealism is the most obvious symptom of the deepness of the problem. I still think that the rearrangement of ontological and epistemological modalities, of necessity/contingency and apriority/aposteriority, by Kripke (1972) and Putnam (1975) brought revolutionary progress here. By establishing the independence of the two dimensions or distinctions, this rearrangement had a most clarifying and liberating effect; it was a break with centuries old entanglements.

At the same time, it opened the opportunity and challenge to think anew about the relation between ontology and epistemology. The main answer that emerged shortly afterwards, this was the other big progress in this field in the 70's, is two-dimensional semantics. It was certainly foreshadowed, but not clearly articulated in the papers of Kripke and Putnam. In a way, all philosophers of language at UCLA worked at that project at that time, culminating in Kaplan's (1977) essay. A different, but equally important interpretation was offered by Stalnaker (1978).

According to two-dimensional semantics, each referring phrase is evaluated, i.e., assigned an extension, along two dimensions, relative to possible contexts (of utterance) and relative to possible indices (of evaluation). Contexts are to be conceived as doxastic alternatives, this was Stalnaker's insight, and thus represent the epistemological dimension, whereas indices represent the ontological dimension. Accordingly, there are two kinds of intensions: horizontal intensions (= Chalmers' (1996) secondary and Jackson's (1998) C-intensions) as functions from indices to extensions (at a given context) and diagonal intensions (= Chalmers' primary and Jackson's A-intension) as functions from contexts to extensions which are defined as diagonalizations of the two-dimensional schemes (= Kaplan's characters) associated with the referring phrases. Horizontal intensions may well be called objective, ontological meanings, and diagonal intensions play the role of subjective, epistemological meanings, which thus diagonalize objective meanings. Hence, diagonalization is, I am convinced, the key to understanding the relation of ontology and epistemology.

This is the rough scheme. It is obvious, though, from my reference to the divergent origins in Kaplan's and Stalnaker's papers and to the still further diverging continuations in Chalmer's and Jackson's work that the proper understanding of two-dimensional semantics is not fixed or even codified, but rather contested and unclear. The situation is aggravated by the fact that there is a lot of philosophical terminology, rigidification and derigidification, response-dependent and response-independent concepts, etc., all of which allude to two-dimensional semantics in some form usually, and unfortunately, left implicit. Naturally, I for my part like best the systematic interpretation elaborated in Haas-Spohn (1995) and Haas-Spohn, Spohn (2001).

What I would wish, then, is a wider and profounder debate about the proper understanding of two-dimensional semantics and about its various philosophical applications, since, as I have indicated, it is not just semantics which is at issue, it is rather the deep relation between ontology and epistemology. Therefore, the issue is bound to have wide-ranging consequences.

For instance, the insight that the usage of the notion of an intension before 1970 and even afterwards has been systematically ambiguous is highly revealing. Does the meaning of a scientific term depend on the theory stated with its help? Yes, as empiricists from Carnap to Feyerabend have emphasized in different ways, provided meaning is understood as diagonal intension; no, as Putnam has fairly objected, provided meaning is understood as horizontal intension.

Possible worlds are ambiguous; according to Wittgenstein they are in some sense maximal states of affairs, and according to Lewis they are in some sense maximal things. Is there a tension? No, the two interpretations complement each other in two-dimensional semantics. Lewisian possible worlds are required as context worlds, and Wittgensteinian possible worlds are to be used as index worlds; it would be a mistake to assume an unequivocal use of possible worlds in two-dimensional semantics (a point in some way reflected also in Chalmers 2002).

Even the notion of truth is ambiguous. There is the correspondence notion of truth and its variants (about which there are most sophisticated debates). And there is an epistemological notion of truth described in variegated, though imprecise ways as coherentistic, as a limit of inquiry, as an evaluational notion, etc. Again, there is no conflict. Correspondence truth is truth at indices; epistemological truth, whatever its most adequate conception, is truth in contexts; and so both notions of truth find their place in two-dimensional semantics.

Might the ideal theory be wrong, as metaphysical realism claims? Yes, of course, in the sense of metaphysical possibility across indices; no, of course not, in the sense of epistemological possibility across contexts.

Or to end up my sample list of applications, take the notion of probability. We may well interpret de Finetti as having proved in his famous representation theorem that subjective probability is the diagonalization (= mixture) of possible objective probabilities.

Of course, each point would have to be argued most carefully. Still, my brief hints should indicate that two-dimensional semantics is capable of providing a comprehensive framework for dealing with the deepest problem in theoretical philosophy and for developing quite a number of most fascinating perspectives. Moreover, it appears to me that all the issues involved in stating the framework and its applications are sufficiently sharpened by the ongoing philosophical discussion, so that the attempt to definitely spell out the framework need not sink into confusion, but can immediately bear rich philosophical fruits. This is my hope at least, and this why I recommend this subject matter to utmost philosophical attention.

References

Blau, U. (forthcoming), *Die Logik der Unbestimmtheiten und Paradoxien*, Heidelberg: Synchron Wissenschaftsverlag der Autoren.

Chalmers, D.J. (1996), *The Conscious Mind*, Oxford: Oxford University Press.

Chalmers, D.J. (2002), "On Sense and Intension", in: J. Tomberlin (ed.), *Philosophical Perspectives 16: Language and Mind*, Oxford: Blackwell, pp. 135–182.

Dawid, A.P. (1979), "Conditional Independence in Statistical Theory", *Journal of the Royal Statistical Society, series B, 41*: 1–31.

Eells, E. (1982), *Rational Decision and Causality*, Cambridge: Cambridge University Press.

Haas-Spohn, U. (1995), *Versteckte Indexikalität und subjektive Bedeutung*, Berlin: Akademie-Verlag.

Haas-Spohn, U., W. Spohn (2001), "Concepts Are Beliefs About Essences", in: A. Newen, U. Nortmann, R. Stuhlmann-Laeisz (eds.), *Building on Frege. New Essays on Sense, Content, and Concept*, Stanford: CSLI Publications, pp. 287–316.

Jackson, F. (1998), *From Metaphysics to Ethics*, Oxford: Clarendon Press.

Kaplan, D. (1977), "Demonstratives. An Essay on the Semantics, Logic, Metaphysics, and Epistemology of Demonstratives and Other Indexicals", in: J. Almog, J. Perry, and H. Wettstein (eds.), *Themes from Kaplan*. Oxford: Oxford University Press, 1989, pp. 481–563.

Kripke, S. (1972), "Naming and Necessity", in: *Semantics of Natural Language*, ed.by D. Davidson & G. Harman, Dordrecht: Reidel, pp. 253–355, 763-769; ext. ed. Oxford: Blackwell 1980.

Lewis, D.K. (1969), *Convention: A Philosophical Study*, Cambridge, Mass.:Harvard University Press.

Lewis, D. (1975), "Languages and Language", in: K. Gunderson (ed.), *Minnesota Studies in the Philosophy of Science, Vol. VII, Language, Mind and Knowledge*, Minneapolis: University of Minnesota Press, pp. 3–35.

McClennen, E.F. (1990), *Rationality and Dynamic Choice*, Cambridge: Cambridge University Press.

Nozick, R. (1969), "Newcomb's Problem and Two Principles of Choice", in: N Rescher et al. (eds.), *Essays in Honor of Carl G. Hempel*, Dordrecht: Reidel, pp. 114–146.

Pearl, J. (1988), *Probabilistic Reasoning in Intelligent Systems: Networks of Plausible Inference*, San Mateo, CA: Morgan Kaufmann.

Pearl, J. (2000), *Causality. Models, Reasoning, and Inference*, Cambridge: Cambridge University Press.

Putnam, H. (1975), "The Meaning of 'Meaning'", in: K. Gunderson (ed.), *Minnesota Studies in the Philosophy of Science, Vol. VII, Language, Mind and Knowledge*, Minneapolis: University of Minnesota Press, pp. 131–193.

Spirtes, P., Glymour, C., and Scheines, R. (1993), *Causation, Prediction, and Search*, Berlin: Springer.

Spohn, W. (1978), *Grundlagen der Entscheidungstheorie*, Kronberg/Ts: Scriptor.

Spohn, W. (1980), "Stochastic Independence, Causal Independence, and Shieldability", *Journal of Philosophical Logic* 9, 73–99.

Spohn, W. (2001), "Bayesian Nets Are All There Is To Causal Dependence", in: M.C. Galavotti, P. Suppes, D. Costantini (eds.), *Stochastic Dependence and Causality*, Stanford: CSLI Publications, pp. 157–172.

Spohn, W. (2003), "Dependency Equilibria and the Causal Structure of Decision and Game Situations", *Homo Oeconomicus* 20, 195–255.

Spohn, W. (forthcoming *a*), "The Core of Free Will", in: P.K. Machamer, G. Wolters (eds.), *Causation: Historical and Contemporary Perspectives. Proceedings of the Pittsburgh-Konstanz Colloquium VII*, Pittsburgh: Pittsburgh University Press.

Spohn, W. (forthcoming *b*), "A Survey of Ranking Theory", in: F. Huber, C. Schmidt-Petri (eds.), *Degrees of Belief. An Anthology*, Oxford: Oxford University Press.

Stalnaker, R.C. (1978), "Assertion", in: P. Cole (ed.), *Syntax and Semantics, Vol. 9: Pragmatics*. New York: Academic Press, pp. 315–32.

Stegmüller, W. (1952), *Hauptströmungen der Gegenwartsphilosophie, Band 1*, 7th edition, Stuttgart: Kröner, 1989.

20

Patrick Suppes

Lucie Stern Professor of Philosophy, Emeritus
Stanford University, CA, USA

Why were you initially drawn to formal methods?

Like a great many people interested in formal methods in philosophy, I was drawn already to certain kinds of formality in my early training in mathematics. I mean by "early training" that which I received in elementary and secondary school, especially in secondary school. By far the hardest math course I took as a high-school student was a course what was in those days called "solid geometry", meaning, of course, three-dimensional geometry. This subject is still a difficult one, especially when taught synthetically. Students of today who are progressing more rapidly through the curriculum will almost certainly, in an American high-school anyway, have a reasonably thorough course in calculus, but this was not the case when I was a high-school student in the 1930s. The second encounter with formal methods that I remember clearly was a course in calculus I took as a sophomore at the University of Chicago (1940–41). The instructor was someone who was himself then young, but became a very well-known mathematician—the topologist, Norman Steenrod. You would never have guessed from the way he conducted the course, and was not something that I learned until much later, that he was a brilliant mathematician. He seemed rather slow, extremely thorough, very thoughtful, but not very quick to give us answers. He would have long pauses when he wasn't sure of exactly how he wanted to say something. Thinking back upon it, he had a big influence because of the careful, detailed, and patient way he drew out of a group of reasonably bright but naive students the epsilon-delta methods for characterizing limits, instead of plunging right in with the compact notation used then in calculus courses. I was intrigued and involved by the methods he tried to teach us to give us a proper foundation for the calculus.

Before going into the army, I declared myself a physics major. For various reasons at that point, I took a break at the University of Chicago and was spending a little more than a year at the University of Tulsa in Tulsa, Okalahoma, where I was born. I remember in the course in differential equations (spring, 1942) I had as a junior at the University of Tulsa, an extended discussion of the reality of infinitesimals. Several of the students with whom I talked got involved in this matter as well, and we had endless naïve discussions of our own about what was really meant by the reality of infinitesimals. I felt challenged by the question in several different directions, was not able to give, of course, a satisfactory answer of my own, and did not think the instructor gave a very good answer either, but this further awakened my latent interest in formal methods. The next occurrence was again back to the University of Chicago where I was an Army Cadet being trained in meteorology. We were given excellent courses on the dynamical equations of the atmosphere and especially on hydrodynamics (1942–43). I was immediately attracted to the kind of reasoning characteristic of the foundations of hydrodynamics taken from a classical viewpoint, exemplified, for example, in the classic book of Horace Lamb (1932/1945), written now about a hundred years ago (1879). These foundations remain tricky today, as the saying goes. Perhaps the outstanding problem in classical mechanics, still not properly settled from a physical standpoint, is that of turbulence. In any case, I was challenged and fascinated by the attempt to give rigorous physical foundations, rigorous in the physical sense, that is, but still formal in the sense of ending up with the standard differential equations.

After the war, I went to Columbia University in New York City as a graduate student, where my mentor was Ernest Nagel. In particular I learned a great deal from his introductory course in mathematical logic using the well-known textbook of Hilbert and Ackermann (1938/1950). I still remember vividly my finding a slight mistake in one of Nagel's formal recursive statements of the definition of a sentence in first-order logic. He graciously acknowledged my pointing out a minor error. Once again, my interests in formal methods were increased. Another influence were the courses I attended while a graduate student in philosophy. These were the graduate lectures in mathematics by Samuel Eilenberg and one and two other members of the mathematics department. Eilenberg was a mathematician of the Polish school, like Tarski, who influenced me later. His lectures were brilliant and wonderful examples of formal methods at work. I still remember the course in abstract-group theory he gave. A number of my friends, also army veterans, who were graduate students in physics, took the course expecting to learn how to use group theory in the analysis of quantum mechanics. They were quite aghast and disappointed at the extraordinarily abstract level of Eilenberg's course—for me, it was a delight. This was also true of his first graduate course in topology.

Finally, when I got to Stanford as a young instructor with a recently received Ph.D. from Columbia in the fall of 1950, I had learned a great deal as a graduate student but not really how to do any formal research. Under the tutelage of J.C.C. McKinsey, who unfortunately died early in 1953, I began in earnest to write formal papers, the first one being a paper on measurement (1951) and the second being the papers on the axiomatic foundations of mechanics that McKinsey and I wrote in the early 1950s. In answering these questions I refer only to dates of papers but without titles. (They can be found in my bibliography on my web site, http://www.stanford.edu/~psuppes/ or in my actual collection of the papers which are also on the web and may be found at the following location, http://suppes-corpus.stanford.edu/index.html.) The completion of my introduction to formal methods, as I think of it in perhaps an artificial way, was, on McKinsey's recommendation, my attending Tarski's graduate seminar at Berkeley (1950–52) to which I went once a week from Stanford. Watching Tarski at work was a lesson of the greatest value in appreciating and understanding at a deeper level what could be accomplished with the highest standards of intellectual clarity.

What example(s) from your work illustrates the role formal methods can play in philosophy?

For me but not for everybody of course, the best way to think about formal methods in philosophy is in providing a foundation for mathematics or for the sciences. I include in the sciences the problem of clarifying the foundations of probability. Much of my philosophical work has been devoted to publishing examples of using formal methods in clarifying, or at least trying to do so, the foundations of various special parts of different branches of science. I'll mention here briefly and give simply the dates of publications, which as I said can be found in my collection of articles on the web. As I mentioned in my answer to the first question, for historical reasons I mentioned first my initial paper on the foundations of measurement (1951) and then the papers with McKinsey on the foundations of classical mechanics (1953), and shortly thereafter a corresponding foundational paper on relativistic particle mechanics with Herman Rubin (1954). In 1956, I studied the role of subjective probability and utility in decision making and gave a set of axioms that I thought were in certain respects superior to those given by Jimmy Savage in his well-known book published in 1954, *Foundations of Statistics*. My paper appeared in 1956 and my claim about the paper as to why it was an improvement from a formal standpoint was the elimination of some unnecessary structural axioms.

I mention next the 1958 paper with Dana Scott on the foundations of theories of measurement in which we proved some formal results on very elementary measurement situations that could not be nicely axiomatized in a finite way. I believe it is fair to say that this paper has had considerable influence over the years.

I next mention various papers I wrote on the foundations of stochastic models of learning in psychology—one of my abiding interests. I particularly like the 1959 paper with Estes on the foundations of linear models and the technical report (1959) we wrote in that same year on a detailed foundational and axiomatic treatment of stimulus-sampling theory, the results of which were not published completely for many years. I also like a paper that has not been much read, published in 1961, on behavioristic foundations of utility in *Econometrica*. This was meant to be a paper to show economists that a much broader and deeper psychological foundation (stimulus-response theory) could be used for deriving the formal properties of stochastic utility functions. I have only recently returned to this work and am now in the process of redoing, more than forty years later, the foundations of utility, again, from this viewpoint, but with a more general set of axioms based upon a wider set of association processes as psychologically fundamental. In 1969, I wrote what was probably my favorite paper in stochastic learning theory, namely, I showed how to derive in a formal way, the theory of finite automata as a basis for regular grammars or, in very good approximation, context-free grammars from stimulus-response theory.

A 1962 article on models of data has had pretty wide circulation. Here I was trying to show how complicated it is to abstract from the details of experiments to a set-theoretical characterization of the data, ready for statistical and other analysis. I remember discussing this with Tarski who felt that there was no real model theory, and, of course in his sense there was none. Data were being prepared, ready for models. But this emphasis on the absolute necessity of abstracting the data, in a very sharp way from endless experimental details, has been a theme that I have returned to continually. This was my first systematic effort at using formal methods on the problem of data.

In 1963, I published a paper I still like on the role of probability in quantum mechanics. I had been studying quantum mechanics ever since I was a graduate student at Columbia. This was the first paper in which I tried to do anything systematic. The formal part of this paper was bringing the role of probability very much to the front, whereas it usually occupies the back seat in most, or at least so in the earlier, foundations of quantum mechanics. A strictly more formal paper from the standpoint of logic was then a 1965 paper on logics appropriate to empirical theories, by which, I really meant quantum mechanics.

In 1970, I published a monograph on probabilistic theory of causality, in which I used things I had been learning for many years about probability, to give what I thought was at least an approximate foundational analysis of many cases of causality. This monograph, which is not very long, has had some influence on what other people have had to say about probabilistic causality.

In 1970 I was 48 years old, and what I have described above gives, I think, a reasonable sense of the kinds of things that I had been involved in, and had spent time on, applying formal methods in philosophy. For my work over the next 45 years, which represents more recent research, I have divided into five areas: foundations of measurement, semantics of natural language, quantum-mechanical entanglement, representations of cognition and perception in the brain, and the nature of freedom. I devote a paragraph or so to each of these topics. They represent a wide—many might well think too wide—spread but reflect a style I had already adopted in earlier years.

Foundations of measurement. My dominate activity was the three-volume work with this title, co-authored with David Krantz, Duncan Luce, and Amos Tversky. Volume I was published in 1971, after a long lag, Volume II in 1989, and Volume III in 1990. This work represents, I think it is fair to say, the most extensive effort in the modern literature to give a systematic treatment of measurement from many different disciplines. It is by no means complete, but it does cover a lot of concepts and a lot of previous research.

Perhaps its largest influence is to be found in subsequent publications by many different authors from many different countries in the *Journal of Mathematical Psychology*.

Semantics of natural language. Beginning in 1973 with my presidential address to the Pacific Division of the American Philosophical Society, I expressed my skepticism of too narrow a view of meaning and concentrated most of the lecture on setting forth examples and principles of what I call congruence concepts for meaning, as an analogue of the many different concepts of congruence in geometry. The example that I found the most important and also the most neglected was that of paraphrase, which seems to me absolutely essential to memory, to conversation, and even to listening to lectures. When we ask someone what he learned at a lecture, he does not repeat it verbatim, but gives a relatively coarse paraphrase. I have recently returned to paraphrase, making it central to computer-assisted instruction in language arts and writing for young students.

In the same year, 1973, I published my first work on the semantics of context-free languages, which in spite of some problems, remain a dominant principal form of formal grammars. In 1980 I extended this analysis to the individual differences I expect in procedural semantics. Each of us has somewhat different semantics at the particular level of actual procedures of producing or comprehending utterances. As part of this program I also wrote a couple of articles, the first in 1979, on logical inference in English and then in the 1980s and 1990s a long series of articles with various people on semantics for robots, including a number of articles with Michael Boëttner and Lin Liang on robotic learning of natural language. Another main collaborator in this period was Colleen Crangle on both the semantics of English and robotic applications.

Quantum mechanical entanglement. My interest in quantum mechanics was revived by working with Mario Zanotti in the 1980s on the logical and philosophical problems raised by the existence of hidden variables. In 1981 we wrote a joint article on when probabilistic explanations are possible, with the answer being that they are not possible when the variables in question do not have a joint-probability distribution. We proved this is also the case when they do not have a common local hidden variable. We continued this work in a number of additional publications on hidden variables. In 2000 Acacio de Barros, a physicist from Brazil, and I wrote a paper on inequalities for three-particle entanglement experiments, an extension of the two-particle experiments familiar from the Bell inequalities. We also approached this topic from a more detailed angle, formally, in another paper on the same subject in 2001. What I found most enjoyable about the two papers with de Barros is that they turned out to be the natural generalization, from a formal standpoint, of the Bell inequalities, replacing bivariate correlations by the expectation of the product of the spins of three particles.

I also like to stress, quite apart from my own interest, that the quantum entanglement of particles, which can be at great distances from each other, is certainly the most puzzling remaining feature in the whole of classical quantum mechanics. What will be discovered in the years ahead at different levels of energy and different circumstances is another matter, but the entanglement experiments can take place in rather standard circumstances here on Earth. Moreover, the concepts involved in these experiments are very much those involved in building quantum computers. So the interest in entanglement continues, and will most certainly continue for the indefinite future, to be an active research focus.

Brain representation of cognition and perception. Having heard in 1996 an excellent lecture on the new technology of magnetoencephalography (MEG), the extension to the magnetic field of the classical electroencephalography (EEG) for the electric field, I became enthusiastic, undoubtedly overly so, on the possibility of using MEG to recognize the representation of words in the brain, with the research being pursued very much on the model of the computer recognition of human speech, a subject on which great progress has been made in the last several decades. That initial enthusiasm was converted within a year into undertaking actual experiments using EEG as well as MEG. I now have published several papers on such representations. This is not the place to enter into the details, but I do want to emphasize a couple of points. First, it seems to me that philosophically it is going to be much more fruitful, especially when it comes to things like language and visual images, to reach for a deeper understanding of brain representations than of mental representations. Think about it. What is your mental representation of the word *anachronism*? Well, my own view is that we have a rather shallow concept of the mental representation of words and, in fact, we are not very conscious of such representations. On the other hand, it is obviously a task worthy of quite considerable research effort to understand both conceptually and empirically how the brain represents language. So what are the brain representations of words and other constituents of languages? This also applies to visual images. How actually do we represent color? If we look at brain signals, can we tell from the brain signal whether you saw in a given context, red or blue? One of the natural ways to show that you have appropriate brain representations, in the spirit of formal methods, is to establish a structural isomorphism between the physical or perceptual representation and the brain representation. So, one of the things to look for is such a structural isomorphism, in the mapping from the perceptual or physical representation to the brain representation of spoken language or visual images. Such structural isomorphisms have not yet been investigated in any very deep way. It is a sign of the still rudimentary character of such research that this is the situation. No doubt much more will be learned in the next few decades. Also, as we come to understand, for example, the brain representations of language and related cognitive matters, I would expect the philosophy of mind to undergo some radical change as well.

In a more general way, my interest in brain representations, has moved me to a broader thesis about philosophy. I have now written a series of papers in the last three or four years centered around what I call the neuropsychological foundations of philosophy. One paper, 2003, with Jean-Yeves Béziau focuses on the computation of truth for elementary empirical sentences, another with the psychological source of Bayesian priors (In Press-a), a third with the role of habits and free associations in rational choice and decision making (2003), and a fourth in the psychological nature of verification of informal mathematical proofs (In Press-b). The basic line of attack is that all of these philosophical matters must be regarded as empirical in character and thus subject to empirical investigation, regimented by psychological and other kinds of empirical theories available. It doesn't mean that we will understand everything about the phenomena, but we will understand more than we did in the past. Certainly, I am critical of Fregean kinds of effort to give a theory of meaning absent of any psychological considerations. It is hard to imagine, from the viewpoint from which I am operating, where else one could find concepts to determine the meanings of ordinary words and sentences, even those of informal sentences about pure mathematics.

Nature and measurement of freedom. Beginning in the last decade, I have written a series of papers on the nature and measurement of freedom, which is in fact the title of the first paper I published on the subject in 1996. I have also offered a course on freedom to undergraduates three or four times during this same period. There are only two points I will stress here. The methodology of my approach to freedom is very much in the spirit of the formal methods already discussed. To begin with, there is emphasis on measurement, and secondly there is an emphasis on what I think is the most missing concept in standard philosophical discussions of freedom, namely, the presence of uncertainty. This is particularly true in discussing freedom in political or social contexts, but I also think it holds for the fundamental psychology of choice of a single individual.

What is the proper role of philosophy in relation to other disciplines?

I have written my answer to this question in several places over many years. Philosophy has no special methodology or special foundational basis to separate it from mathematics and the sciences. The empirical methodology of the sciences must dominate philosophy as well. To understand the mind, for example, there is no privileged way by which philosophers have access to mental representations. In so far as there is access to mental representations of language, for example, it must be found by the methods of empirical psychology and empirical neuroscience. The introspections of the past of many philosophers, among whom I would place Aristotle and Hume as the most important, have certainly contributed a great deal to our intellectual understanding of our mental activities and mental structures, but future progress will depend upon detailed, technical, and disciplined empirical inquiries. I cannot see making much progress by the methods of Aristotle and Hume, and also William James, brilliant and important as they were, they have more or less been exhausted as approaches for finding new results.

What marks philosophers is not having special insight, in particular, what was often thought of as having a special methodology. It is rather that philosophers by taste, and often by training, concentrate on foundational questions. So, for example, investigations in the foundations of mathematics, by and large, use mathematical methods to provide new insight into mathematics. There is not a special brand of methodology called *philosophical methodology* for investigating the foundations of mathematics. What is characteristic, and understood by everybody familiar with the details, is that the methodology for investigating such foundations is just the methodology of mathematics itself. Philosophers who study such foundations are operating in a mathematical way, and they are to be distinguished from mathematicians only by their interest in the particular subject of foundations, just as among other mathematicians we distinguish between individuals interested in geometry, algebra or analysis.

The same viewpoint applies to the sciences. Philosophers who study the foundations of quantum mechanics are not bringing to that study of foundations a new apparatus of a technical nature for studying quantum mechanics. They are using the methods of quantum mechanics augmented by methods brought in from other sciences such as mathematics. A good example in the case of quantum mechanics would be the contribution on the one side of probability theory and on the other of logic. Many of the questions about quantum entanglement entail problems in the foundations of probability. Here is a good example. The Bell inequalities have the interesting feature that when applied just to the standard experiments, they give necessary and sufficient conditions for there to exist a joint probability distribution of the four random variables being observed, those random variables being two on one side of an apparatus say A and B and two on the other side, symmetrically located, A and B. What is observed is one variable from one side and one from another at the same time and the correlation between these two is computed. So for example, we compute the correlation between A and B over a succession of observations or trials. This is only an example of a probability question in quantum mechanics. There are many more.

The same kind of thing applies to the efforts now to build a quantum computer. The rather neglected subject of quantum logic has come to life again and is now an important component of work on the practical problem of constructing quantum computers. Special forms of logic are required for much of what is done in quantum computing, but those special forms of logic are developed using the methods that have been developed by logicians of both philosophical and mathematical bent over the past half century.

So, when asked about the relation of philosophy to other disciplines, my answer is now, and has been in the past, that philosophers are concerned with foundations. They are concerned with the concentrating on the concepts that are fundamental to a given discipline whether it be mathematics, physics, economics, or psychology. The methods they use for these investigations are pretty much the same methods in broad terms that are used by the scientists working in a given discipline. They just use these methods to apply a very focused analysis on the foundations, and of course, it is also correct to emphasize that in many cases they bring to such study concepts used in an another discipline but ordinarily not concepts that have been developed only by philosophers.

There is an important contrast in the current state of philosophy worth noting. Philosophers of physics do not expect to go off on their own in speculations about physics. They understand that the discussion of foundations of quantum mechanics or other parts of physics requires thorough and knowledgeable use of what is known and has been experimentally and theoretically studied by physicists. The situation is very different in the philosophy of mind. It is rather like having a philosophy of physics that is still concentrated on Aristotelian ideas. The philosophy of mind has not yet fully endorsed and adapted itself to what has been learned scientifically about the mind by psychologists and neuroscientists. It is for this reason I predict that extensive changes in philosophy will occur in this century in the philosophy of mind.

What do you consider the most neglected topics and/or contributions in late 20th century philosophy?

My answer here is partly what I said at the end of the third question. What has been neglected in the philosophy of mind are the contributions of psychology and neuroscience to the understanding of the mind and the brain in the last several decades of the twentieth century. This is why I am predicting an intellectual revolution during this century in the philosophy of mind, comparable to what happened in the philosophy of physics in the twentieth century. It sounds almost paradoxical to say that in the twentieth century the philosophy of mind has been neglected, given how much has been written about it, but what has been neglected is the viewpoint that derives from the relevant scientific work.

What are the most important open problems in philosophy and what are the prospects for progress?

I think there are many open problems that will be of great interest in this century, but I cite three that are especially important and in terms of which great progress will be made. The first concerns our conception of the physical universe, the second is about our understanding of how the brain represents the world around it, and the third is the topic of free will, prominent for centuries in philosophical discussion.

Nature of the physical universe. Because of recent research in many different directions in physics, from experiments in quantum entanglement, which challenge the correctness of the special theory of relativity because of the ability to affect, faster than the velocity of light, the behavior of entangled particles separated by indefinitely large distances, to a variety of findings in astrophysics, we will undoubtedly develop a new set of ideas for thinking about the structure of the universe. New concepts concerning space-time and the nature of matter and energy will cause, in many ways, changes in our conceptual thinking as large as any that took place in the twentieth century. If this prediction is correct, our philosophical conceptions of the physical world in which we live will be changed in the kind of fundamental way they changed with the displacement of the Aristotelian and Ptolemaic conception of the heavens, which dominated our world view for fifteen hundred years, to that of Newtonian mechanics, which itself lasted until special relativity and quantum mechanics were developed in the twentieth century. We are now ready for another such conceptual set of changes, and we will find them at first equally mysterious.

Brain representations of the world. There is a long history of speculative ideas about mental representation, but in mental representations we have the kind of freedom we do not have in dealing with the actual processes of the brain that must embody such mental representations. The deep problems we have only begun to touch are the identification of the kinds of structural isomorphisms that exist between our brain representations of our perceptions or our cognitive patterns of dealing with the world. These structural isomorphisms, as we discover them, should show us in detail how the structure, including the processing structure, of the universe as we perceive it, is represented in our brains. As yet we have barely begun the research required to have a detailed understanding of such structural isomorphisms, but as we do, it seems very likely our conception of our own mental lives will change as well. Let me give just two examples. A widely accepted thesis about the structure of spoken language is that sentences are not understood holistically, but are understood by recognizing the words which are their constituents. No one, as far as I know, defends the thesis that we have a purely holistic understanding of sentences. Our conception of how we compute the meaning or truth of even the simplest sentences depends on some kind of process of recognizing the individual constituents that make up sentences. The corresponding question for the brain is how are these constituents isomorphically mapped into the representation of sentences in the brain. The word or phrase constituents of sentences must be mapped into individual representations in the brain, in order for us to compute, in a feasible way, the meaning and truth of sentences. We surely do not do this computation in some completely holistic way.

A second and related example of structural isomorphism is understanding how we recognize or represent in the brain the various natural properties of visual perceptions. Such structural analysis is also needed for perception using the other senses as well. But to take a simple example, consider the perception of a red circle. This simple abstract figure has two properties, one of color and one of shape. How is each of these properties represented in the brain? How do we disentangle the structural isomorphic representation of color from that of shape in the electromagnetic brain waves or signals that reach the cortex and permit us cognitively to recognize and to express that we recognize what we see? The problem when formulated this way in some sense seems simple, but scientifically it is apparently far from being simple. The important point that I want to make is that it is the relation between the constituents, or the parts, and the whole that must be reflected in the structural isomorphism. Finding these isomorphic mappings is a task that is only barely begun, and until greater progress is made our detailed understanding of what the mental, embodied in the brain, really consists of will be poorly understood.

Free will. For me the most important open scandal in philosophy is the problem of free will. I can understand why Hume gave the solution he did to the problem, because he felt he must have an answer that was consistent with the necessary views that held sway, at the time, of the laws of nature. When he said "necessary" he meant in most respects what we mean by the laws being deterministic. We now have a much deeper and more sophisticated understanding of the physics of matter. Determinism is not an idea that has the sway it once did, but we have not properly absorbed what I think is the conversion of the problem of free will from being a traditional philosophical problem to a scientific one. The scientific problem is to give a detailed account of how it is that matter can be intentional in character. In some sense, we all recognize that matter can be animate. This is the great lesson of modern biology. We also need wide dissemination of a thorough analysis of the intentional character of matter. Even though many details are missing, just as they are in case of the evolution of life from inanimate matter, the outlines of the story are pretty clear. The scientific and philosophical mistake was to believe, as Hume, Kant and other great philosophers of the past did, that in some sense the laws of the universe are necessary and deterministic in character. Kant's antinomies were the apex of this tradition. The great problem for philosophy in this area is to disentangle itself from all the arguments of the past that were mistaken and to develop a view of free will that is consistent with modern conceptions of matter, how matter can be intentional, and how it is realized in some very simple intentional processes like elementary conditioning in biologically primitive animals with a relatively small number of neurons.

There is another side to this story, also important from a different scientific angle. This is the realization that there is not really a strong empirical distinction between deterministic and stochastic behavior. This is a new kind of invariance not well enough recognized in scientific or philosophical circles. The main results are beautiful and surprising ones that come out of ergodic theory, which I shall not try to describe here, but just mention some of the consequences that follow from them. An excellent account is to be found in Ornstein and Weiss (1991). I will end with this example, because of its beauty and profundity at the same time. Consider that hallmark of determinism of the past, an ideal billiard table with an ideal ball moving about it periodically and endlessly in exactly the same endless pattern. Now put on that billiard table a convex object in the middle, off of which the ball must be reflected in its course, just as it is from the sides of the table. There must be errors of measurement—one of the great truths of modern experimental physics. And these errors of measurement must be bounded away from zero. Then no matter how many observations we may take of the behavior of this idealized ball, which could be a photon "on a billiard table of mirrors," we cannot decide between the correctness of a stochastic theory of the motion, and that of the classical deterministic theory. The two mathematically formulated theories, one stochastic and the other deterministic, are mutually inconsistent, but due to the existence of errors in the measurement, it is impossible empirically to distinguish one from being more correct than the other. This is a new invariance undoubtedly present in many complex physical systems and of great conceptual importance in the proper view of intentionality and freedom. (A view I defended in a 1993 article on the transcendental character of determinism.)

References

Hilbert, D. and W. Ackermann (1938/1950). *Principles of Mathematical logic*. New York: Chelsea Publishing Company.

Lamb, H. (1932/1945). *Hydrodynamics*. Sixth edition. New York: Dover Publications, Inc.

Hilbert, D. and W. Ackermann (1938/1950). *Principles of mathematical logic*. New York: Chelsea Publishing Company.

Lamb, H. (1932/1945). *Hydrodynamics*. Sixth edition. New York: Dover Publications, Inc.

Ornstein, D. S. and B. Weiss (1991). Statistical properties of chaotic systems. *Bulletin of the American Mathematical Society (New Series)* 24: 11–116.

Savage, L. J. (1954). *Foundations of Statistics*. New York: Wiley.

Suppes, P. Web access to publications, see http://suppes-corpus.stanford.edu/index.html

21

Timothy Williamson

Wykeham Professor of Logic

University of Oxford

University of Oxford, UK

Why were you initially drawn to formal methods?

As a teenager, I enjoyed playing about with formal models of various kinds. For instance, the idea for one of the less trivial proofs in my paper 'On the structure of higher-order vagueness' (*Mind*, 1999) came from my explorations of one-dimensional cellular automata almost thirty years earlier. I liked, and still like, observing how simple rules generate complex behaviour. That combination resembles a characterization Leibniz once gave of what makes the best of all possible worlds the best. Unfortunately, one finds the opposite in some philosophical work uninformed by mathematical instincts: complex rules are used to generate simple behaviour.

As an undergraduate, I studied mathematics and philosophy at Oxford. Before starting I read the logic textbook for the first term, Lemmon's *Beginning Logic*. The language of first-order logic immediately felt in some respects like a better vehicle for thought than English. The natural deduction proof rules impressed me as a wonderfully perspicuous way of articulating arguments, except for a few irritating minor redundancies that Lemmon had added for pedagogical reasons. At last I could see how to argue properly. Some people find rigour oppressive, but its absence is what oppresses me. Rigour came and comes as a longed-for liberation from bluster and bombast, others' and my own.

One of the aspects of mathematics that most intrigued me as an undergraduate was the characterization of apparently elusive concepts by a few simple and precise axioms, as in topology. I tried producing similar axiomatizations myself for other concepts. Something else to be acquired from a mathematical training at university is a strong sense of the aesthetics of definitions. In mathematics, good definitions open up whole new fields of enquiry; bad ones entangle you in intractable complications that lead nowhere. Good definitions are distinguished aesthetically, above all by their elegance. They are not mere disjunctions of miscellaneous disjuncts. Many definitions or analyses on offer in philosophy are recognizable at a glance as hopeless by anyone with a modicum of mathematical sense: they are far too ugly to work. One can be fairly confident in advance that any proposed generalization in which they occur will be subject to counter-examples or trivialization. Of course, the specific objection must still be found, but that is often routine. Those who lack experience of advanced mathematics do not always realize how reliable a guide aesthetics is to structure in the search for truth (it is fallible, obviously, like most guides). Little progress is made in mathematics or philosophy without a strong capacity for abstract pattern recognition; the best definitions are the most patterned. The effect of philosophers' high level of tolerance for ugly definitions and analyses is that the subject risks getting clogged up with gruesome hypotheses. It takes time to eliminate them and their still more gruesome descendants, when their defenders react to counterexamples by adding epicycles. Good judgement is needed to recognize a degenerating research programme; *that* aspect of methodology isn't about to be formalized.

In the summer of my first year as an undergraduate, I got interested in Frege's identification of abstract objects with equivalence classes under suitable equivalence relations, and the non-transitivity of indiscriminability as a challenge to attempts to apply that method to phenomenal qualities: for example, one can have a long series of shape samples in which each member is indiscriminable in shape from the next but the first is easily discriminable in shape from the last. I proved that one could achieve the 'next best thing', or rather that there would always be more than one next best thing. I read Nelson Goodman's *The Structure of Appearance* and later Carnap's *Aufbau*. I did the technical work for my paper 'Criteria of identity and the Axiom of Choice' and sent off a version to *The Journal of Philosophy*. The reply was 'revise and resubmit', but as a naïve undergraduate I mistook that for a rejection with a pat on the head, and put the paper aside in disgust. I had also become sceptical about the reductionist philosophical terms in which it was then framed. Years later, I discovered what the letter really meant, and did revise and resubmit the paper; it was finally published in 1986. That paper was the starting-point for my first book, *Identity and Discrimination* (Oxford: Blackwell, 1990), where I explained the logic of indiscriminability in terms of the interaction between epistemic logic and the logic of identity. The non-transitivity of indiscriminability has continued to fascinate me: both my subsequent books *Vagueness* (London: Routledge, 1994) and *Knowledge and its Limits* (Oxford: Oxford University Press, 2000) explore its less obvious consequences for cognition.

I was an undergraduate and graduate student at Oxford from 1973 to 1980, more or less the years of the 'Davidsonic boom'. The excesses of the manner in which the Davidsonian programme was pursued struck me, and still strike me, as an abuse of formalization. Formal constraints motivated by gnomic sayings were used to close off apparently legitimate avenues of investigation; people with a smattering of logic viewed minor technical points with superstitious awe; ' "Snow is white" is true in English if and only if snow is white' was enunciated as a mantra. I did not object to the valuable project of trying to carry through the programme and overcome the obvious difficulties; what I disliked was the uncritical attitude to Davidson's more obscure arguments, and the treatment of alternative programmes as heresies. Formal methods should be applied in a scientific, experimental, open-minded spirit that was insufficiently evident. I took Saul Kripke's paper 'Is there a problem about substitutional quantification?' as a merited, if harsh, rebuke to a pervasive atmosphere. Of course, not everyone engaged in Davidson's programme was guilty. In my first term as an undergraduate, I had greatly admired the clarity, power and cogency of Kripke's 1973 John Locke lectures. I raced through the 1972 version of *Naming and Necessity* at an absorbed sitting; it is one of the very few books that should constitute irreversible progress in philosophy. Nevertheless, my dislike of Davidsonian orthodoxy alienated me from the philosophical mainstream for some years. In reaction, I read Hegel's *Phenomenology of Spirit* with baffled admiration, and even dipped into Derrida and other post-structuralists without much benefit.

My first idea for a doctoral thesis was to formalize Leibniz's principle of sufficient reason so as to clarify its metaphysical consequences (if any); I even thought I saw a connection with Lévi-Strauss's then-fashionable structuralist anthropology. That all ran into the sand. I switched to Popper's conception of verisimilitude, a measure of the way in which scientific theories can approximate better and better to the truth. I was often annoyed to be asked whether the idea of approximation to the truth had something to do with vagueness; I always answered in the negative, because a sequence of perfectly precise theories can converge on the truth through increasing accuracy and specificity. At the time, I privately regarded the question as a symptom of clichéd thinking and obsession with semantics; I now have to admit that there probably was some subterranean connection with my later work on vagueness, even though the 1980's formed a gap between ending work on verisimilitude and beginning it on vagueness. My thesis was only intermittently formal. It seemed to me that purely formal approaches to verisimilitude failed, for reasons akin to those for which inductive logic cannot be completely formalized. I argued for some very eccentric conclusions, for which my supervisors, David Bostock, Bill Newton-Smith and Michael Dummett, were in no way to blame.

Soon after completing my thesis, I became disillusioned with it. To my publications it contributed only a technical idea about the difference between three-place and four-place similarity relations, out of which grew the paper 'First order logics for comparative similarity' (*Notre Dame Journal of Formal Logic*, 1988). For years I had the feeling that I had wasted so much time on my DPhil thesis (completed when I was twenty-four) that I could never catch up again. I realized that engaging in grandiose projects related only obscurely to what others are doing can be an easy way out. I started writing papers where I had something specific and precise to say, and found that it came very naturally. My first published article was 'Intuitionism disproved?' (*Analysis*, 1982), a formal discussion of the so-called 'paradox of knowability' in the context of intuitionistic logic, a matter on which I have subsequently written several times. Although my philosophical outlook could scarcely be more distant from intuitionism, Dummett's influence made intuitionistic logic hard to take lightly at the time.

My interest in modal logic began when I was an undergraduate, but became serious only through contact with Lloyd Humberstone. I had been trying to use it to formalize questions about the relation between verificationist theories of meaning and verificationist theories of truth, with the box read in terms of verifiability rather than necessity. When I first met Lloyd, in 1986, I told him about this idea; he replied with some technical questions about it to which I did not know the answer. It struck me as ridiculous that I had been trying to squeeze philosophical consequences out of material of which I was not in full technical control. Subsequent correspondence with him forced me to acquire a much deeper understanding of modal logic. The immediate outcome was my paper 'Assertion, denial and some cancellation rules in modal logic' (*Journal of Philosophical Logic*, 1988), followed by a series of others, including our joint paper 'Inverses for normal modal operators' (*Studia Logica*, 1997).

A shorter answer to the question would be that I was initially drawn to formal methods because I found them elegant, objective and easy.

What example(s) from your work illustrates the role formal methods can play in philosophy?

Like other powerful methods, formal methods in philosophy play many different roles. I will illustrate a few.

A degree of formalization often helps to clarify whether an argument is valid, by making its structure more perspicuous. Sometimes it is just a matter of displaying labelled premises and conclusion (the inter-sentential level) and of using a few logic symbols and parentheses to disambiguate scope (the intra-sentential level). For example, I use that degree of formalization in my anti-luminosity argument for the overall conclusion that one can be in any given non-trivial condition without being in a position to know that one is in it, an argument closely related to the non-transitivity of indiscriminability (*Knowledge and its Limits*, pp. 96–8). In that case I display structure in order to make the argument's validity evident. In other cases one displays structure in order to make evident the invalidity of an opponent's argument. To take an example at random, I do that in 'Reply to Machina and Deutsch on vagueness, ignorance, and margins for error' (*Acta Analytica*, 2002). This degree of formalization is widespread throughout analytic philosophy, and requires only the most elementary knowledge of formal logic There are interesting issues about the notorious asymmetry between validity and invalidity with respect to structure – an instance of a valid rule of inference is itself valid, whereas an instance of an invalid rule of inference needn't be invalid— but it does not call into serious question the practical utility of this degree of formalization in establishing validity and invalidity in many cases.

Another obvious use for formal methods in philosophy arises when philosophical claims include mathematical content. Probabilistic epistemology is one of many fields in which that often occurs, because by far our best cognitive control on probability comes from the mathematical theory. My non-subjective Bayesian account of evidential probability is developed in *Knowledge and its Limits* (pp. 209–37). Naturally, arguments for or against a philosophical claim that includes mathematical content are likely to involve mathematical arguments, as one finds throughout probabilistic epistemology.

A less straightforward use of formal methods is to show not merely that a particular argument doesn't work but that its conclusion cannot be validly derived by any argument whatsoever from its premises. In other words, one provides a consistency proof for the combination of the premises with the negation of the conclusion, usually by constructing a formal model in which they are all true. For these purposes, it is no objection if the model doesn't correspond to the intended interpretation of the premises and conclusion. Here is an example. In 'Intuitionism disproved?' (mentioned above), I pointed out that Fitch's famously surprising argument from 'All truths are knowable' to 'All truths are known' is intuitionistically unacceptable. Roy Sorensen later objected that that did not show that there is no intuitionistically acceptable other argument from 'All truths are knowable' to 'All truths are known'. It was a fair challenge, even though most people who had thought about the matter took it as obvious that if Fitch's argument did not bridge the gap from premise to conclusion in an intuitionistically acceptable way, nothing else would either. I therefore constructed models of intuitionistic logic in which 'All truths are knowable' is true and 'All truths are known' false, to meet Sorensen's challenge ('On intuitionistic modal epistemic logic', *Journal of Philosophical Logic*, 1992). Those models are somewhat artificial, and don't pretend to capture the intuitionists' intended interpretation. Nevertheless, they show conclusively that there is no derivation of the specified kind. Someone might still claim that there are other intuitionistically compelling constraints on knowledge and knowability which fail in those models and yet, added to 'All truths are knowable', permit an intuitionistically acceptable derivation of 'All truths are known', but such a hypothesis, unlike Sorensen's, is too vague for formal evaluation until the constraints have been specified: we have a formal specification of intuitionistic logic, but not of intuitionistically compelling constraints on knowledge.

Completeness theorems also have various sorts of philosophical interest. In the study of vagueness, one usually works with a 'definitely' operator such that it is borderline whether something is a heap if and only if it is neither definitely a heap nor definitely not a heap. One can easily write down a few formal principles that most people would accept as valid for 'definitely'; the question is whether all valid principles in the language for 'definitely' are derivable from those few. The answer matters for higher-order vagueness, a graveyard for theories of vagueness: can there be borderline cases of borderline cases and so on up; if so, what is their structure? In *Vagueness* (pp. 270–5), on the basis of the epistemic account of vagueness defended there, I gave a formal proof of a completeness theorem for a logic of 'definitely'. It depended on the plausible but informal assumption that certain formal models ('variable margin models') are legitimate models of vagueness, in the sense that any valid principle about 'definitely' must hold in them; they were not assumed to be the only legitimate models of vagueness. One cannot expect to eliminate such residues of informality. The aim is rather to be as clear and explicit as possible about what informal assumptions are being made.

Another role for completeness theorems is illustrated by the one that Agustín Rayo and I proved for the logic of a quantifier mandatorily interpreted as ranging over everything whatsoever ('A completeness theorem for unrestricted first-order languages', in J.C. Beall, ed., *Liars and Heaps*, Oxford: Clarendon Press, 2003). We wanted to show that unrestricted first-order logic is formally tractable, by providing a sound and complete axiomatization. We also wanted to show that the metatheory of unrestricted first-order logic can be done in a mathematically respectable way, without 'metaphysical' obscurity, by making the completeness proof itself as perspicuous as possible—contrary to some interpreters of Frege, who have suggested that the quantification over all objects whatsoever in his formal language makes it incapable of metalogical treatment because it has no 'outside' to study it from. It turns out that the relevant metalogic needs no such outside.

Some of my work involves model-building of a kind more familiar in the natural and social sciences than in philosophy. The models are based on simplifying assumptions that the theorist expects to hold strictly in few or no cases of interest. Nevertheless, they enable one to study an effect carefully by isolating it from others that usually or always accompany it, making noise through which one cannot hear the message. In *Knowledge and its Limits*, the point of several formal models of knowledge in the appendices is to gain insight into one sort of obstacle to knowledge by working out what knowledge would be like if there were no other obstacles. If the epistemic logician's current interest is in an obstacle to knowledge independent of logical non-omniscience, something can be learnt by assuming logical omniscience even though the assumption is false. Similar issues arise in my 'Some computational constraints in epistemic logic' (in D. Gabbay, S. Rahman, J. Torres and J. van Bendegem, eds., *Logic, Epistemology and the Unity of Science*, Paris: Hermes, 2004). Again, it is hard to build models for the logic of 'definitely' without making many simplifying assumptions (see my symposium with Mario Gómez-Torrente and Delia Graff on margins for error in *Philosophy and Phenomenological Research*, 2002). Although it is difficult to analyse the methodology of such idealizations rigorously, that by itself is not a good argument for regarding them as illegitimate, otherwise parallel arguments would threaten most of contemporary natural science.

The use of formal semantic theories for particular natural languages raises further methodological issues. In 'Knowing how' (*Journal of Philosophy*, 2001), Jason Stanley and I used the best available treatments by linguists of the semantics of indirect questions to argue that knowing how is a special case of knowing that, contrary to Ryle and many others. Some critics have wondered how studying the semantics of the English construction 'knowing how' could lead to conclusions about knowledge itself, rather than just about the English phrase 'knowing how'; any use of linguistic methods to reach non-linguistic conclusions is liable to raise the same question. But it is a mistake to think that the method in use is purely linguistic. The formal semantics tells one that satisfying 'knows how to F' in English is equivalent to having a corresponding piece of propositional knowledge. One's competence as a speaker of English tells one that satisfying 'knows how to F' in English is equivalent to knowing how to F. It follows, without any confusion of use and mention, that knowing how to F is equivalent to having a corresponding piece of propositional knowledge, a conclusion about knowledge, not about the English language. In a similar way one can defend other uses of formal linguistic methods to reach non-linguistic conclusions.

The preceding remarks should give an impression of a rather miscellaneous variety of roles that formal methods play in philosophy, and within almost every role a complex, subtle interplay of formal and informal considerations: for that is how things are, and should be. In particular, it should be clear that informal methods are also essential to philosophy, for formal methods, like all others, easily mislead when applied without good informal judgement.

What is the proper role of philosophy in relation to other disciplines?

Philosophy has many different proper roles in relation to other disciplines.

Perhaps the most obvious role is that for any discipline D (including philosophy itself), there is a potential and usually actual legitimate sub-discipline of philosophy, the philosophy of D, which reflects on the aims and methods of D. The relationship may be reciprocal: both the philosophy of sociology and the sociology of philosophy are legitimate branches of enquiry. The question obviously arises whether the philosophy of a non-philosophical discipline D can contribute to D itself, perhaps by criticism of its current practice, or only to philosophy. Some philosophers of D may call for the abolition of D: for instance, when D is psychoanalysis. We can predict in advance that practitioners of D will not take kindly even to constructive criticism from philosophers; that does not prove that the criticism is unmerited. Berkeley was right to complain that contemporary explanations of infinitesimals were muddled ('ghosts of departed quantities'); Abraham Robinson's rehabilitation of infinitesimals by means of non-standard analysis did not show that those explanations were satisfactory after all, but instead replaced them by a better one less revisionary than the Cauchy-Weierstrass approach. Practitioners of a mature non-philosophical discipline D may tend to feel that philosophers cannot even make a positive contribution to D, for example by articulating assumptions or clarifying distinctions. It is reasonable to be wary of attempts to improve D by philosophers who have never practiced D itself at an advanced level; second-guessing the experts is a dangerous game. Nevertheless, the experts are not omniscient even in their own domain; there is no good reason to think that philosophy cannot in principle contribute to other disciplines. After all, someone may be a properly trained practitioner in both philosophy and D; their philosophical training may help them to articulate assumptions and arguments within D. If so, the same contribution can in principle be made by a philosopher who has acquired a serious knowledge of D without practicing D.

A picture used to be widespread of philosophy as an essentially 'second-order' discipline in relation to 'first-order' disciplines such

as physics, biology and history: physicists, biologists and historians develop and apply concepts to the world; philosophers then
analyse those concepts. I have argued elsewhere that many philosophical problems are not about concepts or words ('Past the linguistic turn?', in B. Leiter, ed., *The Future for Philosophy*, Oxford:
Clarendon Press, 2004). They are as first-order as the problems
of physics, biology and history. For example, the dispute between
three-dimensionalist and four-dimensionalist accounts of our per-
sistence over time concerns our general underlying nature, not
words or concepts, even though we may need to discuss words
and concepts to resolve the dispute. It is myopic to pretend that
other disciplines cannot contribute to the solution of philosophical
problems. Philosophers of time cannot simply ignore the implications of special relativity—although the bearing of the physics on
the philosophical issues may be less direct than is sometimes imagined. Equally obviously, philosophers of mind cannot simply ignore
the findings of experimental psychology. In some areas, philosophy
merges seamlessly into other disciplines, or overlaps them. Logic is
a branch of both philosophy and mathematics; it cannot be separated into mutually exclusive contributions from mathematics and
philosophy. Some philosophers of physics do very highly theoretical physics without thereby ceasing to do philosophy. Philosophers
of biology engage cooperatively with biologists in debates about
the nature of evolution. In such cases, philosophy gives something
to other disciplines as well as receiving from them.

In my own case, I have published two joint papers with the
economist Hyun Shin, who was himself trained in both economics
and philosophy as an undergraduate at Oxford. For one of our
papers, he saw how to use my ideas about margins for error to
prove a result about the robustness of simple conventions ('How
much common belief is necessary for a convention?', *Games and
Economic Behavior*, 1996). The other emerged from a discussion
between us of the relation between provability interpretations of
modal logic and computational constraints on knowledge ('Representing the knowledge of Turing machines', *Theory and Decision*,
1994). It would be ludicrous to ask whether they were papers in
economics or philosophy, as though the disjunction were exclusive.
I have also collaborated with the cognitive psychologist Dan Os-
herson in designing experiments on the psychology of vagueness
(with Nicolao Bonini and Riccardo Viale, 'On the psychology of
vague predicates', *Mind and Language*, 1999). Superficially striking differences of disciplinary style, culture and manner of pre-

sentation often mask deeper similarities and overlaps of questions and arguments.

Some philosophers are completely seduced through their contact with other disciplines. There is a phenomenon of philosophy-hating philosophers enamoured of some other science; they despise philosophy for its lack of discipline and progress. Their work easily degenerates into pop psychology, pop biology, pop physics or whatever it is. It may still serve an auxiliary role in facilitating the communication of ideas between their favourite discipline and philosophy. But in drawing implications from that discipline for philosophy they tend to make large bridging philosophical assumptions, often of a reductionist kind, which they fail to support, state or even notice because they look down on the traditional philosophical discipline of the careful articulation of arguments. Philosophy has most to offer other disciplines when it retains its self-respect and distinctive character as a discipline in its own right, not a mere cheerleader for science.

Nevertheless, one major task for philosophy is to interpret the wider implications of other disciplines (taken separately or together) for common-sense and our overall picture of the world. Many of the main debates in philosophy concern the relation between the scientific image and the manifest image, for example in metaphysics and philosophy of mind. It is not good enough to assert that the two conceptions are somehow at different 'levels' and therefore cannot be inconsistent with each other. It is just that the issues are too important and too subtle to be left to crude scientism.

What do you consider the most neglected topics and/or contributions in late 20th century philosophy?

Very many trivial topics and contributions are *justly* totally neglected, in the sense that no attention is or should be paid to them. No doubt the question concerns which topics and contributions are the most *unjustly* neglected. I'll also take it that how much attention should be paid to a topic or contribution depends on the current state of understanding, not just on its intrinsic nature. Theoretical advances may subsume a topic or contribution under a more general one, after which the former deserves much less attention than it did when it appeared in isolation. A topic is not unjustly neglected when it cannot even be conceived, or available methodologies do not permit any progress to be made on it. The problem of the independence of the continuum hypothesis was not unjustly neglected in the middle ages; it was simply beyond the horizon. In this sense, cases of unjust neglect are wasted opportunities.

Various particular anomalies come to mind. Why has the philosophy of history almost disappeared from view? Does the prevailing treatment of aesthetics as far less philosophically central than ethics derive from a residual streak of puritanism in Anglo-American culture, according to which art is less than fully serious? Why do so many epistemologists and metaphysicians marginalize mathematics, rather than treating it as the paradigm of knowledge that it surely is? In each of these cases, philosophers may be displaying more general cultural prejudices of our time.

Another source of bias is the concentration of power and influence over analytic philosophy in a small number of American and British departments. An analytic philosopher networked into continental Europe has to write a much better paper to have the same level of impact as an analytic philosopher networked into a few leading Anglo-American departments. Philosophical fashion is set by the few and followed by the many; the few are more interested in their friends' ideas than in those of people they have never met. They are more willing to believe that their friends are doing important work. Those in the know use the right buzz words and engage with the right modish articles on the basis of the right fashionable assumptions; others struggle to keep up, fearing that they are out of date but not knowing in exactly what respect. These are entirely unsurprising and human phenomena; nevertheless, the result is unfairness. The rapid growth, qualitative as well as quantitative, of analytic philosophy in continental Europe has narrowed the credibility gap and will narrow it further. Although philosophical leadership will never be evenly distributed, I look forward to a less narrow geographical concentration than presently obtains—something more like the current situation in mathematics.

A form of methodological neglect also deserves mention here. There is scope for many more applications of a model-building methodology in philosophy than one currently finds. If you can construct a non-trivial, mathematically precise model and show that your philosophical hypotheses hold true in it, you have earned them a special right to be taken seriously, for many philosophical theories cannot pass even that elementary test: they are either too vague to be so tested, or suffer from inconsistency or some almost equally bad form of collapse. Moreover, by adjusting suitable parameters in the model, one can calculate the consequences in a simple case of a range of hypotheses. Definite progress can be made. Of course, many philosophers lack the formal skills required for model-building. But if you can state your hypotheses precisely, you may well find that a logician will be only too pleased to build a model for you—or prove that there is none. Philosophy will benefit from an attitude that looks more actively for opportunities for model-building. It will increase the scope for the kind of creative play that is good for the development of children and of every intellectually serious discipline.

What are the most important open problems in philosophy and what are the prospects for progress?

An initial reaction is: how many closed problems are there in philosophy? But of course philosophy is so tolerant of dissent that even if a philosophical problem is solved, an ingenious philosopher can always challenge an assumption of the solution and still be counted as doing philosophy. Thus, as Austin noted, philosophical progress tends to be constituted by the creation of new disciplines, such as logic and formal semantics, less tolerant of philosophical dissent. I suspect that this gradual hiving off of bits of philosophy once philosophers have brought them under sufficient theoretical control will continue.

I don't expect dramatic changes in the philosophical landscape, but rather incremental clarifications, the elimination of some bad ideas and the introduction of a few good ones. Philosophy seems to be in a period of 'normal science' rather than Kuhnian revolutionary change. Of course, it is difficult to foresee such revolutions because as soon as they are foreseen they thereby happen, like the downfall of communism in eastern Europe.

My deepest hope for progress is in methodology. Again, I don't expect anything dramatic: just a gradual improvement in generally accepted standards for precision of statement, accuracy of argument, distrust of hectoring, and similar intellectual skills or virtues. The philosophical community can bring about that sort of change if it has the collective will to do so, for example through the training of doctoral students. A mathematical analogy might be the enforcement of ε, δ-methods in nineteenth century analysis from Cauchy onwards. Like the fine-tuning of an experimental method, such changes can enable one to test hypotheses too close to a host of alternatives to have been previously tractable, as Frege's work shows. A small improvement in methodology can make a large long-term difference in results. As for where the results will come in philosophy, I trust that the answer is: everywhere. Let's try making the improvements; then we'll see.

Much of my current work concerns the philosophical methods. Philosophers' uncritical talk of philosophy as relying, for better or worse, on 'intuitions' often manifests the misconception that our evidence in philosophy consists of psychological facts about ourselves rather than facts about the philosophical topic itself. In consequence, scepticism about philosophy gains more credence than it deserves. The sceptical arguments are really just variants of traditional arguments for scepticism about our knowledge of the external world. In both cases, the evidence needs to be reconceived in less psychological terms. After all, it is a rather implausible relic of logical empiricism to conceive our evidence for theories in natural science as consisting of our own psychological states; why should the evidence for philosophical theories be so different? I hope that a better understanding of philosophers' actual method will also contribute to the refinement of those methods, but of course the connection is by no means automatic. At any rate, we can be sure that the methods will never amount to a decision procedure for solving philosophical problems.

About the Editors

Vincent F. Hendricks is Professor of Epistemology, Logic and Methodology and member of IIP — Institut Internationale de Philosophie. He is the author of many books including *Mainstream and Formal Epistemology*, *The Convergence of Scientific Knowledge*, *Feisty Fragments*, *Logical Lyrics* and *500 CC: Computer Citations*. Other books include *Self-Reference*, *Proof Theory*, *Probability Theory* and *Knowledge Contributors*. Editor of *Synthese* and *Synthese Library* he is also the founder of ΦLOG—*The Network for Philosophical Logic and Its Applications*.

John Symons teaches philosophy at the University of Texas at El Paso and is an associate member of l'Institut d'Histoire et de Philosophie des Sciences et des Techniques, Université de Paris 1. In addition to numerous articles, he is the author of two books on Daniel Dennett's philosophy, *On Dennett* and *Daniel Dennett: Le Naturalisme en Chantier*. Other books include *Quantifiers, Questions and Quantum Physics: Essays on the Philosophy of Jaakko Hintikka* and *Logic, Epistemology and the Unity of Science*. Symons has edited *Synthese* and *Synthese Library* since 2002 and has represented Ireland in the Institut Internationale de Philosophie since 2004.

About Formal Philosophy

Formal Philosophy is a collection of short interviews based on 5 questions presented to some of the most influential and prominent scholars in formal philosophy. We hear their views on formal philosophy, its aim, scope, the future direction of philosophy and how their work fits in these respects.

> This is a fabulous collection. Hendricks and Symons have performed an important service to the entire philosophical community. The interviews are not only rewarding in and of themselves but they will help the reader understand what has been going on and has been achieved in the past fifty years.
>
> — **Ernie Lepore**, Rutgers

FORMAL PHILOSOPHY

WWW.FORMALPHILOSOPHY.COM

Why do you do philosophy that way? Do you believe all philosophy could be done that way? Do you think it should be done that way? These are questions one seldom asks, except perhaps at dinner. Yet there is a lot one could learn from the answers, especially when they come from philosophers who do have a distinguished way of doing their job. *Formal Philosophy* identifies one such way and collects the answers of its eminent practitioners—not the quick answers one might give

over an entrecôte, but the answers one gives when seriously prompted to reflect upon their daily profession.
An enticing, provocative, completely novel way of sur-
veying the landscape of contemporary philosophy.

— **Achille Varzi**, Columbia University

Index

Printed in the United Kingdom
by Lightning Source UK Ltd.
106991UKS00001B/346-378